D1519494

Have you reached your peak?

Sure it's a tough climb.

All the way along are diverging paths, always one more difficult, holding the promise of greater fulfillment. And the other option is available: to stop, relax and take in the view, head back.

Yet, for reasons not fully known even to yourself, you do go higher, give more, perform to greater intensity. You make sacrifices—maybe missing sleep, or friendship, or a family meal. And when you've made it, you tip your hat to those challenges in your life which built up your strength.

Quotation and Jacket Design Courtesy of Signode Industries

CLIMB YOUR OWN MOUNTAIN

THE ULTIMATE SUCCESS GUIDE
By John F. Zaccaro

NEW HORIZON PRESS
Far Hills, New Jersey
Distributed by Scribner Book Companies, Inc.

Copyright 1985 by John F. Zaccaro

No part of this book may be reproduced in any form including electronic or mechanical means or information storage and retrieval systems without permission in writing
from the publisher.

Manufactured in the United States of America

Library of Congress Cataloging in Publication Data
Zaccaro, John F.
Climb Your Own Mountain: The Ultimate Success Guide

Bibliography: P.

I. Title
ISBN 0-88282-014-1

DEDICATION

To my mother and father, who gave me the
love and confidence to leave the "base camp"
for the many summits awaiting me.

"Truth is the Summit of Being!"
RALPH WALDO EMERSON

This book is about Summits and Truths
and my personal climb to each.

Table of Contents

Preface

I have been working since I was a boy of six. In fact, as I think about it, I cannot remember not working. I am a perfect example of work-ethic offspring resulting in work-ethic adult.

My grandfather was the honorary mayor of Italian Harlem. His son, Joe, my father, came to New York from Italy, via Argentina, in 1914, at the age of 14. There was no man on earth prouder of being an American, than was my father. His philosophy regarding his adopted country was a simple one . . . "America, the land of plenty, has enough for everyone, providing its children are as generous with it as it has been to them." This was the posture he maintained for the sixty-two years he spent loving this country and rearing four sons and two daughters to honor their country and God. He married my mother, Ray, in 1930, and together they proceeded to work hard to better the lot of their offspring. The lessons I learned from them are many, with the most indelible being that each generation must become more educated, more financially solvent, and develop more enthusiasm for the gift of life than the one preceding it.

My memories are of an education obtained from days shared with my parents, enriched by visits to New York's many museums, Central Park, the Metropolitan Opera and Radio City. The countless perfunctory things I do today to make my professional and personal life a reflection of success and happiness, are all influenced by lessons learned as a child in a home with little money, but filled with love and laughter.

My five brothers and sisters and I are all goal-oriented, setting our aim always for the top of the mountain. This credo was impressed upon us in countless ways and through hard work, dedication, stick-to-itiveness we've succeeded. It has been etched in my memory since I was a toddler that the "energy pot" for life is like the tomato sauce pot, my mother kept full and never off-limits. If you were hungry you only had to dip into it. How much you took from it was measured only by how much you put back. "To me, America is like that." If you were hungry for knowledge, the "energy pot" would feed you . . . energy was knowledge . . . it was the substance by which those like my family the naturalized citizens became part of the American dream. Their dreams have been passed on to me and now I hope to pass them on to you.

When I was eight years old, I was guilty of unionizing the altar boys in our local parish. After one winter of getting out of a warm bed at 5:00 a.m. to run five city blocks through the cold and the snow to serve the 6:00 a.m. mass, I decided that there had to be a better way to arrange things. When the circuitous route I had charted through the alleys and basements of buildings, failed to relieve the massive discomfort of this morning ritual, I swore never to do it again. I solved the problem by having a talk with all the young novices, convincing them that they would get bonus points for volunteering for the early morning mass. While I never really explained to them that the bonus points would ultimately come from heaven, I never again had to serve early morning mass. Salesmanship is one of my "birthskills." This has been obvious almost since I was old enough to talk. I have always been able to sell practically anything to anyone, always making them feel they have gotten a bargain. Ever since, children and adults alike, have shown a desire to share in the energy I have been blessed with. Throughout my life, I have been constantly on the move, taking little or no time to rest. I do not refer here to transiency (I have only moved my family once in eighteen years) or job-hopping; I just like to have several things going on at the same time to keep me busy. Even as a child, I couldn't sleep more than four hours a night . . . staying still bored me. Nothing has changed. . . . "standing still" continues to bore me and I still need very little sleep.

I grew up in New York during the war years, in Italian Harlem around 120th Street. The entire island of Manhattan was my playground. In 1948, my family moved to Long Island when it was still a place of potato truck farms and space . . . a far cry from my beloved and teeming Manhattan but a distinct and unique experience of another aspect of America's multifaceted geography and populace.

I graduated from Malverne High School on Long Island and attended Springfield College in Massachusetts on a scholarship, graduating in 1956. While at Springfield, I worked as a teaching assistant; the cute female undergraduates whom I tutored, made my life just a bit happier. I worked my way to Europe and spent a summer sightseeing. I received a postgraduate fellowship to Brandeis University and, following that experience, I took an interim teaching job at a private school in Manhattan. While in New York, I met, courted and married Joyce Foss, a beautiful singer, who was then working on Broadway in the musical, THE MOST HAPPY FELLA. Immediately after our marriage, we left New York for Atlanta, where I attended Emory University on a graduate fellowship. I supplemented my college scholarship, and my love of the good life, by doing everything from working as a professor's assistant, to teaching ballroom dancing.

Through my high school and college years, I was very involved in the theater . . . thinking that down the road, I might pursue it as a profession. "While we lived in Atlanta, I attended Emory University. . ." my wife and I owned and operated a successful ballroom dance school. From ground zero, until we departed Atlanta for California, the "Zaccaro School of Dance" had redoubling enrollments. More often than not, I would teach Joyce the steps to that day's lesson just minutes before the class started. Joyce was carrying our first daughter, Jessica, when we did the "tango" all the way to California . . . the promised land, and we have never looked back.

We were in California less than three months when I signed my first contract as an actor with a theatrical agency; I was working professionally within days of signing the contract. My gift for doing voices and accents kept me quite busy in television and movie work. When I wasn't portraying a bad guy on the "Untouchables" or the "Roaring Twenties," I was in western gear riding tall in the saddle in a myriad of different television shows. I worked at Warner Brothers in television shows such as "Maverick," "Hawaiian Eye," "Sunset Strip," and "Cheyenne," among others. During a show called "The Alaskans" I began doing character roles, and found myself busy at most major studios. I sang and acted on the stage of the classic Pasadena Playhouse. While on television sitcoms, I got riddled with machine gun bullets, fell off horses, down elevator shafts and received a black eye from the actor presently playing James Bond (Roger Moore). In one segment of the "Combat" television show, a cute brown and white puppy I carried into battle as a mascot, urinated on my chest for ten straight takes, moistening the gun powder charges in my vest, causing them to go off with a fizzle instead of a bang . . . It was all just part of a day's work. In all, I worked in over 150 television shows and motion pictures, the last of which was *The Other Side of the Mountain,* in 1976. On occasion a business client will ask me if I have a "double" who used to be an actor . . . as he or she saw someone looking just like me on the late show or some old T.V. rerun. Often I just smile and don't reveal the past. It was all exciting and fun, but only the beginning of the real career challenge ahead of me.

I was at the peak of my theater career, when I found another center stage in the selling world. My sales and marketing activities, pursued concurrently with my acting career, made me somewhat of an enigma to the casting agents. Strangely enough, the two complemented each other. I got many jobs because the casting agents were impressed with my enterprise . . . impressed by the fact that I wasn't sitting around idly living from one acting job to the next one, as so many actors seem to do. They were totally amazed when I would turn down an acting job if it interfered with my sales career.

I had started selling stereo equipment at the time it first became the "latest craze," and that gave me an entree into the homes of directors, fellow actors, casting agents, etc. I never failed to take advantage of that entree or any other opportunity which presented itself . . . in an unobtrusive way of course, and in this way I ended up with many jobs that were far beyond that warranted by my experience and credits. Between the two careers, I kept very busy.

My selling eventually led me into a wide range of enterprises, covering everything from construction and floor coverings to commodities and solar energy. In several of these enterprises, I became president of the corporation.

As my life plan has developed, I seem to have settled into the niche of market consulting, taking a product, and developing it from the ground floor up, for a company. Most of these endeavors have been highly profitable, some earning me over a million dollars but the most important thing to me, is that they have been exciting and personally rewarding and it is the essence of these experiences I want to share with you. For I believe they prove that real success is within the reach of all those who don't limit themselves and are willing to undertake the challenges of climbing arduous but stimulating, symbolic mountains.

Foreword

Over the years, in the course of my career, I have presented scores of sales and motivational seminars, reading widely in an attempt to make my seminars a catalyst to greater motivation for each person attending them. The catalyst for this book was a vacation trip to the Triangle X Guest Ranch at the base of the Teton Mountains in Moose, Wyoming. Day after day, year after year, I was drawn more and more to the majestic Tetons. I wanted to experience them to the fullest . . . to become immersed in them . . . and ultimately, to climb them.

From the beginning, I've been aware that the physical ascent of a rugged peak is a graphic and parallel example of any struggle towards a successful goal. For twenty years as I have continued to read, study and climb mountains, I realize that a number of my climbing experiences are analogous not only to some particular "truth" in my life, but to those found in the books written by the people who have been my personal guides in scaling the heights of success. In this book, I have selected what I believe to be crucial information in preparing you for a climb to your personal heights of prosperity. The authors come from many fields of expertise; you will share in the wisdom of scientists, businessmen, doctors, ministers, professors, philosophers, an acting coach team. Despite their diverse occupations all share certain common denominators of success.

So that I might develop the analogy of mountain climbing and success in an orderly fashion, I have divided CLIMB YOUR OWN MOUNTAIN into four sections; however, it is not essential to read the chapters in the order they are presented as this book is designed to accommodate the hectic schedule of today, by allowing one to take the good from one chapter at a time, whenever there are a few spare minutes.

The first section emphasizes the possibility of taking your destiny into your own hands, and the rewards to be gained when you do so. The second section delineates some character traits that could make the difference between success or failure. Section three then gives some practical and definitive techniques which can be used to better control your thinking and your actions. Section four points out some obstacles that might be encountered along the way, with suggestions to help you avoid or remove them.

The theme of CLIMB YOUR OWN MOUNTAIN is taken from a quotation by Ralph Waldo Emerson, "Truth is the summit of being." Philosophical credos such as this have highly-complex meanings. They are gestalts of ideals, which in and of themselves could be studied by scholars over a lifetime. Yet if we segregate those complexities into their various components, we can find many simple, elemental truths. Emerson does break his theories down a little more than most counselors by saying "To know yourself is the single most important truth for a successful life," and this single concept contains for me the kernel of my own beliefs. Some of the components of "knowing yourself" are knowing your relationship to the universe, and to your fellow man. When you understand that, or even get a glimmer of those relationships, you are on your way to leading a successful life. Quite often, however, a person with 20/20 vision in one area (where he will be experiencing success) will have to resort to a "seeing-eye dog" in other areas. For example, it would never occur to some businessmen to apply the same tactics they might use to save a foundering business to save a foundering marriage. Yet true success is never achieved without a balance in all areas.

The principles you are being exposed to in this book can be applied to all phases of your life. To be both happy and successful there should not be one standard or code of behavior for your personal life and another for your business life. Among the people who have reached summits: J.C. Penney built his personal life and his business success around the Golden Rule. David C. Prosser advises you to run your life like a business. I believe the components of your life must blend effectively to reach your highest peak of success and that includes taking a spiritual awareness into your business; using the universal laws of success such as the law of magnetism to attract customers or clients, and stopping to consciously give thanks and see beauty all along the way.

I have tried to "practice what I preach" in my own life. In Section I, I offer a suggestion, based on my career experiences, to outline a marketing plan for "your" life. In this book, you have the benefit and wisdom of eighteen life consultants ready to help you outline your future plans and ascent.

Some of this material you may have read previously . . . if so, you may want to read it again. If this is your introduction to "self motivation" you are on the threshold of an adventure which can lead you to heights you've only dreamed of, never realizing that in your dreams and desires is the seed to sow actuality. As you get to know yourself better, you will realize you can trust yourself and your inner guide. Success will come to you when you trust yourself enough to take the risks that must be taken in order to grow. Trust yourself enough to make choices. Trust yourself enough to be independent, flexible and honest with yourself. Trust yourself enough to live in the present and see life as it really is. Trust yourself enough to recognize your birthskills. . . . you can then concentrate on developing those traits which will benefit you most in your life climb. Trust yourself enough to set a goal based on your desires. A true desire will usually stay with you until you do something about it . . . and the fulfillment of it is usually inherent in the desire.

It takes courage to do any of these things; however, *right now* you have the hidden attributes which will enable you to reach for your own summit. CLIMB YOUR OWN MOUNTAIN is specifically designed to assist you in revealing them and answering your quest for a more productive and rewarding life.

Acknowledgments

In the final analysis, a great many people are responsible for this book, as I am the sum total of all I have met. The following list, while far from complete, acknowledges some of those people who have had a significant influence on my life; who have helped me set my directions and get my bearings as I have made my life's climb.

My wife, Joyce, who brings love and understanding to our base camp and without whom no summit would be complete; my daughters, Jessica and Dina, who have supported and loved me through the peaks and valleys; my brothers and sisters, Sal, Joe, Katherine, Bernie and Anne-Marie, all of whom have been a source of strength, love and fun.

The "Sisters of Charity," who were tested to their utmost during my elementary school days, and my mentors at Springfield College, Dr. Egon Bergel, Dr. Frederick G. Bratton and Dr. William Palmer.

The following business associates, from whom I have learned by observing, listening to and working with, whose assistance and friendship have been invaluable to me: Stan Mattox, *Mattox Industrial Real Estate;* Merle Brown, Larry Chandler, Jerry Barnes, George Shegog, and Ross Morrison, *Sealed Air Corporation;* Frank Marshall, *Teledyne-Water-Pic;* Barton Leach, Pastor, *Third Presbyterian Church* of Pittsburgh, PA; Jim Edmiston, *Polaris Vac-Sweep,* John Molinaro, *Ramona Savings and Loan;* Ben VandenBossche, *Double E Structures;* Roger Rasbach, *Roger Rasbach & Associates;* Terry Koch, *Colamco Industries;* Robert Ellington and Don Gough, *Heldor Industries;* John de Elorza, *John de Elorza and Associates;* and Charles Morgan, *United Foam Corporation;* with a special mention to William Danforth, William R. Young, III, *Young Ideas Advertising Agency,* and the ''Jolly Island'' boys, who know who they are.

Lynn Stalmaster, Hugh Benson and Lea Stalmaster, casting agents and producers, who kept me working in the theater.

In addition, I have had the privilege of being friends and associates with three men whom I consider to be leaders in their fields and whom I must acknowledge for their contributions to my business and personal success; the late Charles K. Fletcher, founder of *Home Federal Savings;* T.J. Dermot Dunphy, President of *Sealed Air Corporation;* and the late Harold ''Duke'' Ellington, Chairman of the Board and founder of *Heldor Industries.* They have helped me in my metaphorical climb, My literal climbs have been aided by Bob Gaines, *Vertical Adventures,* without whom I might never have discovered my love for the mountain; Jim Bridwell, who pushed me to a summit where circular rainbows greeted us; Ken Jern, *Exum Mountain Guides,* as much a part of Wyoming as the Grand Tetons; George Dunn, *Rainier Mountaineering,* with whom I shared an incredible night on Rainier.

I would also like to acknowledge the following who have assisted me in the actual preparation of this book; first and foremost, the authors without whom this book would not have been possible, with a special thanks to those who graciously took the time to see us in person or talk to us over the telephone; W. Clement Stone, Dr. Laurence Peter, Donald Prosser, Ari Kiev, and M.R. Kopmeyer, as well as the others whom I have not met, but feel I know quite well through their written words; Claude Bristol, Terry Cole-Whittaker, Dr. Wayne Dyer, Emmet Fox, Napoleon Hill, Maxwell Maltz, Edward P. Morgan, Donald Norfolk, Nena and George O'Neill, James C Penney, Neil and Margaret Rau, Merle Shain and Leon Tec, as well as Dr. Norman Vincent Peale. These authors have been my personal guides, along with many others who have helped keep me on the trail. I would like to have included them all, but could not as the list is too long.

I would also like to thank Joan Gosnell, historical specialist for J.C. Penney Company and Mr. Andy Svenson, as well as the following publishing houses for kindly granting permission to use the works we selected; Prentice Hall, with a special thanks to Alice Corring and James Bradler; Simon & Schuster, Wm. Morrow and Company, M. Evans and Company, Success Foundation, Oak Tree Publications, Harper and Row, and De-Vorss & Company.

Lastly, my appreciation to my friend and assistant, Edith Nielsen, whose belief in me has been unwavering, whose enthusiasm, self-reliance, confidence, discipline and commitment to excellence, have given me the support to climb my own mountain . . . and without whom this book could not possibly have been written.

SECTION I

Quests
And
Questions

CHAPTER ONE

Why Climb?

Why do I climb mountains? Why make the climb? Why not sit in the shade and comfort of the front porch swing? . . . for that matter, why does anyone do anything? Obviously, for wide and varied reasons relating to satisfying our most basic and important human needs. Through the ages man has pursued the upper limits of his capabilities to gain what A.H. Maslow called self-actualization.

We will not only dwell on these questions in this section, we will explore the answers I feel lie in the basic assumption that man explores the unknown, subjects himself to stress and sets out for the foothills (his goals), in order to achieve some approximation of "self-actualization;" for some it is to "gain authenticity," or as I have experienced it . . . a "summit feeling."

You simply cannot live fully without such experiences. Feel free to use the feelings and messages of those who have climbed before you, taking the ones that have the most intuitive meaning for you; use them to construct your personal marketing plan, the plan by which you sell yourself to yourself, as well as to others.

These reasons for making the decision of whether to climb or not to climb will be discussed and illustrated with chapters, or portions of chapters, from *Peel Your Own Onion* by David Prosser, *Your Erroneous Zones* by Dr. Wayne Dyer; and *The Stress Factor* by Donald Norfolk.

The message woven into the content of their philosophies is:

1. That we have the choice to be what we wish to be
2. That we have the choice to do what we wish to do
3. That it is obligatory that we make a choice . . .
4. That we must trust ourselves to make a choice.

My First Summit

These were the messages that were in my mind when I decided I could climb mountains. After weighing all the parameters, it became obvious that my first major climb should be Mt. Rainier in Washington State. What was also glaringly obvious was that I would have to "pull out the stopper" when it came to conditioning. The few days I had spent in my first lessons in Wyoming had left an indelible mark on my stamina . . . or rather, my lack of it.

When I stand up straight, I am, at the tallest, six feet, so you can see why the 212 lbs on that frame made it more appropriate for me to seek out "line backing" as a hobby, rather than technical mountain climbing. The truth of it was, I couldn't handle that weight on the mountain. I dreaded cutting down on the red meat at Smith and Wollensky, my favorite steak house in Manhattan, but knew it had to be done. Diet was the first event in my personal triathelon. I lost thirty-two pounds in seventy days. The second event of my triathelon was a rigorous and dogmatic exercise schedule at the gym. For six

months, I worked out a minimum of four to five times a week
. . . each session lasting at least ninety minutes. I began to hurt
in places *Gray's Anatomy* had not even heard of.

My third event was running and. . . . *the steps.* I started
jogging again . . . first one mile, then two, then three miles a
day, and so on, until my jogging became running. Then I added
a new dimension to the training routine . . . *steps* . . . *steps*
. . . *steps* . . . *and more steps!* . . . fifty-five of them at the
high school stadium. I would run down them, then back up,
two or three steps at a time, forcing myself to do one thousand
steps a day. My discipline was dogged   and it was working.
My new weight of one hundred eighty pounds began to firm
up . . . the rigors I experienced in my many weekends of rock
climbing at Joshua Tree and Yosemite, were getting easier. The
aches and pains were disappearing, but more important, as I
learned to accept the difficulties of training for the necessity
they were, I began to develop climbing techniques important
to the peaks that lay ahead of me. While I did miss my sauces,
wines, Mt. Gay Rum and St. Pauli Girl, I was ready to trade
them all in permanently if only I could forego *the steps*. I hated
them then and I hate them now, and yet without them, I
wouldn't have made it to the ten-thousand foot level, which
was our base camp on Rainier. Even with *the steps*, I was hard
pressed to make it.

When we left Paradise Lodge at the five thousand foot level,
it was a cold and clear day in the Cascades. The sky had a few
passing clouds in it, just enough to remind us that Rainier was
in charge of the region's weather and could change its mind
without a moment's notice.

Near the eight-thousand foot level, I developed severe leg
cramps. I tried surreptitiously to rub them out, but it didn't
work; when I tried to walk them out, the pain became so
intense that my knee joints locked. Nothing I tried relieved the
pain. The leg cramps came and went and when they arrived

for the last time, they stayed around for the next six hours.

I had a decision to make. I was sure that if I told my guide he would make me turn back, but I felt it was my pain, therefore my decision. I made the choice to go on. I had come to the point in my life where the development of my "birthskills" was being put to the extreme test; there was no doubt in my mind that without those damn steps, I would have been forced to quit. Running the steps had taken an average set of leg muscles and hardened them for the challenge before me that day, and for the climb to follow. I had come to reach the summit and settling for less than the completion of my goal would have meant settling for less than what my "birthskills" were capable of. I could not accept that. Every sense told me I had the skill . . . and the desire. I had to trust myself and go on, in spite of the pain, uncertainty and fear.

The weather had been growing slowly hostile. First, we encountered hours of limited visibility . . . white-outs in the middle of late morning . . . then fierce winds would whip up the moderate snow fall into a frenzied blizzard, and then it would clear up again. The worst result was that the fresh powder made the "plodding" through the snow fields more difficult by the minute. Soon the boot tracks of my guide in front of me, were thigh deep . . . "post-holing" as it is graphically called.

As the pain got worse and constant, I started dealing with it by playing number games in my mind, mentally counting to the number "thirty-eight". Keeping my head down in the dense fog, wind, and snow . . . barely seeing the boot holes of my guide just two feet in front of me, I plodded up the mountain. When my count reached thirty-eight, I would look up to see the progress I had made. Seeing little, I would start the counting sequence all over again. After an hour or two of the "thirty-eight" game, I began to recall every telephone number I had ever known. I found I could even recall my grandfather's telephone number of some forty years ago.

For the six hours that the ordeal lasted (the pain never did subside during that time) I substituted the acknowledgment of pain with the thought processes of past happy times . . . times without pain.

When we did finally reach the summit, my determined and unrelenting training program . . . and my "choice" of continuing up the mountain, in spite of the pain . . . were vindicated. It was a supreme moment of exhilaration, more than I had bargained for . . . a "summit feeling" too beautiful to describe . . . it was even worth *the steps*. I have since then reached other summits, and will reach more, but never again will I experience quite the same thrill that shook me to my depths, that I felt on my first summit.

CHAPTER TWO

To Reach a Goal

I believe that amazing feeling of achievement on reaching a mountain's summit is duplicated in other areas by those who strive to conquer towering peaks of achievement.

After graduating from the University of Minnesota, David C. Prosser began his professional career as an industrial engineer with companies such as Green Giant and 3M Corporation; the management techniques he pioneered led to a successful career as a management consultant and business entrepreneur. He spent ten years prior to the publication of *Peel Your Own Onion,* refining his remarkably effective business planning system to teach individuals how to run their lives more effectively. He is now working on a second book which will show businessmen how to use his method to make their businesses more successful. In 1985, he sold his temporary help agency to his employees and divested himself of all his other entrepreneurial businesses to devote his full time to a new company concerned with employer/employee benefits of workman compensation. We were talking to Mr. Prosser the day he had just closed the sale of one of his last businesses and the excitement singing across the telephone wires about the start-up of his new business, gave me a big clue to the secret of his successes. At an age when most people are ready to think about retiring, he is making another new beginning. To me, that is the most salient comment he could make about his philosophies, beliefs, and successes. Instead of stagnating awaiting death, he has just given himself a new goal; a new mountain to climb.

Goals are Necessary to Success
In his consultation work, Mr. Prosser discovered that those businesses which were most successful, were those which clearly identified their specific functions and then translated them into goals. As they achieved one goal however, they would discover another one beneath it . . . like "peeling an onion," as they pulled away one layer or challenge, a new one lay beneath it. The closer they got to the center of the onion, the more effective they became as a functioning business. In my opinion, no better analogy exists for your personal climb than peeling away the goals of your life which have been achieved, making the next one visible.

Mr. Prosser's first chapter, entitled "Goals," presents many essential ideas for climbing your own mountain. A basic assumption of this chapter is that all people have the same basic goals, though they are often identified by many different names or phrases by every author, philosopher, psychologist, or teacher, who has taken the leap (successfully or not); that basic goal is to work toward achieving as much of your full potential as possible. . . . realizing of course, that full potential is a goal no one ever reaches, yet you cannot let that stop you from seeing just how far you can go. The attempt at reaching for your potential takes place by setting and reaching a goal at a time . . . a series of "pitches" up the mountain . . . each with its own sense of accomplishment. This feeling of accomplishment which accompanies a quantum leap in your life, I choose to call the "summit feeling," although, as you will see, it encompasses much more than that.

Mr. Prosser suggests that if businessmen would apply the same techniques to running their lives that they apply to running successful businesses, they would find a totally new, well-balanced, happier and more productive way of living. A working example of this idea was the success of my late mentor, "Duke" Ellington (no, not the musician, but the much loved and respected president of Heldor Industries). Duke was an inspiration to me because he so totally applied his business acumen to his daily living. The profit in his business was measured in dollars, but his self-profit was in the pleasure he gave to others with his homespun wisdom, his concern and love for his fellow man, and for just being "Duke," If this principle works for even one person, it can work for all.

Setting a Goal

The most difficult part of reaching a goal, for a company, and an individual, is setting one. As a marketing consultant, each time I take on a new client, I do a complete marketing plan for the company. This plan delineates the company's goals and clarifies them by reducing the "generic ultimate" of "wanting to be successful" to its elemental parts and defining what that success really entails. The plan will take into consideration all of the parameters of the product, the company, and the marketplace in which it will be competing; then projections are made as far ahead as five to ten years. In this way, the company can see, quite graphically, what is involved and can then make a decision as to whether the chance for success is worth the time, money, energy, and risk involved.

By developing a personal marketing plan, you will be able to make more valid choices in all areas of your life. What we

accomplish is quite dependent upon the choices we make
. . . or don't make . . . as we encounter crossroads in our
careers and our relationships. We cannot avoid making
choices, even not choosing is making a choice, so it is logical
to give ourselves any edge we can that will head us in the
direction we would like to be going.

My personal five-year plan is every bit as detailed as the
plans I prepare for my clients. It gives me a framework on
which to hang my decisions. I am constantly aware, however,
that as events evolve, my goals will change, just as they do in
my business. This is as it should be. Rigidity is self-destructive;
however, any change should be a logical progression, with one
step leading to another; peeling away one layer to see the next,
being conscious always, that there is a vast difference between
being flexible and being wishy-washy.

As part of my five-year plan, I have one major goal in the
area of mountain climbing; this lofty goal is truly a "generic
ultimate," which is shared in common with all who are obsessed with climbing mountains; that goal is to climb the highest peak they are capable of climbing. Just as no one ever
reaches his full potential, or becomes fully "self-actualized,"
I know that I might never totally achieve that particular goal,
but it is the criterion upon which I base my decisions about
training and climbing.

When I prepare a "marketing plan" for a climb, I don't
choose a peak until I have weighed all factors such as the
difficulty of the climb, time factors, financial considerations,
availability of professional guides, etc. Analyzing, then combining these various ramifications will help me make my decision as to which peaks or goals are realistic ones for me at the
time.

The goals we select for our life climb can be arrived at the
same way. We can start with one major "generic ultimate"
and work our way backwards, or else start with a small desire

which turns into an all-encompassing and consuming goal as we gain confidence, self-assurance and direction.

A Leisurely . . . or a Strenuous Climb

The point I'm stressing here is that without a goal, you don't have a starting point. If you're just out for a stroll and enjoy ambling through the flowers, that's all right too. (We should never become so goal-oriented that we can't enjoy the scenery on the way up). Enjoy the compensations and gratifications of the climb itself, but be aware that without a summit goal, all you might get out of your stroll is a breath of fresh air.

Your First Summit

Inevitably, there will be moments in your life when you will be faced with pain, uncertainty and fear. Even in the best managed businesses there will always be risks and hazards that must be faced and dealt with. All business plans make allowances for the unexpected and more often than not, it is those very risks which lend excitement to what might otherwise have been a very prosaic endeavor. If the unpleasantness is faced, looked at squarely and courageously dealt with on a rational level, you will be able to climb over it and see the summit. No matter how many times you must deviate from your route, keep your eyes on the top of the mountain, using the summit as your landmark, so you don't lose sight of your goals.

And so I offer the following steps which the successful people I have known and studied have used as a success formula. If *you* practice using these steps, no matter how tedious or difficult the mental training may seem, these *steps* will lead you to conquer your own summits.

1. Set your goals.
2. Devise the strategy for reaching them.

3. Make a start.
4. Keep your eyes on the top of the mountain.
5. Enjoy the going.
6. Experience the reward of the "summit feeling."

Book Title: Peel Your Own Onion
Author: David C. Prosser
Publisher: Everest House
Chapter: Goals

Goals

A successful business is goal-oriented. So is the individual—
though the goal is not always sharply defined or well understood and is frequently obscured by false goals. A business
establishes goals it wishes to achieve within a specific time—
usually one year for short-term goals and five years for long-
term goals—and then plots a course of action to achieve these
goals.

When they write down their goals, businesses describe several things—such as what percent profit they're going to make,
how many dollars of sales they will achieve, and what kinds
of products they will produce. They also describe what kind
of relationships they are going to have with their employees,
with government, with their community, and whether or not
they are going to be good citizens. These goals are quite well
defined, but they are different for every business.

PEEL YOUR OWN ONION, By David C. Prosser, Copyright © 1979, Reprinted by permission of author.

People, like businesses, have goals, but a number of noted psychologists believe that all individuals have the same common goal. This goal has been given different names by different people, such as the term "self-actualization" used by the brilliant psychologist the late Abraham Maslow. *Self-actualization is the profit you are striving for in life.* Each of us will get a different amount of profit; we will be more or less self-actualized than each other, depending on the environment we are working in, our skills, and our ability to plan.

In her best-selling book *Passages,* [1] Gail Sheehy uses the term "gaining authenticity" in describing something similar to Maslow's self-actualization. Sheehy says this means knowing your potential and having the strength of will or ego to work toward fulfilling this potential.

Maslow arrived at his conclusions about a common goal by undertaking a rather remarkable study: Instead of looking at the mentally ill to understand our behavior, Maslow examined the lives of very successful people to see what they had in common. From these studies he concluded that all humans are inherently motivated, to greater or lesser degrees, to move up a common scale of needs toward self-actualization. He contended that this self-actualization is reached when an individual is using all of his abilities to the fullest.

Maslow believed that only a small percentage of people achieved a high level of self-actualization, even though we all have the desire, from birth, to seek it. He also said that one of the rewards of self-actualization is that you will experience more pleasure and less pain in your life. He didn't say that maximum self-actualization will give you *only* pleasure and *no* pain, but that you will experience more of the former and less of the latter.

Since I have converted business techniques to the matter of how individuals can run their lives better, I prefer to use a business-type term to describe the common goal: self-profit.

Essentially that is what is going to happen to you as you peel away your layers of knowledge and understanding—you are going to realize profits for yourself. The more you know about yourself, the more you will be able to help yourself to achieve a happier, more productive—and profitable—life.

The profits of a business are often measured in dollars, but yours will be measured in personal growth and more pleasure and less pain in your life. You will discover an increase in your creativity, and in your zeal for life.

There are, of course, businesses with a great deal of creativity that are, nonetheless, not very healthy psychologically. You may recall several years ago that a high official in our government was implicated in a scheme whereby large sums of money were borrowed by a company against nonexistent commodities in huge storage tanks. There was a lot of creativity in that scheme, even though it wasn't used for healthy reasons. The same can be true of individuals. There are countless examples of artists and writers who have produced very significant works but who were not mentally healthy. Their self-profit was low, even though their creativity was abundant. So creativity—while it is important in achieving a high degree of self-profit—is not by itself an assurance of such an achievement.

One of the other important elements in self-profit is the ability to deal with reality—to see life as it is and not as you might like it to be. There was a company not far from where I live that used to make yo-yos. For years and years it turned out yo-yos by the hundreds of thousands. It continued to do so even when the market for yo-yos started to decline. Rather than acknowledge that the yo-yo craze had run its course, and diversify into other products, the company ignored all of the signs and continued to grind out yo-yos. The people who ran that company clung stubbornly to the belief that the demand would bounce back, which ran right into the stumbling block of reality. The people who ran that company aren't there anymore. The old yo-yo plant now makes mattresses, and there is a huge pile of yo-yos in the local dump.

Many individuals are the same way. They keep building yo-yos when the world wants frisbees. But not the people who are working toward maximizing their self-profit. They see life as it really is; they are more objective and less emotional in their observations than most people.

You might ask, "What is the maximum self-profit?" I don't know. I don't know of anyone who had found it. Nor do I know of any business that has reached its maximum profit. A few decades ago some people started a little sandpaper business in Minnesota, and at each step in the growth of that business there were stockholders who unloaded its stock, figuring that now it had reached its potential. Now 3M Company has over $3 billion in sales annually and it is still growing.

I don't think there is any limit to your self-profit, either. There is always a layer beneath the layer you peel away. As you peel away each layer, you are getting closer to something, and I think that "something" is a more complete, more fulfilled life. You are growing while you are peeling. Conversely, if you don't peel, you won't grow.

The companies I know that are the most profitable are not necessarily those with the fewest problems. It often takes a risk to make a profit, and risk-taking leads to problems. That, too, is a characteristic of the people striving to maximize their self-profit. They take risks and they get in trouble. They have problems like everyone else—probably more of them than the individual who leads the "safe" life of constant routine and few challenges. But because of their objectivity and their ability to look at reality, they are not emotionally wrecked by every problem. More often than not they will view problems as opportunities, and set out to take advantage of these.

Self-profit seems to be greatest among individuals who do

not make a big distinction between work and play; they are not the kind who go to a nine-to-five job and then come home and sit in front of the television, drinking beer. Typically their work —not some exterior stimulant—provides them with excitement and pleasure.

The profitable companies and the profitable individuals might also be described as independent, flexible, spontaneous, open, disciplined, courageous, and humble. They usually have respect and confidence in their own abilities, and they don't follow the herd. If they are opposed to a popular stand, they usually let their opposition be known.

Some of the individuals Maslow studied and considered to be highly self-actualized were Thomas Jefferson, Eleanor Roosevelt, Albert Schweitzer, Ralph Waldo Emerson, Robert Benchley, and Benjamin Franklin.

You don't have to be a well-known politician or statesman or author to achieve significant self-profit. Above all, you don't have to be perfect. Everyone has warts. The people I know who have a high level of self-profit have feelings of guilt and self-doubt at times. They have temper outbursts like you and I, and they may even do things that put a temporary limit on their self-profit. I know a person who is a very creative and highly respected television producer who is doing all kinds of marvelous things with his life—but once or twice a year he goes on a tremendous bender that takes him out of action for several days. During the course of this binge he has a peculiar habit: He telephones famous people, or just people he knows, all over the world. In one night he can run up a phone bill of several hundred dollars. Sometimes he even arranges conference calls involving people in different parts of the country— or the world.

It's not the loss of the time or the money spent on his horrendous telephone bills that lowers his self-profit, but rather the feelings he is left with when he sobers up. He has an awful lot of remorse and guilt—especially over the telephone calls—and he must first deal with this before he can again be effective in those activities of his life where his self-profit lies.

There are many similar stories of individuals whose strivings for self-profit have been blocked by alcoholism. Alcoholics Anonymous is filled with them. The real accomplishment of AA has been to help individuals to lower the barriers between the individual and his self-profit.

I have observed that some highly motivated and highly profitable businesses also will, on occasions, act in ways to stifle their own profitability. I know of one company that has been successful for five years in fabricating steel for large buildings; the company will never be highly profitable because of ongoing strife with its union workers. This company is highly respected for its workmanship and integrity, and it has become ensnared in self-limiting games with the employees' union. Neither the management of the company nor the union leaders discuss how to maximize the profits for the benefit of both company and workers. Instead it is a them-versus-us contest every single time a new contract comes up. This adversary relationship, this pulling apart from within, is all that prevents the company from getting on with maximizing its potential. Labor-management issues are difficult matters, but I know of other companies similar to the steel fabricating company that don't have these problems because they don't have unions. From the outset, the management of these non-union companies decided that their profit potential would be determined in large part by the motivation of and rewards to their workers. So they offered their workers incentives such as profit sharing. They expressed concern for their employees in many other ways, and the employees saw no need for a union.

I'm not expressing anti-union sentiments; rather I'm trying to point out how even a successful business can place limitations on its profitability through self-defeating actions. There are more companies in no-growth, low-profit situations than there are dynamic, growing, highly-profitable companies.

Almost invariably when a psychologist describes successful, high-profit people the word "creative" comes into play. This would seem to indicate that only persons with a certain level of creativity can achieve high self-profit or else that creativity is in all of us and that the ones who learn to use it to its fullest will get the most self-profit. From my own observations I favor the latter—even though I have run across a number of people who say, "Oh, I'm not creative like she is." There is never any evidence to support this. Creativity isn't related exclusively to art or music or acting or writing, as so many people believe. A carpenter or a plumber or a housewife can be creative in finding new ways to solve old problems.

I don't think a person exists who has no creativity, but I know there are a lot of individuals who do not know how to use what they do have. These individuals are like businesses that fall into lifelong ruts, never seeking new challenges, new products, or new markets as long as they can survive comfortably without change.

There is no one class of people blessed with the creativity and ability to achieve great self-profit, and another class incapable of getting there. The road to self-profit is an endless road upon which all of us are traveling. The further we go, the better conditions are for us. But everyone is at a different place on this road.

I know a number of people who have traveled very far, indeed, along this road. They are very talented and very successful in their work, and they are willing to pay the price to achieve a great degree of self-profit. That price, as I have observed it, usually consists of plenty of hard work and risks. They are willing to take the risks of change, the risks of being creative, and the risks of failure.

I see very close correlations between the individuals and businesses that have achieved great self-profit. Those businesses that are most open to change and that are willing to take risks are the most profitable. Such a company will be highly actualized.

The individual with these same characteristics also will be highly actualized—which is *his* profit. But just because all people do not possess these same characteristics does not mean they will have no self-profit at all. They just haven't gotten as far along the road. To be sure, some people never do travel very far along that road, but still they are on it. They will profit according to how far they do get, which in turn depends on a variety of factors—not the least of which is how hard they want to work.

As you achieve greater self-profit you will have greater ability to see life clearly. If you are seeing life clearly only part of the time, you are limited in your self-profit. Many books have been written on how we do not see things that would be painful to acknowledge, and hear only what we want to hear, and say one thing when we mean another.

It appears evident that to achieve substantial self-profit is to grow beyond the need for such self-deception. The person with a driving goal for greater self-profit usually has sufficient self-esteem and self-confidence to deal with reality, no matter what it may bring.

Now, it might occur to you that if each of us has this same built-in goal of self-profit, why it is that some individuals never seem to make progress along the path toward achieving it? That question plagued me, too, and after some research I became convinced that some individuals—like some businesses—get into acting in negative, losing ways, as opposed to positive, profitable ways.

I have prepared a diagram (Figure 1) that shows what I believe happens in self-loss. There are three ways in which

SELF-LOSS CHART

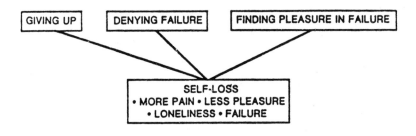

Figure 1

individuals ultimately move along into self-loss: They give up, they deny their failures, or they find pleasure in their failures.

In the first—giving up—the individual turns away from self-profit because of some difficulty or pain he has encountered in life. It is easier to be a failure than a success. Even though he ultimately finds pain, also, in having given up, he had adopted the negative attitude that he is deserving of this pain.

You can see a lot of people around you giving up, but some of the most visible examples in our society today are the teen-agers who aren't making it in school. Because they have not been motivated to succeed, they fall behind and begin to get bad grades. Even though this failure may be painful, too much discipline and effort are required to turn things around. When that happens, they have begun to give up. As they continue down this negative pathway, they experience greater and greater self-loss.

A second pathway to self-loss is for a person who experiences failure in life (as we all do from time to time) to begin denying his failure. Whatever went wrong was someone else's fault. These people busy themselves building excuses and rationalizations for their failures, because there is pain associated with failure. If they can place the blame for the failure somewhere else, they reason, then the pain will go with it. This self-deception doesn't work for long, of course, and the pain returns. Individuals caught up in this are so busy denying their failures that they have precious little time to build some successes.

A third road to self-loss is to find pleasure in failure. These individuals admit their failures and welcome new ones. Each new failure reinforces their belief that nothing they can do will ever change things. So they, too, try to block out the pain and increase their pleasure, usually through the use of drugs or alcohol or compulsively self-destructive behavior of another kind—like gambling to excess.

People who act in criminal ways, or misbehave in ways that are detrimental to the people around them, or hurt other people, are doing negative things that can lead to self-loss.

They will have less pleasure and more pain. They will be lonely and they will be failures. They will be emotionally motivated, rather than rationally motivated. Rather than the ever-expanding, beautiful world that opens up to the person achieving self-profit, the individual moving toward self-loss will find a smaller personal world, with little beauty or joy in it.

Businesses also get into acting in losing ways. There is a little roofing company in my hometown that was polluting the air in its neighborhood for years and years, despite public outcry. The company must have received over one hundred tickets and fines for polluting. The neighbors would complain and take the company to court, and the company fought the courts and everyone else. The courts finally brought them up on charges. The company had to pay large fines and eventually it went broke. That is what I call negative action. That company had a choice between taking a negative or a positive pathway and it chose the negative. It could have acknowledged its wrongdoing and found a way to correct it, and it probably would have survived. If it had chosen this positive pathway, I am sure the community would even have gotten behind the company and helped it overcome whatever hardships were associated with cleaning up its pollution.

I think another good example of negative action is the business the Mafia runs. Some people might think the Mafia is successful because it makes a lot of money, but I think *The Godfather*, [2] which describes the business and social life of the Mafia, indicates how much pain and how little pleasure is in that business. I can't help but feel that all those people in that business hurt, and they hurt greatly.

Each of us acts in negative ways from time to time, but that doesn't mean we are lost causes or that we are evil. It usually means that we have some problem we haven't worked out, which is causing us to act that way. If you are spending a great amount of time in negative actions so that they seem to be controlling your life, then you should consider ways to give up these negative influences and get back on the road toward self-profit.

A woman who was in one of my life planning groups is the perfect example of a type of negative action that is rampant in our society—overeating. At one time, this woman had been thin and beautiful, but she began to eat compulsively as a means of avoiding an unhappiness in her life. She allowed this overeating to control her life and as she got heavier and heavier she became negative about everything. Eventually she weighed over three hundred pounds.

One day someone from a weight-control organization got her to go to a meeting, and she began to look at her compulsiveness and what it was doing to her life. She came to realize how negative this compulsiveness was and that it was preventing her from reaching her full potential—so she replaced it with more positive behavior. She lost the weight, got down to 130 pounds, and began to like herself again. She then began to work on her love needs, which had been missing in her life, and ultimately on the other basic needs which must be met if the individual is to move forward toward self-profit. Her personal life became more rewarding, and her business life improved immensely. Her sales commission earnings tripled because she stopped acting negatively and got into positive pathways.

From what I have observed, people who act in negative ways must abandon those ways before they can make any substantial progress toward their goal.

A second major roadblock to moving along the pathway toward self-profit is the pursuit of false goals. You probably know people who establish as their goal in life the accumulation of great material wealth. If only they had a million dollars in the bank, the birds would sing again, the color would return to the flowers, and there would be laughter in the air. They cannot see or hear beauty in their obsession over their goal. And what happens when they achieve their goal? Most often they still aren't happy. If material riches were the ultimate goal, why is it we so often hear about wealthy individuals being unhappy and into crime and other inappropriate behavior?

Many women in our society were raised to believe that the only true and good life for a woman consisted of getting married and raising a family. Having done that, why are so many of these women today experiencing great unhappiness with their lives?

Making money and raising a family are not our ultimate goals in life. They are subgoals that may help us achieve our ultimate goal, which is the greatest possible self-profit. But they are not primary goals, no more than signing a new contract for a million dollars in new orders is the primary goal of a business.

The real purpose of the business is to come in at the end of the year with an annual report that shows it made significant strides toward achieving its long-term goal. That year's activities are important, to be sure, just like your success in creating a happy and healthy family situation is important. But in each case these are simply subgoals or intermediate goals related to the achievement of a long-term goal.

When a business is repeatedly reporting increased profits, a lot of good things are happening to it. People are buying its stock and talking about it and praising its management. The business likes to have glowing reports in the newspaper about its increased profits.

If you were to publish a newspaper on people who were reporting their self-profit, you would—just like a business— look for a number you could put on that self-profit: "Joe Smith Reports 15 Percent Increase in Self-profit for the Year." Joe made some real progress toward his goal, and as a result everyone wants to buy his stock. People want to be his friend and be around him because he's a dynamic, interesting, assured man.

The general manager of a business that reports a good increase in profits is very likely to get a raise from the board of directors. That is his bonus for helping to move the company along toward its goal. The same thing is going to happen to you. You are going to feel better, you are going to really be turning in some great results, and the significant people in your life are going to like that and have greater appreciation of you. They are going to be excited about you, and you are likely to develop closer friends and more people who really care about you—and want to be with you because you're not into negative living. They will know you are not out to destroy them and you are not going to pollute their environment like the roofing company did to its environment.

As you consider this discussion about goals, there is another important psychological insight you should be aware of: the path toward maximum self-profit has an infinite succession of plateaus. Shortly after you achieve some objective (reach a plateau), you will find that new challenges pop up and off you go toward an even higher plateau. There is no end to it, as you will discover when you move along with your life plan in action. Life will become an exciting series of adventures, calling forth from you all of the creativity you were born with.

And always you will be striving for that common goal of all people, variously called self-actualization or gaining authenticity or self-profit. As you begin making real progress toward that goal, a lot of good things will happen to you. It is going to be fun to be alive. You're going to like to wake up in the morning and put your feet on the floor and charge off into the day.

Once you are working successfully toward your goal, you are going to become a blue-chip enterprise.

Peel Your Own Onion may be obtained by writing to author at DAVID C. PROSSER & ASSOC., 7550 France Ave. South, Suite 214, Edina, MN 55435

CHAPTER THREE

For The Adventure and The Challenge

Another unique achiever, Dr. Wayne Dyer, is a brilliant counselor and therapist who admits unabashedly that he has done, and continues to do, everything he has ever wanted to do in life, has achieved all of his goals, and continues to set new ones. He insists this is something we can all accomplish and supports his premise through logic and case histories from his own files. He has been a professor of Psychology at St. John's University in Queens, New York, and is the author of several textbooks, in addition to his motivational books which include *The Sky's the Limit, Pulling Your Strings, Gifts From Eykis* and his latest one, *What Do You Really Want For Your Children?* He is also one of the leading motivational speakers in the country.

What We See Is What We Get
When I first glanced at *Your Erroneous Zones* some eight years ago, I thought it was a sex-education book. Being a red-blooded Italian, I wanted to learn more about my

"erogenous zones." When I discovered my mistake, I laughed at myself all the way to the cash register, because, of course, once having glanced through it, it had to go home with me. My wife and I had a good laugh together when I told her about it, then a few more as we started reading and sharing *Your Erroneous Zones.* In Dr. Dyer's words, "While I do not believe that mental health should be treated in a flip manner, neither do I support the notion that it must be a humorless enterprise," however, Dr. Wayne Dyer's theme is that the way we "choose" to look at a situation can make all the differences as to whether it is a positive or a negative influence in our lives. The "erroneous zones" are defined as "areas of self-destructive behavior" and Dr. Dyer has written each chapter as if it were a counseling session. A particular "erroneous zone" is explored in depth in three stages;

First . . . a look is taken at the historical antecedents for the behavior in our culture (a person can then understand why he gets trapped in a self-defeating zone), then details are given as to specific behavior for that "erroneous zone."

Second. . . . he examines reasons why a person hangs on to behavior which doesn't make him happy. This includes a look at the psychological support system a person will erect to maintain self-defeating behavior rather than give it up.

Third . . . each chapter concludes with some straightforward strategies for eliminating self-nullifying behavior.

There are two central ideas that recur:

The first emphasizes you have the ability to make choices about your emotions . . . *"that you are the sum total of your choices,*:

The second urges you to *"take charge of your present moment."*

It was very difficult choosing just one chapter from this book, which I consider to be one of the finest of its genre, however, the chapter "Exploring the Unknown" covers an area I feel strongly about. Reaching out to the unknown has enriched my life so greatly I become almost messianic in my zeal to encourage others to experiment in that direction.

Expect the Unexpected

In any new venture, I not only expect the unexpected, I look forward to it as the ingredient that adds the spice. Our civilization has grown and developed as a result of the unexpected. Many of the world's great discoveries and inventions came about by accident during a search for something else. . . . and there is always someone ready to take an unexpected discovery into a tangential unknown, thereby illuminating other hidden surprises.

Twice in my personal business career I have been the recipient of a product which was incidentally developed for use in another technology. On both occasions, I trusted my business sense enough to take a slight detour in my existing life style and make a choice; after soliciting and obtaining the international marketing rights for both of those products, they became world-wide successes. One of them was the Solar Pool Blanket for swimming pools. The pool blanket was an extension of Sealed Air Corporation's highly successful air-filled bubble packaging material which is used world-wide to transport breakables. Serendipity set in and I was off and running. I would never have been able to achieve the success we did with the Sealed Air Solar Pool Blanket without the cooperation and invaluable assistance of the corporation and the executives at the helm. T.J. Dermot Dunphy, (Chief executive officer of Sealed Air Corporation, a multinational company whose most famous packaging product, is known popularly as "the bubble sheets children of all ages love to pop,") exemplifies the executive we've been discussing, one who is willing to take a risk with the unexpected and the unknown, one with the skill to turn the unexpected to advantage. His door is always open to the new. I can sell the proverbial "refrigerator to an Eskimo" but if I have nothing to vend . . . I have no job. Sealed Air worked with me constantly to improve the pool blanket which is, by the way, made of an impregnable form of those famous bubbles, and then to add new items to the Pool Division they had created to manufacture the blanket. Because of this success we shared, I would not hesitate to go to Dermot with a "find" or to suggest new applications of his existing products. In the ten years I have known Dermot, we have always mixed personal reflections and laughter with our business discussions; the charm of Dermot's Irish ancestry is a welcome diversion in the hectic pace of the corporate world, and in my opinion, has been a major factor in Sealed Air's successful growth from a corporation which had sales of approximately five million dollars and a small operating loss to a corporation which today has sales of almost two hundred million dollars.

Reach for a Star
Many have deplored America's venture into the unknown of outer space as a fool's errand, or a super stunt, shouting of the many ills that need to be cured on earth before we should even think of reaching for a star. Unfortunately, those deprecating voices found responsive ears and the space program was cut back, yet ironically, it is in space where some of the greatest progress towards curing some of the literal ills of the world are being made; for example, space provides the pure milieu essential to the development of serums beyond a purity now available on earth. You get a better perspective when you

realize that the annual cost of the Apollo program was the same as the annual expenditure for cosmetics or cigarettes; even in its present reduced state, the list of spin-offs from the space programs, which are bettering the life of all on this space ship we call earth, goes on and on. It is never a waste to reach for a star . . . at the very least you might reach the top of the mountain.

Be Flexible

We can map out a route, knowing exactly where we are going, and still meet with the unexpected . . . or we can follow the same route day after day, wearing blinders, refusing to acknowledge the unexpected until it hits us in the face, but the rigidity of this approach stifles creativity. I know some who consider rigidity and implacability to be signs of strength that prove they have will-power, or character, or whatever; yet the philosophical definition of what characterizes the most highly-evolved person, is the ability to adapt, to flow with a situation, to meet the unexpected.

What Is There to Fear?

Exploring the unknown should not be based upon success or failure. Anytime we are experiencing to the fullest, that is instant success. If we have a fear of loss, realize that the only thing we can be sure of is "change," and that things will pass out of our realm. How we view the "change" makes the difference of whether it is one for our advancement. I never judge a change as good or bad . . . it is just a change, and I look for the expected and the unexpected good in it. If something goes out of our life or our experience, it is because it is no longer in harmony with our inner beliefs and goals. The secret is to arrange our inner landscape correctly, then the outer changes happening to us, will conform to our inner beliefs and be satisfying and productive steps forward.

If we have any fears, they can be looked at logically and non-judgmentally, and then can usually be seen as useless gear to be discarded. I have left many figurative base camps littered with debris I refused to take along as excess baggage on my upward climb. Unfortunately, fear and anxiety are readily available to all of us (in fact, someone is always trying to gift you with some). Good judgment easily outdistances fear and anxiety . . . items which you'll never find in my backpack. If you don't pack them in the first place, you'll never face the decision of whether to leave them at the base camp.

Establish a Base Camp

Before the attempt is made to scale a top peak, a base camp must be established. The climber knows he must not be burdened with equipment he won't need on the ascent or at the top. At the base camp he leaves tents and other gear judged to be extra weight and superfluous to the climb. He knows this gear will be waiting for his comfort and well-being when he returns from the peak. It is his safety zone from which he can explore out in any direction. It will help us in our personal climb if we establish base camps, as well as recognizing the ones already in place. I consider my home to be my base camp. I'm lucky in having a partner there who, in essence, "keeps the fire going" while I go exploring. The fact that I have this base camp to return to, gives me a sense of security which allows me to reach out farther than I could without it. I'm very appreciative of the support which I have always received from my lovely wife, Joyce, and my two beautiful daughters, Jessica and Dina.

There are times when the sense of being alone on the mountain is overwhelming; it is times like that when I recall the back-up crew who helped me to get there, and who are plugging for my success; you too should take notice of the loyal "Sherpas" who have given you the support and encouragement to start your climb; without them, a base camp can be a very frightening place.

Don't Underestimate Curiosity

In the final analysis, I believe that my greatest assets are my insatiable curiosity and a tremendous energy level. Combined, they have propelled me into scores of adventures. If I lived to be a thousand years old and expended my energy to the utmost, I doubt if I would be able to explore and experience everything my curiosity questions. Don't underestimate curiosity . . . it becomes a reality when you are willing to familiarize yourself with the unfamiliar. Since you don't have a thousand years, live your life on the premise that right now is the only moment you will have and experience as much as you can for as long as you can . . . to simplify . . . see the world as yours.

Trust Yourself

If you tend to avoid making decisions for fear of the unknown or the unfamiliar (whether it is a small thing or a big one), your life style will be safe, but about as bland as the chalk that climbers use on their hands for greater friction on the rocks. I challenge you to trust yourself . . . to live life to the fullest . . . experience to the utmost. Dare to do! Choose to do!

Book Title: Your Erroneous Zones
Author: Dr. Wayne Dyer
Publisher: Harper & Row, New York
Chapter: Exploring the Unknown

Exploring the Unknown

Only the insecure strive for security.

You may be a safety expert—an individual who shuns the unknown in favor of always knowing where he is going, and what he can expect when he gets there. Early training in our society tends to encourage caution at the expense of curiosity, safety at the expense of adventure. Avoid the questionable, stay in areas that you know, never wander into the unknown. These early messages can become a psychological barrier that prevents your own personal fulfillment and present-moment happiness in countless ways.

Albert Einstein, a man who devoted his life to exploring the unknown, said in an article entitled "What I Believe" in *Forum* (October 1930),

The most beautiful thing we can experience is the mysterious. It is the true source of all art and science.

YOUR ERRONEOUS ZONES By Wayne W. Dyer Copyright © 1976 by Wayne W. Dyer Reprinted by pernission of Harper & Row, Publishers, Inc.

35

He might also have said it is the source of all growth and excitement as well.

But too many people equate the unknown with danger. The purpose of life, they think, is to deal with certainty, and to always know where they are headed. Only the foolhardy risk exploring the fuzzy areas of life, and when they do, they end up being surprised, hurt, and worst of all, unprepared. As a young scout you were told to *Be Prepared.* But how can you prepare for the unknown? Obviously, you cannot! Therefore avoid it and you'll never end up with egg on your face. Be safe, don't take risks, follow the road maps—even if it is dull.

Perhaps you're getting tired of all that certainty, knowing what every day will be like before it has been lived. You can't grow if you already know the answers before the questions have even been asked. Probably the times you most remember are those in which you were spontaneously alive, doing whatever you wanted, and delightfully anticipating the mysterious.

We hear the cultural messages of certainty throughout life. They began with family and are reinforced by educators. The child learns to avoid experimentation and is encouraged to avoid the unknown. Don't get lost. Have the right answers. Stay with your own kind. If you still cling to these fearful encouragements to security, now is the time to break free. Get rid of the idea that you can't try out new and doubtful behavior. You can if you choose to. It begins with an understanding of your conditioned reflex to avoid new experiences.

Openness to New Experiences

If you believe in yourself fully, no activity is beyond your potential. The entire gamut of human experience is yours to enjoy, once you decide to venture into territory where you don't have guarantees. Think of the people who are regarded as geniuses and were spectacularly effective in their lifetimes.

They weren't people who could do only one thing well. They weren't individuals who avoided the unknown. Benjamin Franklin, Ludwig van Beethoven, Leonardo da Vinci, Jesus Christ, Albert Einstein, Galileo, Bertrand Russell, George Bernard Shaw, Winston Churchill, these and many like them were pioneers, adventurers into new, unreliable areas. They were people, just like you, set apart only in that they were willing to traverse areas where others dared not tread. Albert Schweitzer, another Renaissance Man, once said, "Nothing human is alien to me." You can look at yourself with new eyes, and open yourself up to experiences that you've never even considered as a part of your own human potential, or you can do the same things, the same way, until you reach your coffin. It is a fact that great men remind you of no other, and their greatness is generally discernible in the quality of exploration and the boldness with which they explored the unknown.

Opening yourself up to new experiences means surrendering the notion that it is better to tolerate something familiar than to work at changing it because change is fraught with uncertainty. Perhaps you've adopted a stance that the self (you) is fragile, and easily shattered if you enter areas where you've never been before. This is a myth. You are a tower of strength. You are not going to collapse or fall apart if you encounter something new. In fact, you stand a much better chance of avoiding psychological collapse if you eliminate some of the routine and sameness in your life. Boredom is debilitating and psychologically unhealthy. Once you lose interest in life you are potentially shatterable. You won't choose that mythological nervous breakdown if you add a little spicy uncertainty to your life.

You may also have adopted the "if it's unusual I must stay away from it" mentality, which inhibits your openness to new experiences. Thus, if you see deaf people using sign language, you watch with curiosity but never attempt to converse with them. Similarly, when you encounter people who speak a foreign language, rather than work it out and attempt somehow to communicate, you very likely just wander off, and avoid the vast unknown of communicating in other than your own spoken language. There are uncountable activities and people who are considered taboo merely because they are unknown. Thus homosexuals, transvestites, the handicapped, the retarded, nudists and the like, are in the category of the obscure. You are not quite certain how to behave, and therefore you avoid the entire business.

You may also believe that you must have a reason for doing something; otherwise what's the point of doing it? Balderdash! You can do anything you want just because you want to, and for no other reason. You don't need a reason for anything that you do. Looking for a reason for everything is the kind of thinking that keeps you from new and exciting experiences. As a child you could play with a grasshopper for an hour, for no reason but that you liked it. Or you could climb a hill, or take an exploratory trip in the woods. Why? Because you wanted to. But as an adult, you have to come up with a good reason for things. This passion for reasons keeps you from opening up and growing. What freedom to know that you don't have to justify anything to anyone, including yourself, ever again.

Emerson, in his Journal of April 11, 1834, observed

Four snakes gliding up and down a hollow for no purpose that I could see. Not to eat. Not for love . . . But only gliding.

You can do whatever you want because you want to and for no other reason. This kind of thinking will open up new vistas of experience and help to eliminate the fear of the unknown that you may have adopted as a life-style.

Rigidity vs. Spontaneity

Take a hard look at your spontaneity. Can you open up to something new or do you rigidly hang onto your accustomed behavior? Spontaneity means being able to try anything, at the spur of the second, just because it is something you'd enjoy. You may even discover that it's something you don't enjoy doing but you did enjoy attempting it. It is likely that you will be condemned as irresponsible or incautious, but what does the judgment of others matter when you're having such a marvelous time discovering the unknown. There are many people in high places who find it difficult to be spontaneous. They live out their lives in a rigid fashion, oblivious to the absurdities they blindly follow. Democrats and Republicans support the statements of top party leaders and vote the party line. Cabinet officials who speak spontaneously and honestly are very often ex-cabinet officials. Independent thinking is discouraged, and there are official guidelines for how one should think and speak. Yesmen are not spontaneous men. They desperately fear the unknown. They fit in. They do what they are told. They never challenge but rigidly adhere to what is expected of them. Where are you on this dimension? Can you be your own person in this area? Can you spontaneously take the avenues that don't always lead to a sure thing?

The rigid never grow. They tend to do things the same way they've always done them. A colleague of mine who teaches graduate courses for teachers frequently asks the old-timers, who have spent thirty years or more in the classroom, "Have you really been teaching for thirty years or have you been teaching one year, thirty times?" And you, dear reader, have you really lived 10,000 or more days or have you lived one day, 10,000 or more times? A good question to ask yourself as you work toward more spontaneity in your life.

Prejudice and Rigidity

Rigidity is the basis of all prejudice, which means to *pre-*judge. Prejudice is based less on hate or even dislike for certain people, ideas, or activities than on the fact that it's easier and safer to stay with the known. That is, people who are like you. Your prejudices seem to work for you. They keep you away from people, things and ideas that are unknown and potentially troublesome. Actually they work against you by preventing you from exploring the unknown. Being spontaneous means eliminating your prejudgments and allowing yourself to meet and deal with new people and ideas. The prejudgments themselves are a safety valve for avoiding murky or puzzling provinces and preventing growth. If you don't trust anyone you can't get a "handle on"; it really means you don't trust yourself on unfamiliar grounds.

The "Always Having a Plan" Trap

There is no such thing as planned spontaneity. It is a contradiction in terms. We all know people who go through their lives with a road map and a list, unable to vary their life a single iota from the original plan. A plan is not necessarily unhealthy, but falling in love with the plan is the real neurosis. You may have a life plan for what you'll do at age 25, 30, 40, 50, 70, etc., and then you simply consult your agenda to see where you ought to be, rather than making a new decision each day and having a strong enough belief in yourself to be able to alter the plan. Don't let the plan become bigger than you.

Henry was a client of mine who was in his middle twenties. He suffered desperately from the having-a-plan-neurosis, and as a consequence he missed out on many exciting life opportunities. When he was twenty-two he was offered a position in another state. He was petrified about the move. Would he be able to make it in Georgia? Where would he live? How about his parents and friends? The fear of the unknown literally immobilized Henry, and he turned down what might have been a chance at advancement, exciting new work and a brand new environment, in favor of staying where he was. It was this experience that brought Henry to counseling. He felt that his own rigid adherence to a plan was keeping him from growing, and yet he was afraid to break out and try something new. After one exploratory session, it was revealed that Henry was a veritable plan freak. He always ate the same breakfast, planned his clothing days in advance, had his dresser drawers arranged perfectly by color and size. Moreover, he imposed his plan on his family as well. He expected his children to have things in their place and his wife to conform to a rigid set of rules that he had laid down. In short, Henry was a very unhappy, albeit organized person. He lacked creativity, innovation and personal warmth. He was in fact, a plan unto himself, with his goal in life to get everything into its proper place. With counseling, Henry began to try some spontaneous living. He saw his plans as manipulators of others, and as convenient escapes from wandering into the risky unknown. He soon eased up on his family and allowed them to be different from what he expected them to be. After several months, Henry actually applied for a job in a firm that would require him to move frequently. The very thing that he originally feared became desirable. While Henry is by no means a totally spontaneous person, he has effectively challenged some of the neurotic thinking that supported his previously planned-out existence. He is working on it every day, and learning to enjoy living, rather than living out his life in a ritualized fashion.

Security: Internal and External Varieties

A long time ago you learned how to write a high school theme or essay. You were taught that you need a good introduction, a well-organized body and a conclusion. Unfortunately, you may have applied the same logic to your life, and come to see the whole business of living as a theme. The introduction was your childhood wherein you were preparing to be a person. The body is your adult life, which is organized and planned out in preparation for your conclusion, which is the retirement and happy ending. All of this organized thinking keeps you from living your present moments. Living according to this plan implies a guarantee that everything will be okay forever. Security, the final plan, is for cadavers. Security means knowing what is going to happen. Security means no excitement, no risks, no challenge. Security means no growth and no growth means death. Besides, security is a myth. As long as you are a person on earth, and the system stays the same, you can never have security. And even if it weren't a myth, it would be a horrible way to live. Certainty eliminates excitement—and growth.

The word security as used here refers to external guarantees, possessions such as money, a house and a car, to bulwarks such as a job or a position in the community. But there is a different kind of security that is worth pursuing, and this is the internal security of trusting yourself to handle anything that may come down the pike. This is the only lasting security, the only real security. Things can break down, a depression can wipe out your money, your house can be repossessed, but you, you can be a rock of self-esteem. You can believe so much in you and your internal strength that things or others will be seen as mere pleasant but superfluous adjuncts to your life.

Try this little exercise. Suppose that right now, this second, as you are reading this book, someone swooped down on you, stripped you naked, and carted you off in a helicopter. No warning, no money, nothing but yourself. Supposing you were flown to the middle of Red China and dropped in a field. You would be up against new language, new habits, and new climate, and all you would have is yourself. Would you survive or collapse? Could you make friends, get food, shelter and the like, or would you simply lie there and moan about how unfortunate you were to have this catastrophe visited on you? If you need external security, you'd perish, for all of your goods would have been taken away. But if you have internal security and are not afraid of the unknown, then you would survive. Security can then be redefined as the knowledge that you can handle anything, including having no external security. Don't be trapped by that kind of external security, since it robs you of your ability to live and grow and fulfill yourself. Take a look at those people without external security, people who don't have it all mapped out. Perhaps they are way ahead of the game. At least they can try new things and avoid the trap of always having to stay with the safe.

James Kavanaugh in *Will You Be My Friend?* writes tellingly about security in his little poem called "Some Day."

> Someday I'll walk away
> And be free
> And leave the sterile ones
> Their secure sterility.
> I'll leave without a forwarding address
> And walk across some barren wilderness
> To drop the world there.
> Then wander free of care
> Like an unemployed Atlas.*

*Los Angeles: Nash Publishing Corp., 1971.

Achievement as Security

But the "walking away" to "be free," as Kavanaugh puts it, is difficult as long as you carry around the conviction that you must achieve. Fear of failure is a powerful fear in our society, one inculcated in childhood and often carried throughout life.

You may be surprised to hear this, but failure does not exist. Failure is simply someone else's opinion of how a certain act should have been completed. Once you believe that no act must be performed in any specific other-directed way, then failing becomes impossible.

There may, however, be occasions when you will fail in some given task according to your own standards. The important thing here is not to equate the act with your own self-worth. Not to succeed in a particular endeavor is not to fail as a person. It is simply not being successful with that particular trial at that particular present moment.

Try to imagine using failure as a description of an animal's behavior. Consider a dog barking for fifteen minutes, and someone saying, "He really isn't very good at barking, I'd give him a "C." How absurd! It is impossible for an animal to fail because there is no provision for evaluating natural behavior. Spiders construct webs, not successful or unsuccessful webs. Cats hunt mice; if they aren't successful in one attempt, they simply go after another. They don't lie there and whine, complaining about the one that got away, or have a nervous breakdown because they failed. Natural behavior simply is! So why not apply the same logic to your own behavior and rid yourself of the fear of failure.

The push to achieve comes from three of the most self-destructive words in our culture. You've heard them and used them thousands of times. Do your best! This is the cornerstone of the achievement neurosis. Do your best at everything you do. What's wrong with taking a mediocre bicycle ride, or going for an average walk in the park? Why not have some activities in your life which you just do, rather than do to the best of your ability? The do-your-best neurosis can keep you from trying new activities and enjoying old ones.

At one time I counseled an eighteen-year-old high school senior named Louann, who was imbued with the achievement standard. Louann was a straight A student, and had been since she first set foot in a school. She worked long tedious hours on her school work, and as a result she had no time for being a person. She was a veritable computer of book knowledge. Yet Louann was painfully shy around boys, never even having held hands let alone dated. She had developed a nervous twitch which came into play whenever we talked about this side of her personality. Louann had placed all of her emphasis on being an achieving student at the expense of her total development. In working with Louann, I asked her what was more important in her life. "What you know, or how you feel?" Even though she was a valedictorian, she was lacking inner peace and was actually very unhappy. She began to place some importance on her feelings, and because she was such an excellent learner, she applied the same rigorous standards to learning new social behaviors as she had to her school work. Louann's mother called me a year later and told me that she was concerned because her daughter had received her very first "C" in a college freshman English class. I recommended that she make a big production out of it, and take her out for dinner in celebration.

Some Strategies for Coming to Grips with the Mysterious and the Unknown

• Make selective efforts to try new things even if you are tempted to stay with the familiar. For example, at a restaurant order a new dish. Why? Because it would be different and you might enjoy it.

• Invite a collection of people to your home who represent

widely divergent points of view. Go with the unknown rather than your typical clique of acquaintances wherein you can predict everything that will take place.

• Give up having to have a reason for everything you do. When someone asks you why, remember that you don't have to come up with a reasonable answer that will satisfy them. You can do what you decide just because you want to.

• Begin to take some risks that will get you out of your routine. Perhaps an unplanned vacation with no reservations or maps, where you just trust yourself to handle whatever might come along. Interview for a new job, or talk with someone that you've been avoiding because you were afraid of not knowing what might happen. Take a new route to work, or have dinner at midnight. Why? Just because it's different and you want to do it.

• Entertain yourself with a fantasy in which you allow yourself to have anything you want. No holds barred. You have all of the money to do anything you want for a two-week period. You'll find that almost all of your mental meanderings are indeed attainable for you, that you don't want the moon or the unreachable, but simply things that you can achieve if you eliminate the fear of the unknown and go after them.

• Take a risk that might involve some personal upheaval, but which would be intensely rewarding to you. For several years a colleague of mine had told his students and clients about the need for trying the unknown in their lives. But in many ways his advice was hypocritical since he stayed with the same university, consulting work and comfortable life-style. He had stated that anyone could handle new and different situations, but he continued to stay with the familiar. In 1974 he decided to live in Europe for six months because it was something he had always wanted to do. He taught two courses for an overseas graduate program in educational psychology and learned first-hand (experientially rather than verbally) that he could handle the doubtful. After three weeks in Germany, because of his inner security, he had as many opportunities to conduct workshops, work with clients and give lectures as he had in New York where he was comfortable with the familiar surroundings. Even in a remote village in Turkey, where he lived for two months, he was busier than he had been in New York. At last, out of experience, he knew that he could go anywhere, at any time, and be effective, not because of the external circumstances, but because he could handle the unknown, exactly as he handled the known, with his own inner strength and skills.

• Whenever you find yourself avoiding the unknown, ask yourself, "What's the worst thing that could happen to me?" You'll probably see that the fears of the unknown are out of proportion to the reality of the consequences.

• Try to do something silly like going barefoot in the park, or skinny-dipping. Try out some of the things that you've always avoided because you "Mustn't ever do such things." Open your own personal horizons to new experiences that you've previously avoided because they were silly or inane.

• Remind yourself that the fear of failure is very often the fear of someone else's disapproval or ridicule. If you let them have their own opinions, which have nothing to do with you, you can begin to evaluate your behavior in your own, rather than their terms. You'll come to see your abilities not as better or worse, but as simply different from others.

• Make an attempt to do some things that you've always avoided, with the sentence "I'm just not good at that." You can spend an afternoon painting a picture and have a hell of a time. If the end product is less than masterful, you haven't failed, you've had a half day of pleasure. On my living room wall is a painting that is aesthetically horrible. Everyone who visits comments or painfully avoids commenting on how bad it really is. In the lower left-hand corner are inscribed the words, "To you, Dr. Dyer, I give you not my best." It is from a former student who had avoided painting all of her life because she'd learned a long time ago that she was bad at it. She spent a weekend painting just for her own pleasure and it is one of my most prized gifts.

• Remember that the opposites of growth are sameness and death. Thus, you can resolve to live each day in a new way, being spontaneous and alive, or you can fear the unknown and remain the same—psychologically dead.

• Have a talk with those people in your life who you feel are most responsible for your fear of the unknown. State in no uncertain terms that you intend to do new things, and check out their reactions. You may find that their incredulity is one of the things that you've always worried about in the past, and as a result you chose immobilization over those disapproving looks. Now that you can handle the looks, state your Declaration of Independence from their control.

• Instead of "Do your best in everything" as a credo for you and your children, try "Select the things that are important to you, and work hard at them, and in the rest of your life, just do." It's O.K. not to do your best! In fact, the whole "Do your Best," syndrome is a myth. You never do your absolute best, nor does anyone else. There is always room for improvement, since perfection is not a human attribute.

• Don't let your convictions keep you stagnant. Believing something out of past experience and hanging onto that belief is an avoidance of reality. There is only what is now, and the truth of the present may not be the truth of the past. Assess your behavior not on what you believe, but in terms of what is and what you experience in the present. By allowing yourself to experience, rather than coloring your reality with beliefs, you'll find the unknown a fantastic place to be.

• Remember, nothing human is alien to you. You can be anything you choose. Imprint this on your mind and remind yourself of it when you fall into your typically safe evasive behavior.

• Become aware of avoiding the unknown as you are doing it. At that moment begin a dialogue with yourself. Tell yourself it's okay if you don't know where you are going at every moment of your life. Awareness of routine is the first step in changing it.

• Deliberately fail at something. Are you really less of a person for losing a tennis game or painting a bad picture or are you still a worthwhile individual who just enjoyed some pleasant activity?

• Have a conversation with a member of a group that you've avoided in the past. You'll soon discover that your prejudices, when challenged by you, are keeping you stagnant and uninteresting. If you pre-judge anyone, you prevent yourself from dealing with them honestly since your viewpoint has already been established. The more different kinds of people you encounter, the more likely you are to remark to yourself how much you've been missing, and how foolish your fears have been. With these insights, the unknown will become an area for ever-increasing exploration rather than something to shun.

Some Final Thoughts on Fearing the Unknown

The above suggestions represent some constructive means of fighting fear of the unknown. The whole process begins with new insights into your avoidance behavior, followed by actively challenging the old behavior and moving in new directions. Just imagine if the great inventors or explorers of the past had feared the unknown. The entire population of the world would still reside in the Tigris-Euphrates Valley. The unknown is where growth resides. Both for civilization and for the individual.

Think of a road with a fork in it. In one direction lies security, in the other the great uncharted unknown. Which road would you take?

Robert Frost answered the question in *The Road Not Taken.*

> Two roads diverged in a wood, and I—
> I took the one less traveled by,
> And that has made all the difference.

The choice is yours. Your erroneous zone of fear of the unknown is waiting to be replaced by new exciting activities that will bring pleasure to your life. You don't have to know where you're going—as long as you're on your way.

CHAPTER FOUR

To Harness Stress

Sometimes in order to scale new heights we must harness the anxiety and stress within us so that they yield further energy. Donald Norfolk has been deeply involved in stress management for many years. He was a great admirer of Dr. Hans Selye, who is considered to be one of the world's leading authorities on stress, based on his experiments and research conducted in his Montreal laboratories. In addition to organizing study groups in relaxation therapy for doctors and psychiatrists, Mr. Norfolk has conducted "Learn To Relax" weekends for businessmen and their wives, plus Stress Seminars for Senior Executives. His further credentials include frequent contributions to numerous radio shows, including his own program, "Your Very Good Health."

Donald Norfolk's book, *The Stress Factor,* points out that stress is a necessary ingredient in our lives, that indeed it "prods" us into action . . . that anxiety improves performance until a certain optimum level has been reached. Beyond that point, performance deteriorates as higher levels of anxiety are attained . . . the goal is to find your optimum stress level. Mr. Norfolk cites studies done both in Europe and America, confirmin ˙ ˙¹ at stress is a world-wide phenomenon. He covers a myriad oɪ situations which can cause stress, including our self-defeating behavior, then he gives suggestions on how to handle it as it arises; he reinforces the idea that the choice of how to handle it is ours. Some topics covered include: learning to express your feelings, realizing your goals and abilities, the value of exercise, how colors, temperatures and lighting affect stress, coping with change, turning work into play and many more subjects. Finally, he emphasizes the wisdom of a healthy retreat from time to time and offers guidelines for this relaxation from stress. In other words, allow yourself a break from the humdrum and the stress in your life will not get used to hanging around. Kick it out . . . share your stress with a consuming hobby or activity. My hobby is mountain climbing. The relief of stress is simple for me when I prioritize my life so as to leave room for my hobby. Whatever your hobby is, stamp collecting or mountain climbing, don't just dabble in it. Give it the same depth of interest and intensity you display in your business or profession. Whatever you are into, model trains, toy soldiers, tennis, whatever you fancy . . . you have the choice to dabble in it, getting little out of it, or to become involved and enjoy the experience to the fullest.

Stress Can Be Productive

Because of my energy, curiosity and my desire to excel and experience life to the fullest, I sometimes play the game at hand too intensely. The resultant stress must be handled constructively or it becomes a negative force which takes a toll on my health, as well as on the patience of my loved ones. As Mr. Norfolk points out, we tend to forget that a certain amount of stress can be productive. One such experience happened to me as I attempted climbing Mount Rainier.

Rainier is a massive mountain; how well I remember viewing it from United's 727 . . . enroute to my April Fool's Day climb. As we flew over Mt. St. Helens, it was still spewing a steady steam of ash into the high sky, I realized that by comparison, Mt. St. Helen's . . . and for that matter, all of the other Cascades, seemed miniscule compared to the dominant boss of the range, Rainier. Fully half of its 14,410-foot elevation jutted up out of the cloud layer below our plane, while other clouds ringed the peak . . . making its own weather . . . defying those who would scale it in late winter. Here is a mountain that is peaceful in spring, summer and early fall, putting out a welcome mat to visitors from all over the world, reserving its bad temper for those who would dare to trod across its vast snow fields, tip-toeing around its numerous crevasses, while trying to avoid the sure doom of its thundering avalanches. The adventure and the challenge of those next days will live with me forever.

The stone hut on Rainier where we holed up before the last ascent to the top, had been built in 1910 . . . as Spartan as it was, after my day long battle with leg cramps in knee-deep snow, it seemed like a luxury lodge at Vail or Sundance. I was content to accept the rest and warmth as well-earned. The many cups of hot cocoa and schnapps had lulled me into a quiet that was foreign to my nature and yet I felt quite comfortable with it. I settled down in my sleeping bag . . . the schnapps and my new-found tranquility emitting a glow matched by the tiny flames that danced in the propane stove. I fashioned a dream in my mind of peak conquest to shut out the tick-tocking of the loud alarm clock set to arouse me and my guide at 2:00 a.m. He snored in his self-assurance, while I mentally prepared my worry list for tomorrow. "Let's see," I thought. . . . "I may have to scratch the angry weather from my worry list. It sounds like it has let up." My last look outside had revealed a sky too white to possibly have a black hole in its heavens . . . a sky so blanketed with stars that it was impossible to discern a gap between the star masses; truly, it looked as if the sky were a reflection of the snow on the mountain which covered everything save the sheerest vertical walls . . . Secondly (as I went on with my worry list), I'm certain that the batteries for our miner's hat lamps won't last the three hours necessary to light our way across the darkened snow fields on our way to our first pitch toward the summit. . . . do I have enough schooling in ice arrest using my ice-axe? . . . what if the snow covers our hut. Our hut was like a single snowflake on the vast mountain, nestled in a small encampment below the brooding peak above. As I mentally recorded my worries, I knew that some of them were very real indeed.

As my worries blended in with the relaxing schnapps, I took a last look at the clock. It was 8:00 p.m. George had been asleep for an hour. I began to breathe in when he did, exhaling in unison with him . . . counting an army of black sheep outfitted like a four-legged ski patrol . . . on skis, gliding effortlessly over slightly hilly terrain . . . jumping in synchronization. I finally fell asleep, only to be awakened by a thunderous sound reverberating in the tiny stone hut. I jumped out of bed, realizing that the sound I was hearing was pounding on the heavy Dutch steel door that sheltered us from the outside world. Between the pounding, I could hear the wind howling fiercely; the short respite from the terrible weather of yesterday was over. (Well, I thought, the weather made the worry list after all.)

Before I could reach the door, George was there hurriedly untying the rope that secured the top portion of the door to the hut wall. "Christ," he said, "its 1:00 a.m. Who the hell can be out in this?" The rope was frozen stiff by the sub-zero cold of the outside. We both grappled with the door, as George muttered, "There's no way you can find this hut in this storm. Only something subhuman or crazy is out there." We both drove our shoulders against the steel door, pushing back the accumulated drifts against it. A large figure stood before us in the opening, imposing its eerie presence upon us. I raised my ice-axe . . . no third world visitor was getting my bunk.

At first glance, it looked like nothing more than a block of ice, then the flashlight beaming against it revealed a face with eyes too frozen to move in their sockets, and a beard with a mass of icicles clinging to it. What a sight . . . he to me . . . and I to him as I stood there brandishing my ice-axe. Before I could wield my axe in defense against this thing from the ice age, it spoke. My God, I thought, The Abominable Snowman speaks English . . . and Cockney to boot.

"Blimey, old chap, would you mind if I stepped in a moment. Its a bit nippy out here." he said, standing there in a raging storm . . . geared up for the Arctic . . . ski poles in one mittened hand and the other thrust forward to shake the hand of his saviors . . . he introduced himself as Lieutenant Ian something or other. George and I were so dumbfounded, we just stood there on the wet stone floor, clothed only in layers of long johns, too speechless to offer hospitality to this British Army officer who, as it turned out, was on loan to the U.S. Army at Ft. Lewis to teach Artic survival to our troops.

After being engulfed by his steady stream of "Blimey, this . . ." and "Blimey, that. . . ." we surrendered the doorway and pulled him into the shelter of the hut, now grown cold and filling quickly with snow. "A miracle," I voiced, and the lieutenant and George agreed. A little while longer on the mountain and Rainier would have added an Englishman to its climber's cemetery. Ian was warming to the cup of hot water in his gloveless hands, when he exclaimed at the top of his voice, "Blimey, Terrell is still outside!" Ian had been inside the hut a full two minutes before he collected his senses enough to remember his climbing companion, who was standing in his own block of ice a few strides beyond where we had first seen the Yetti-like figure of Ian. We dragged Terrell inside and helped them both thaw out before we greeted a dawn which would see these two travelers, as well as George and me, lost in a white-out for two solid days in the grasp of mighty Rainier.

Geologically speaking, many mountains are themselves the result of stress. Remember the dinosaurs who could see over the hills in their way, stayed at sea level and became extinct . . . while early man journeyed over the hills to seek the new challenges ahead, and survived. Because of the great technological advances made in the 20th century, we seldom come into direct conflict with the raw forces of nature. With concrete cities and highways, we can go for years without touching the soil itself. In fact, we spend so much time indoors, encased in our little protective shells, that we are often intimidated by the bigness, the crudeness and by the earth itself. Find an empty field to walk in, or drive to a lonely hillside, and see how uncomfortable the majority of you feel. Technology has, for the most part, robbed us of a chance to be honed and sharpened by hand-to-hand combat with the elements. Prehistoric man had to have a healthy respect for the physical universe, based upon his inability to control so very little of it . . . even to build adequate shelters to protect himself, he had to rely upon his inherent instincts, which were as natural to him as they were to the animals in his world. Even though civilization has progressed technically to the point where it has pretty much eliminated the daily struggle for survival, man has paid a high price for his sanctuary. Be assured that we still incorporate a natural intuition which is attuned to the deep rhythms of the earth; not to share in the harmony is a costly mistake.

I Find Strength in the Mountains

I go to the mountains to renew my personal ties with the earth. When I'm climbing, I'm in close physical contact with this wonderful planet on which we live. I gain serenity and peace of mind from this communication. I've climbed in snow, rain, wind, thunder and lightning, and have felt revitalized by my confrontation with the most basic elements of this earth, even at their most terrifying. When I'm on the mountain, its because I choose to be there. I've picked the challenge . . . it hasn't been thrust upon me . . . and it is my challenge alone. Yes, its a stress situation, but it is a different kind of stress than I usually deal with, and changing the stress from a mental one to a physical one helps me to maintain a balance in my personal life and affairs. When I'm hanging by my fingertips from a crack in a cliff, everything takes on a different perspective and I find I can return to my every day world with a better sense of priorities and proportion.

Learn to revel in the opportunity to match yourself against the forces of nature, whether it is a physical combat or a mental one, and to win by meeting the challenges head-on. This is a part of your heritage . . . a linkage . . . if you will, with your ancestors whose understanding of the soil gave them the courage not only to exist, but to thrive in the adversities of their physical universe.

Can We Avoid the Lightening in Our Personal Climb?

The immediate danger when climbing on the "Grand" in the Tetons, is the ever-present danger of lightning strikes as you get close to the top. In our every day life, the closer we get to the top (our goals), the more dangers (challenges), we encounter, and the more vulnerable we seem to become; yet the final push is the most important one of the climb . . . the one that separates the "men from the boys" or the "women from the girls." That is the time we need the courage and the staying power the most. If we have prepared well, we'll know how to weather the lightning striking around our heads and we will act appropriately. Seeking a deceptively false sanctuary could turn out to be a trap from which we might never be able to extract ourselves. Meeting the challenge head-on is where the growth takes place. Sometimes, we may have to "back-step" a little, or get completely out of the area, but it is really only a question of correctly apprising the challenge, then trusting yourself to be capable of making the right choice, based on correctly gauging the situation and taking the appropriate corrective action. The best test of rightness is the feeling of well-being which accompanies it . . . that feeling of knowing "this is exactly the way it should be". If we heed the signals, our intuition can guide us through the lightning bolts and the storms . . . the stresses . . . which we will inevitably encounter in our climb.

Book Title: The Stress Factor
Author: Donald Norfolk
Publisher: Simon & Schuster
Chapter: Back to Nature

Back To Nature

Man is by nature a pastoral animal. Despite several centuries of industrialization he is still not adapted to the city's crowded clangor. It took the fringe-toed lizard thousands of years to adapt to life in the Arizona desert—to develop webbed feet built like snow shoes to prevent their sinking into the soft ground, nostrils which swing shut like trap doors to keep out the drifting sand, and eyelids which intermesh like zippers to protect the eyes when sandstorms blow. Man's full adaptation to the peculiar demands of contemporary life will also take millennia to achieve. The process of urbanization has occurred too rapidly for our mental well-being. At the beginning of the nineteenth century four-fifths of the British population lived in the country. Then the great urban migration began and by the end of the century only one of every five lived in rural districts. The new urbanities gained prosperity, but were dispossessed of their traditional work, customs and roots.

THE STRESS FACTOR By Donald Norfolk Copyright © 1977 by Donald Norfolk Reprinted by permission of SIMON & SCHUSTER, Inc.

During the twentieth century life has become increasingly complex and artificial. Inhabitants of a modern city block, like Chicago's one-hundred-story Sears Building, need never leave their concrete pen to battle with the elements. Everything required for their daily existence—department stores, restaurants, banks and cocktail bars—is included within the apartment complex. Montreal has its underground city, the vast Place Ville Marie with its dozen subterranean cinemas and theaters, 330 shops, and 64 restaurants, snack bars and cafés. Here, far removed from green fields, bird song and natural sunlight, it is possible to work and play in a totally controlled environment. America is even developing underground schools, which their advocates say are easier to clean and have the additional advantage of screening the children from outside distractions. Now more than ever youngsters will have to rely on biology textbooks to learn about the birds and bees.

Undoubtedly we will survive in these inimical conditions. Humans are extremely tolerant animals and are known to put up with a level of noise, dirt, discomfort, frustration and misery that would be intolerable for a rabbit or mouse. In fact in many ways we are *too* tolerant for our own good. As Professor René Dubos says in *Man Adapting,* "Life in the modern city has become a symbol of the fact that man can become adapted to starless skies, treeless avenues, shapeless buildings, tasteless bread, joyless celebrations, spiritless pleasures." But we pay a price for this easy acceptance.

It is likely that much of to-day's mental stress arises because we are as yet ill-adapted to an industrial way of life. Zoologists have noted that the health of animals frequently deteriorates when they are moved from a natural environment and placed in captivity. Autopsies show that the frequency of arteriosclerosis among mammals and birds at the Philadelphia Zoo has increased ten- to twentyfold in the last forty years. This is attributed to the "social pressures" resulting from overcrowding, loss of territory, and the general restriction of activities. Social rivals cannot escape from one another when they are in captivity. After a fight they still have to see each other and this can lead to perpetual conflict. Similar stresses occur in man and in the *Human Zoo* ethologist Desmond Morris suggests that it is more realistic to compare the behavior of man with that of other caged animals. In their natural habitat wild animals do not mutilate themselves, murder, suffer stomach ulcers, become obese, develop arteriosclerosis or form homosexual pair-bonds. In captivity they do all of these things. So does contemporary man in his concrete zoo. As Morris says, "The modern human animal is no longer living in conditions natural for his species. Trapped, not by a zoo collector, but by his own brainy brilliance, he has set himself up in a huge, restless menagerie where he is in constant danger of cracking under the strain."

To alleviate this strain we long to return to the simplicity of the arcadian life. Much of this yearning is at a purely subconscious level. Town dwellers seek to reestablish their links with nature by keeping parrots and tropical fish, growing exotic indoor plants and cultivating town gardens and window boxes. On he weekend there is a mass migration of city dwellers into the great outdoors, where they hike, picnic, sightsee and visit zoos, wildlife parks and nature reserves. Those who can afford it buy a house in the country. (By 1971 20 percent of urban households in America and Sweden had a second home in the country, but only 1 percent in England.) For five days of the week an executive will struggle to keep his family in the material comforts of the city, then on the weekend he escapes into the country to rediscover his grass roots and practice the primitive arts and crafts of human survival—chopping wood, making fires, mending broken fences and mowing overgrown grass. The wealthy will now pay a king's ransom to hunt, shoot and fish—activities which once were the necessary chores of survival in peasant communities. Middle-class wives, tired of the monotony of synthetic convenience foods, are returning to baking their own bread from whole wheat, stone-ground flour. In their spare time they weave, throw pots and make wine.

This atavistic trek is probably most noticeable in the young, who are less attracted by convention and more willing to throw overboard the accretions of two centuries of urbanization. Not for them the regimentation, the military hair cuts, stiff collars and ties and formal suits. They are happy to go vegetarian, experiment with macrobiotic food or eat only compost-grown vegetables and fruit. They are prepared for a while at least to dress simply, to live in self-supporting communes and to have few material possessions other than a shirt, a pair of jeans and a sleeping bag.

Enlightened civic planners are also playing their part by preserving city parks, creating garden cities, and planting protective green belts around existing industrial towns. So too are architects, like Finland's Alvar Aalto, who blended structures into their natural environments. He used curved structural beams to reflect the sun's rays and give diffuse natural lighting in museums, and designed buildings to incorporate natural outcrops of rock rather than insisting that the site should first be dynamited. One of Aalto's guiding principles was that man must remain in closer contact with nature.

This may for him have been chiefly an aesthetic consideration, but it is equally well a sound psychoprophylactic principle. Doctors have reported what appears to be a close causal link between town dwelling and symptoms of psychosocial distress. The prevalence of crime, divorce, desertion, mental breakdown and suicide is higher in towns than in the country, and is particularly high in large, rapidly expanding industrial cities. To escape this source of stress we need occasionally to regress to a simple, pastoral way of life. People spending weekends in the countryside give a number of reasons for their love of the great outdoors. Some go to revel in the scenery, others to enjoy a break from routine and convention, to live for a while at a slower pace, to exchange artificial values for real values, to recharge batteries, to have a few moments peace and quiet, or to escape from difficult or demanding human relationships. A closer examination suggests that an occasional return to nature confers six main benefits:

- *It establishes a healthy sense of perspective.* When we contemplate the vastness of the universe it is difficult to have an exaggerated sense of one's own importance. It is humbling to discover that even if every one of the world's three billion inhabitants were six feet tall and a foot-and-a-half wide they could still be packed together in a box no bigger than a half-mile square, pushed over the top of the Grand Canyon and totally lost from sight.

  We are often dazzled by our technological genius, by our ability to create massive generators and nuclear reactors, and yet the motive power of industry is a puny thing compared with the tremendous forces liberated by earthquakes, tempests and electrical storms. In one minute, for example, an average hurricane expends more energy than the United States consumes in half a century.

  Faced with these awe-inspiring statistics our day-to-day anxieties seem trivial. They may loom large to us today, but tomorrow they will fade from sight and in a year they will probably be completely forgotten. Compared with the infinite world of nature we and our petty problems are but grains of sand.

- *It induces a feeling of timelessness.* Observation of the world around us should inspire a spirit of patience and calm. We are slaves to haste, but nature refuses to be hurried. Nothing can speed the sunrise, nothing can hasten the rhythm of the tides or the annual rebirth of the flowers. We alone have introduced rush and bustle into the world. We no longer allow things to happen at the leisurely pace at which trees grow, rivers flow and seasons change. Everything has to happen in the shortest possible time and tomorrow it must be quicker still. But when we study the world of nature we are less inclined to stick to rigid deadlines and more willing to let things develop in the fullness of time.

- *It creates a sense of permanence.* When society is in a state of constant flux it is comforting to be reassured of the permanence of the world around us. Mother earth makes up for the vagaries and wild eccentricities of man by being simple, solid, sane and utterly dependable. *Terra firma* has become our hallmark of everything solid and secure. Simple things are described as being "down to earth," and the return to sanity after a period of madness a "coming back to earth." We feel secure when we have our feet firmly planted on the ground, particularly if it happens to be our native land or our own backyard. As Anthony Trollope said, "It is a very comfortable thing to stand on your own ground. Land is about the only thing that can't fly away."

- *It encourages a spirit of quiet meditation.* Most great men have drawn strength and inspiration through communion with nature. As the Psalmist said, "I will lift up mine eyes unto the hills from whence cometh my strength." Generations later Roman citizens climbed the Janicus mountain to seek inspiration. John the Baptist went out into the wilderness to contemplate, and the prophet Mohammed climbed Mount Hira to meditate.

Conrad Russell, when looking back on the life of his father Bertrand Russell, Nobel-prize winning philosopher, scientist and author, remembers his lifelong communion with nature. He loved the sea and hills. "I remember him, at ninety-five, swinging over the steps of the balcony at Plas Penrhyn for the sheer delight of the view of Snowdon in the afternoon sun. Above all, I remember him spending hours watching the movement of water in waterfalls One of my earliest memories is of watching him standing under a waterfall in California, and one of my latest is of him gazing rapt at the fall of water through the rapids of Aberglaslyn in North Wales." And his favorite proverb was "Men of wisdom love the sea; men of virtue love the mountains."

In today's frenetic world men of sanity love nature in all its myriad forms.

- *It engenders a feeling of unity and harmony.* In the process of civilization man has become increasingly divorced from his pastoral setting. An unhealthy schism has developed between man and the world he inhabits. This is seen by theologians as a spiritual disaster. As Cardinal Newman says, "The human race is implicated in some terrible aboriginal calamity. It is out of joint with the purpose of its Creator." To psychologists the rift is regarded more prosaically as a common cause of alienation and distress. As writer Charles Reich says, "Man was uprooted from his supporting physical and social environment and, like a polar bear in a city zoo, he would from then on suffer an alienated existence." When we return to the world of nature we heal the rift and end this unnatural alienation. This relieves the underlying tension and can be a source of unparalleled delight. This is the basis of the mystical experience, those rare moments of ecstasy when time stands still and we seem to be at one with the universe—a condition variously described as "cosmic consciousness," "the transcendental experience" or by Freud as the "oceanic feeling." These moments rarely come when we are engaged in conscious thought, but when we are relaxing and at peace with the world. The writer John Buchan tells in his autobiography of one such experience. It happened when he took an early morning dip and then basked contentedly in the sunshine while his breakfast cooked. Suddenly, he recalls, "scents, sights and sounds blended into a harmony so perfect that it transcended human expression, even human thought. It was like a glimpse of the peace of eternity." Feelings like that may be encountered sitting quietly beside a mountain stream, or lying in a flower-strewn meadow, but they are rarely experienced in night clubs, casinos, dance halls or restaurants.

- *It simplifies life.* Our way of life has become increasingly complicated. We would find it difficult to imagine life today without cars and centrally-heated homes. But cars bring traffic jams, breakdowns and parking problems, and homes mean mortgages, repairs and utility bills. The more we need the more we have to worry about. The poor man has no cause to worry about stock market plunges, or tax increases. We worry less if we take the wider, cosmic view and realize that we can flourish with a fraction of what we have today. After all our forebears managed without sugar until the thirteenth century, without buttered bread until the sixteenth century, without soap until the seventeenth, gas and electricity until the nineteenth, and cars, canned food and airplanes until the twentieth.

Some people will rediscover their grass roots by going for long country walks. Others will fish, watch birds, grow orchids or study geology. Camping is another pastime that meets this primeval need. It is an activity which gives city dwellers an opportunity to escape from their time-obsessed lives and have the freedom to camp when and where they wish, eat when they will, dress as casually as they please and enjoy the soothing sight of green grass and the soft smells and sounds of the countryside. Charles Lindbergh, writing nearly half a century after he made his solo cross-Atlantic flight, said, "Man must feel the earth to know himself and recognize his values." He himself made this contact by going on regular camping trips. "The great difference between a tent and a house," he wrote, "is that a tent introduces you to the earth, while a house separates you from it. . . . In a sleeping-bag, after an ember-cooked meal, you feel free of civilization's elaborate accoutrements and realize the basic simplicity of life. The only essentials are a covering for your body, a shelter from the weather and a little food."

Gardening is another favored retreat. Author Alicia Bay Laurel in her book *Living on the Earth* gives this recipe for relaxation: "Find a little bit of land somewhere and plant a carrot seed. Now sit down and watch it grow. When it is fully grown, pull it up and eat it." In that simple cycle lies the essence of life. It is difficult to worry about inflation while carefully thinning out a row of carrot plants, impossible to be hurried while waiting for pears to ripen and not easy to turn over the soil and reveal a healthy crop of Idaho potatoes without experiencing a sense of real satisfaction. That is why avid gardeners tend as a breed to be relaxed, patient and optimistic. As Bertrand

Russell once observed, "Every time I talk to a savant I feel quite sure that happiness is no longer a possibility. Yet when I talk with my gardener, I'm convinced of the opposite."

Other ideas for atavistic regression were suggested by a group of Japanese government officials, university professors, journalists and sociologists who set out to study the best ways for their countrymen to use their leisure time to help them cope with the stresses of their everyday working lives. They recommended a return to the traditional pastimes of bonsai (dwarf tree culture), ikebana (flower arranging) or even simply "listening to the sigh of the wind in the trees."

Whatever way is chosen we can find relief from stress by temporarily returning to a simpler way of life more closely attuned to our rustic origins. Then we experience the *vis medicatrix naturae,* the healing power of nature.

SECTION II

Gear Needed
For the
Climb

CHAPTER FIVE

Equipment

In Section I, we questioned the basic reasons for making your climb. It is now time to start the preparations. An old Italian proverb states. . . . "In order to start you have to begin, in order to begin, you have to start." So let's start by assembling our gear. This must be done very carefully and thoughtfully because at some point in your climb, a tool you may have left behind may make the difference between success and failure.

The right gear, or tools, makes the difference between doing a project successfully or just so-so, or worse yet, failing completely to accomplish what you set out to do.

I climbed the "Grand Teton" the first of August, which meant that the only snow climbing we would be doing would be across snow fields and one permanent glacier. We didn't add the awkward ice-axe to our already over-loaded backpacks, even though we would need them; the guide knew that there would be axes cached on either side of the glacier. Unfortunately, the previous climbers had failed to return the axes to their usual place. We were at an impasse. Crossing the steep snow field without an ice axe, or a tool of some sort, would make the climb much more difficult and dangerous. Again, I had no desire to turn back, particularly since we had already hiked and climbed for seven hours and knew that after we were across the snow field and glacier, it was a mere two hours to the base camp.

We decided to back track to a stand of trees where we could find a pole to help me cross the glacier, but at the last minute, we spotted climbers on the other side of the snow field with axes. We proceeded across the first snow field. . . . wearing flimsy tennis shoes which had been perfect for the hiking portion of the trail. When my feet started freezing, I realized once again how important the right gear is. Why hadn't I listened to my own intuition and not that of my guide.? My boots, which would have been superfluous, and heavy to carry, for 95 percent of the climb, would have been perfect and much appreciated on those few icy, frozen stretches of the climb. My "rock" climbing shoes were in my backpack and represented even less protection from the snow and ice. Leaving my water-proof boots at the cabin for fear of the extra five pounds they weighed, was foolhardy indeed. Those two hours crossing the snow and ice in a near-freezing rain, were memorable, but for the wrong reasons. Never again would I approach a major climb without the right tools.

Fortunately, the borrowed ice-axes made the most difficult pitch a success. How often do we find ourselves at the edge of a snow field without the proper tools? . . . and what do we do about it? Do we grab a pole when a little more effort would lead us to discover an ice-axe? I've been as guilty as anyone in choosing the lazy way. When I don't have a true picture of the encounter I usually end up in trouble.

Don't substitute nervous laughter for knowledge and enthusiasm that says, "I've done my homework." Its a fine line sometimes. Don't use imitation of a role model as your own personality. It doesn't work because its not the correct application of the tool. Don't cross the ice-field in tennis shoes.

In putting together any survival kit, we must first concern ourselves with basic items, the most rudimentary and common-sense tools coming first; the remainder of the space, if any, is then filled with items you feel are necessary for your comfort. Tim Kneeland, in his pocketbook *"Wilderness Survival,"* . . . stresses the following points in his "General Rules of Survival"

1. Be prepared to face the worst, while expecting the best. Become as self-reliant as possible (but don't dwell on the worst.)
2. Try to maintain *Full Control Over Your Mind At All Times.* Your mental attitude (your analytical problem solving ability and your will to survive) controls more than 90 percent of a situation. Don't let fear or panic cause bad judgment or mistakes.
3. Regardless of personal belief, most people confronted with survival have found great strength in asking for God's help.
4. You can live through almost anything. Most survival is simply an inconvenience. It is the individual who turns it into a life or death situation.

Kneeland's rules are applicable to any situation you might encounter on your metaphoric climb. In one way or another, this message of survival (success) is reiterated in every article used in this section. The underlying message conveyed by books such as *Enthusiasm Makes the Difference* by Norman Vincent Peale, *Psycho-Cybernetics* by Maxwell Maltz, *Strategy for Success* by Ari Kiev, *When Lovers are Friends* by Merle Shain, along with the essays on *"Love"* by Emmet Fox, *"Desire"* by M.R. Kopmeyer and *"Role Model"* by Lionel

Barrymore, is to evaluate your needs, assemble the necessary gear (including knowledge), then trust yourself to move ahead in a positive manner. If we packed everything that has been suggested over the centuries, for our metaphorical climb, we would surely require a C-52 or Hannibal's elephants; for the present, these are the basic items I would put in my back-pack.

1. Enthusiasm
2. A personality geared and ready for success
3. Self reliance
4. Commitment
5. A role model to follow
6. Love
7. Desire

The chapters in this section are based on the traits above, but there are many more that could and should be included, such as perseverance, laughter and faith . . . make your own list of those important to you in reaching your goals.

CHAPTER SIX

Enthusiasm

Norman Vincent Peale is one of the most prolific writers of our generation, with at least thirty books to his credit. He is also editor and co-publisher of the magazine *Guideposts,* in addition to being a prominent radio host. He was born in Ohio, the son of a physician turned minister. He is pastor emeritus of Marble Collegiate Church in New York City. Dr. Peale's first books were published in the 1930's, but the book that first brought him wide public recognition was *The Power of Positive Thinking;* in 1953, it was number-one on the non-fiction best seller list, dropping to number two in 1955 and number five in 1956. By 1956, it had been on the Best Seller list longer than any other book in any category except the Bible and some textbooks. He has been seen and heard on hundreds of radio and television stations and he also lectures several times a week. Dr. Peale, it seems, is the epitome of his message, in fact, its best student.

How Dr. Peale Turned a Weakness into an Asset

For some reason, Dr. Peale grew up with a gigantic inferiority complex, which, by his own admission, he has never completely gotten over; but he has refused to let it cripple him. He has, in fact, turned it into his greatest asset.

He had always wanted to be an orator, even though he could hardly prevent himself from choking up if called upon to recite in class. This continued in varying degrees, until his sophomore year at Ohio Weslyan College, when a chance admonition from one of his professors angered him; this proved to be precisely what he needed to heal himself. He called upon the lessons learned from his father, and moved ahead with the business of his life. He still has "stage fright" before any lecture, wondering about his ability to deliver a message, and yet he goes out to the lecture platform and talks in an entertaining and inspirational manner for an hour without any notes.

In his book, *Enthusiasm Makes the Difference,* Dr. Peale uses a format which relies heavily on case histories. His years in the ministry have given him reams of source material which he uses to advantage. This explains, in large measure, the appeal of his spoken and written words. A problem, along with its solution, is much easier to understand and relate to when the human element is introduced. When you read of the scores of apathetic losers drifting aimlessly and lackadaisically through life, who are turned into dynamic go-getting successes by changing their attitudes so as to insert enthusiasm into their lives, you become a believer in Dr. Peale's simple teachings.

Enthusiasm Makes the Difference will tell you that enthusiasm is one of the most powerful motivators in making things happen . . . that it can work miracles on your problems . . . that it can cancel fear, worry and stress. Enthusiasm is a powerful tool to take along with you . . . a must for the backpack.

My Personal Encounter with Dr. Peale

The main impression you take away from a meeting with Dr. Peale is his enthusiasm for living, which is extremely infectious; that is why I was very pleased when he released *Enthusiasm Makes the Difference* in order to share his secret with us.

In 1963, I was working on a motion picture called "One Man's Way," which was based on the life story of Dr. Peale. I was going through a decisive period in my life at this time, awkwardly approaching the challenges before me, in truth, I was trying to find my way, all the while feeling very sorry for myself. That, of course, doesn't work. I was pensive about continuing in the motion picture business. In the five short years I had been working at it, I had been relatively successful. I was a quasi-regular at Warner Brothers, working virtually every week in one T.V. series or another, with an occasional movie in between. What was at the crux of it all, was the fact that I could foster little real enthusiasm for the business. Maybe it had come too easy; I'm not really sure, but this I am sure of, my encounter with Dr. Peale was timely and productive. The part I had in the movie was non-descript. When Dr. Peale visited the set, he was quite busy as "the" technical advisor on the picture and had little time for chit-chat. They had just finished lighting a scene where Dr. Peale (as portrayed in the movie by Don Murray), was a newspaper reporter about to encounter a suicide; it was the scene I was involved in. While rehearsing was going on, I received a phone call on the set. Dr. Peale was near the telephone and overheard my side of the conversation, which was less than enthusiastic. My agent had arranged another spot for me in a movie just about like the one I was in . . . and was very pleased with himself because he kept me working. He was not the least bit concerned with the quality of my work, only the quantity. When I hung up the telephone, I found a receptive ear in Dr. Peale . . . he became an extension of the conversation which had gone on before, almost as if he were part of the scenario. He had this incredible air of receptivity which made it seem so right and natural to be talking to him. I guess this is the mark of a good counselor. I told him how non-rewarding most of my work in show business was and that I had much more enthusiasm at the thought of striking out into the business world. He listened very attentively and then in a few short words made me realize that my enormous energy and enthusiasm was God-given and that I should not settle for less than their full development. He pointed out that this present moment in my life was just a little foot-hill which, with my energy and birthskills, could easily be vaulted over. He helped me see that my real summits were ahead of me. That meeting was quite instrumental in the focusing of my enthusiasm and energy on my life plan, which soon thereafter veered toward the course I have plotted ever since.

Enthusiasm Can Be Generated

Enthusiasm is energy. How do you generate it when it isn't there? Where is the switch you throw to activate the inner light? That is the time when you use that small, but important adage, "Act as if you were and you will be." Things are never quite what they seem to be . . . and this is part of the "which came first . . . the chicken or the egg." Which comes first . . . the smile or the happiness that causes it? Don't spend too much time worrying about it, but if you are really interested, experiment with it. When you feel the lowest, put a lilting bounce in your step . . . put more expression into your voice . . . and a smile on your face. I think you will be surprised at the result.

The "I don't care" attitude, when its used in a detached manner, is one of the most self-defeating actions going. Make yourself care . . . find something in every situation that becomes important to you.

What is the other side of the enthusiasm coin? Is it disinterest

. . . depression, criticism, hesitancy, fear, deprecation, boredom? Unfortunately, its all of them. Separately and collectively, they are all very limited ways of approaching life . . . and all caused by being self-centered. Listen to those who practice any of these self-defeating actions and you will find that every other word they use is "I". "I want it!" "I don't have it because life is unfair and cruel to me." "Why should I try? It doesn't do me any good. I never get anyplace anyway." Be aware that life doesn't really care one way or the other. The creative force that flows through you has no concept of good or bad; its only purpose is to create as you direct it to, with your conscious mind which is the contact point between the inner environment and the outer. If you look upon all as gray, you will have more gray created for you. But if your actions say you are determined to achieve your highest good, you will have the help of your creative inner nature.

Enthusiasm means you are aware of your place in the universe and accept it with joy and without fear.

Book Title: Enthusiasm Makes the Difference
Author: Norman Vincent Peale
Publisher: Prentice-Hall, Inc.
Chapter: Enthusiasm That Never Runs Down

Enthusiasm That Never Runs Down

I shall never forget the night I met Miss Nobody. After making a speech in a West Coast city, I was shaking hands with people who came up to greet me, when along came a young woman who gave me a limp handshake and said in a small, timid voice, "I thought I'd like to shake hands with you, but I really shouldn't be bothering you. There are so many important people here and I'm just a nobody. Forgive me for taking your time."

I took a look at her and said, "Will you do me a favor? Please remain a few minutes. I'd like to talk with you."

In some surprise she did as I suggested. When I had finished greeting the others, I said, "Now, Miss Nobody, let's sit down and have a little visit."

"What did you call me?" she asked in surprise.

"I called you by the only name you gave. You told me you were a Nobody. Have you another name?"

From the book ENTHUSIASM MAKES THE DIFFERENCE By Norman Vincent Peale
© 1967 By Norman Vincent Peale Published by Prentice-Hall, Inc., Englewood Cliffs, NJ 07632

"Of course."

"I thought you must have," I said. "One reason I wanted to talk with you is to find out how anybody can get the idea she's a nobody. Another reason is that referring to yourself this way is in my opinion an affront to God."

"Oh, Dr. Peale!" she exclaimed, "you can't be serious. An affront to God?"

"You are a child of God, created in His image. So it really bothers me, it hurts me, to hear you say you're a nobody." And I asked, "Tell me a little about yourself."

She proceeded to describe her circumstances and problems. She talked haltingly, but with evident relief at being able to confide in someone. "So you see," she concluded, "I've quite an inferiority complex and sometimes I get terribly discouraged. I came to hear you tonight hoping you might say something that would help me."

"Well," I answered, "I'm saying it to you now: You are a child of God." And I advised her to draw herself up tall each day and say to herself, "I am a child of God."

She looked at me with a lovely smile and promised to follow that advice. And she added, "Pray for me."

And I did. I prayed that the Lord would help her to acquire real enthusiasm about herself and some proper self-confidence as well.

Recently I was speaking in the same area and an attractive young woman approached me asking, "Do you remember me?"

"Have we met before?" I asked.

"Yes, we have. I'm the former Miss Nobody."

Then I remembered. And I knew that she had fared extremely well since our first meeting. I could tell it from her manner and the sparkle in her eyes even before she had time to report anything in words. She had discovered her extension powers as a child of God.

This incident underscores an important fact. You can

change! Anybody can change! And even from a dull nobody to an enthusiastic somebody.

In addition to "Miss Nobody," I have seen many people change and change greatly. They cease to be defeated and unhappy people and become altogether different in nature, so they are hardly the same individuals. Less attractive qualities have given way to better ones and their personalities have been dramatically brought out and enhanced. As a result they enter upon a life so full of happiness and success and creativity that people around them marvel. And they themselves marvel. And why not? For it is a marvel.

In the years that we have taught creative living through spiritual practice, I have seen people who were literally packed full of hate changed into people equally full of love. I have watched defeated individuals shed anxiety as they absorb the amazing secret of victory. I have observed people who suffer from fear transformed into courageous, worry-free persons.

ENTHUSIASM WILL IMPROVE YOUR PERSONALITY

There is another important form of change, one perhaps more complicated, related as it is to complex moods, to the cyclic rise and fall of emotional reaction. It is the change from apathy to enthusiasm, from indifference to exciting participation; it is an astonishing personality change which sensitizes the spirit, erases dullness and infuses the individual with a powerful motivation that activates enthusiasm and never allows it to run down.

Most people acknowledge the possibility of personality change in connection with hate, fear and other common forms of conflict, but seem to doubt that they can be made over into enthusiastic persons. They argue, "Sure I would like to have enthusiasm, but what if you just haven't got it? You cannot make yourself enthusiastic can you?" This is always said in anticipation of an of-course-you-can't agreement. But I do not agree at all. For you can make yourself an optimist. You can develop enthusiasm, and of a type that is continuous and joyous in nature.

The important fact is that you can deliberately make yourself enthusiastic. Actually you can go further and develop a quality of enthusiasm so meaningful and in such depth that it will not decline or run dry no matter what strain it is put to. It has been established by repeated demonstration that a person can make of himself just about what he wants to, provided he wants to badly enough and correctly goes about doing it. A method for deliberately transforming yourself into whatever type of person you wish to be is first to decide specifically what particular characteristic you desire to possess and then to hold that image firmly in your consciousness. Second, proceed to develop it by acting as if you actually possessed the desired characteristic. And third, believe and repeatedly affirm that you are in the process of self-creating the quality you have undertaken to develop.

MAKE USE OF THE "AS IF" PRINCIPLE

Many years ago the noted psychologist, William James, announced his famous "As if" principle. He said, "If you want a quality, act as if you already had it." Try the "As if" technique. It is packed with power and it works.

For example, let us suppose you are a shy and diffident individual with a miserable inferiority complex. The procedure for change into normal extrovertism is to start visualizing yourself not as you think you are, but rather as you'd like to be, a person confident and assured, able to meet people and to deal with situations. Once the thought or image of what you desire to be is deeply imbedded in your consciousness, then deliberately start acting in a confident manner, as if you are competent to handle situations and personal encounters. It is a proven law of human nature that as you imagine yourself to be and as you act on the assumption that you are what you see yourself as being, you will in time strongly tend to become, *provided* you persevere in the process.

This law of self-assumed personal change has been demonstrated by many and diverse people. For example, the famous religious leader John Wesley was terrified in a violent storm on the Atlantic as he sailed to America in the seventeenth century. But some people aboard the wildly tossing ship were calm and confident during the storm. Wesley was so impressed by their imperturbability that he asked their secret. It proved to be simply a serene faith in God's providential care. When Wesley sadly confessed that he did not have such faith, one of them said, "It is a simple secret. Act as if you do have such faith and in time faith of that character will take hold of you." Wesley followed the advice and ultimately developed such powerful faith that he was able to overcome the most difficult situations. So therefore if you are afraid, discipline yourself to act as if you had courage. If you are tense, deliberately act as if calm and assured. Shakespeare, whose insights into human nature have scarcely ever been equalled, supports this method. "Assume a virtue if you have it not," he tells us in Act III of *Hamlet.*

Another outstanding illustration of the law of acting "As if" and as you desire to be is that of Frank Bettger, a top insurance man. In his book *How I Raised Myself from Failure to Success in Selling* * Mr. Bettger tells of his early experience as a professional baseball player on a minor league team from which he was summarily discharged. The manager regretted letting him go since Frank possessed the basic qualifications of a good player. But though competent, he was dropped for one reason only—lack of enthusiasm.

*Copyright 1958, Prentice-Hall, Inc., Englewood Cliffs, N.J.

Bettger, signed by another team at a lower salary, continued to play the same desultory kind of game. Then one day he encountered a famous oldtime professional who asked, "Frank, don't you really like baseball? You have real ability, but you are totally lacking in enthusiasm, and until you get that you will never go ahead in this sport, or for that matter, in anything else in life. You must have enthusiasm. It's a primary requisite for success."

"But," complained Bettger, "what can I do? I haven't got enthusiasm. You just can't go out and buy it in a store. You either have it or you don't. I haven't, so that's it, I guess."

"You're wrong, Frank," said the older man urgently. "Make yourself act enthusiastic. It's as simple as that. Act with enthusiasm, play ball with enthusiasm, and pretty soon you will have enthusiasm. Once you're fired with conviction your natural talents will take you to the top in this sport."

Finally Frank Bettger's chance came. He was taken on by the New Haven ball club, and when he went out to play that first day he resolved to take his old friend's advice and act as though he was charged with enthusiasm. He ran like a man electrified. He threw the ball so hard it seared the gloves of other players. He swung like mad at the ball and actually made some hits. He literally burned up baselines; all this, while the temperature was over ninety in the shade.

The New Haven newspapers the next day asked where this terrific new player Bettger came from. He was a human dynamo, they reported. Soon they were calling him "Pep" Bettger. As he continued to play with such vigor he found himself feeling like a new man. And why not, for he was just that. He became such an enthusiastic player, that a scout for the St. Louis Cardinals spotted him and before long he was playing in the National League.

Later, having taken up a career in insurance, Bettger was once again plagued by apathy and he was once more courting failure. Then he recalled how he had deliberately cultivated enthusiasm, and applied the same "As if" principle to his insurance work. The result was that he rose to the top in this selling field as he had in baseball. Mr. Bettger's experiences demonstrate that enthusiasm can be cultivated and developed by deliberately thinking and acting with enthusiasm. You too can activate yourself into enthusiasm by use of the "As if" principle. What you are comes to you. This remarkable principle is thus stated by Emerson, "A man is a method, a progressive arrangement; a selecting principle, gathering his like unto him wherever he goes." So act as you want to be and you will be as you act.

MENTAL VENTILATION LETS IN ENTHUSIASM

Another practice important to the development of optimistic attitudes is that of mental ventilation. A mind full of gloomy foreboding thoughts makes difficult the cheerful and spirited quality of thinking that stimulates enthusiasm. This is true also of such dark closed thoughts as hate, prejudice, resentment and general dissatisfaction with people and world conditions. Discouragement and frustration form a heavy cloud-blanket over the mind and condition mental attitudes accordingly. Mental ventilation, then, is a highly important step in reconditioning the mind to accept the creative thought climate in which enthusiasm may develop and finally become the dominant factor.

This concept of mental ventilation was first suggested to me some years ago by Mr. A. E. Russ, an old friend who operated a drugstore on lower Fifth Avenue near Twelfth Street in New York. Mr. Russ, a member of my church, had a remarkable gift of native wisdom and insight. He was a natural philosopher, a keen and discerning thinker, a voracious reader, and a successful businessman. His spiritual life had depth, the kind which results when personal suffering emerges into understanding and victory. He knew how to help people and communicate to them a sense of meaning in life, as is evidenced by my personal experience with him.

Discouragement was once somewhat of a problem for me and it would occasionally plunge me into pretty low feelings. Though enthusiastic and optimistic by nature, I was sometimes given to depressions. During such low periods, it seemed that nothing went right. In those days I preached at Marble Collegiate Church on Sunday nights as well as Sunday mornings. (Later the morning congregations grew to such proportions that it became necessary to give the same sermon twice on Sunday morning; the evening service was handled by associates.) But at the time of which I write, I felt I had done particularly badly in my sermon one Sunday evening. Avoiding as many people as possible I plunged out into the dark misty night and walked glumly down Fifth Avenue toward my home.

Passing Mr. Russ's drugstore, I decided on an impulse to go in to see him. He was making sodas at the fountain, so I sat at the counter and watched him. "How come you are making sodas?" I asked, "Where is your regular counterman?"

"He left me, so I'm shorthanded," he replied.

"Tell you what," I said. "I preached a terrible sermon tonight. Can't imagine why I ever took up preaching in the first place. I'm a flop. How about giving me that soda jerk job?"

"Sure, why not?" replied Mr. Russ without a change of expression. "Come around the counter and make a soda for me. I want to see how good you are before taking you on." So Mr. Russ sat at the counter while I donned an apron and proceeded to put together a chocolate ice cream soda. It had a fairly good head on it, I thought. I laid a straw against it as I'd seen the experts do and put it in front of him. He took a long draw while I waited for the verdict. Removing the straw from his mouth he said, "Better stick to preaching."

Climbing down off the stool he locked the front door. "Closing time," he explained and then added, "Come into my back room and let's talk." He led me into those mysterious recesses behind the drug area to which druggists retire to compound prescriptions. There, I must say, he made up a "thought prescription" for me for which I have been grateful through the many years that have passed since that gloomy night.

Mr. Russ began to tell of his personal battles with discouragement. As I listened to his story of difficulties, reverses and sorrows, my depression seemed trifling indeed. "But I can tell you honestly," he declared, "that since I began a certain mental and spiritual practice I have never had any lasting discouragement. And I'm sure you will agree I'm on the enthusiastic side."

"I don't know a man of more genuine enthusiasm than yourself. What is this mental and spiritual practice which helped you?"

"Daily mental ventilation," he replied. "That's what did it and, I may add, still does it. Keeping the mind free of darkness is a day to day job."

He went on to emphasize the importance of the process of daily mind-emptying. "If you allow dark thoughts, regrets, resentments and the like to accumulate, your whole psychology can in time be so adversely affected that a major effort may be required to bring it back to a normal state of balance." I knew he was right, for our religio-psychiatric counseling service at the church was even then working with the pathetic problem of a man who had, as he himself put it, "accumulated a putrifying mass of old unhappiness in the mind." Weeks were required for our ministers and psychiatrists to cleanse and restore his psychological equipment to proper working order.

Since then I have used the mental ventilation system employed daily by Mr. Russ, both personally and in other cases, and with such effective results in stimulating new enthusiasm that I set it down here for the benefit of all who may read this book. He "emptied" his mind at the end of every day to prevent unhealthy thoughts from lodging in consciousness overnight, for he knew such thoughts can take root quickly if allowed to accumulate even for as long as twenty-four hours.

This mental emptying took the form of a recapitulation of unpleasant incidents that had occurred during the day; a sharp word, an insinuating remark, an hostile act by some other person. Also, a review of his own mistakes, errors or stupidities. To these he added disappointments, frustrations and every form of unhappiness that had clouded the preceding hours. He held all these in a strong mental view, deliberately drawing from them all the experience and understanding they had to give. Then he "lumped" them together and mentally "dropped" them out of consciousness, saying as he did so these therapeutic words: "Forgetting those things which are behind, and reaching forth unto those things which are before . . ." (Philippians 3:13)

Mr. Russ stated that when he first began to use his "lumping" and "dropping" practice, the mental accumulation, as he put it, readily "lumped" but just did not "drop." However, the continued application of a determined and disciplined mental effort resulted in due time in a remarkable ability to forget the useless and unhealthy material that had previously cluttered his mind, siphoning off zest and enthusiasm. In these procedures, Mr. Russ made use of the law that one can do practically anything he wants with his thoughts, provided he consistently continues the effort.

"You cannot possibly realize until you try it for yourself what a powerful upthrust of joy surges through your being when you find that you can actually 'lump' and 'drop' those pesky enemies of a happy mind," he declared. "Ventilate—that's the answer. Ventilate. Let them go; throw them out, 'lump' and 'drop'—ventilate the mind.

"Now take yourself," he exclaimed, "you say you've had

a bad evening; that you preached a disappointing sermon. All right then; analyze it carefully. Determine what you did that may have been wrong. Learn something from your analysis. Then 'lump' and 'drop'—Ventilate. The old enthusiasm will bounce back.''

He punched me affectionately on the chest as we said goodbye. I went home and at once started practicing Mr. Russ's mental ventilation system. It took some time and some doing over many days, but finally I got the hang of making my mind obey me. Then it was easy. Believe me, this method is a sure-fire secret of having boundless enthusiasm.

TELL YOURSELF ALL THE GOOD NEWS YOU KNOW

A vital element in developing enthusiasm is the manner in which you start the day. You can pretty well condition a day in the first five minutes after you wake up. Of course, some people are naturally slow starters and for them it takes time to become fully awake and adjusted to a new day. But even so, careful attention to the matter of setting the tone of a day in the early hours is likely to have a determinative effect.

Henry Thoreau, the American philosopher, used to lie abed for awhile in the morning telling himself all the good news he could think of; that he had a healthy body, that his mind was alert, that his work was interesting, that the future looked bright, that a lot of people trusted him. Presently he arose to meet the day in a world filled for him with good things, good people, good opportunities.

This good news technique each morning can help make your day, despite the fact that there may be disappointing news that must be faced. Still, the more good news you tell yourself, the more such there is likely to be. The practice will also help you take bad news in your stride. At any rate, that which the mind receives upon awakening tends to influence and to a considerable degree determine what your day will be.

One man whose enthusiasm is always in evidence, even when the going is rough, has his own method for beginning a day. He takes a few minutes before breakfast for what he calls a "quiet time." This consists of reading a brief spiritual or inspirational piece and is followed by three or four minutes of quiet during which he affirms and practices a quiet state of mind. Regardless of how busy his program for the day, in those few minutes no hurry or haste is permitted, even in thought.

He then pictures every person he expects to contact during that day and prays for each one. "Then I commit the day to God and get going," he says. And he really does get going. Everyone he touches is revitalized by this man whose boundless enthusiasm seems never to diminish. And a principal reason for its vitality is that his practice of spiritual motivation at the start of each day infuses him with new zest.

EVERY MORNING A NEW SET OF FACTS

Apprehension about the day ahead is characteristic of some people, particularly if they find difficult and trying problems looming ahead. They view the prospect with distaste, perhaps even fear, so they have little enthusiasm for the exciting challenge that problems present. But I do admire the attitude of a friend toward each day. He has experienced some tragic trials and reverses in his lifetime, enough in fact to completely destroy many men. But he says, "A reversal is not a disaster, merely an incident in a total business career." He approaches each day on the principle that you get a new set of facts each morning. Then you convince yourself that you are going to take this new set of facts, be happy with it and do something constructive with it.

This man, whose enthusiasm and ability are considerable, declares, "There are only two kinds of days for me: Some days

I'm happy. Other days I'm hysterically happy." The policy of taking hold of a new set of facts each morning and being happy about it seems to be a real factor in sustaining high-level enthusiasm. It has been said that every tomorrow has two handles. You can take hold of either the handle of anxiety or the handle of enthusiasm. The continued choice of handle determines the character of your multiplying days. Choose enthusiasm daily and you are likely to have it permanently.

HOW TO HAVE CONTINUING ENTHUSIASM

The problem of sustaining enthusiasm is often difficult, especially for older persons. The natural enthusiasm of youth may take a fearful battering as the years add up. Disappointments, frustrated hopes and ambitions, the drain-off of natural energy all conspire to dull excitement and enthusiastic response.

But such deterioration of your life force need not occur. In fact, it will happen only if allowed to happen. You can arrest the decline of spirit; you can be perpetually motivated by enthusiasm despite age, pain, sickness, disappointment and frustration.

I have known people who have remained enthusiastic until the end of their lives and then seemed to go out of this world with flags flying, the light of enthusiasm for life still in their eyes. Nothing could ever happen to destroy the precious gift of enthusiasm.

In thinking of such energetic and enterprising people, Huxley's insight comes to mind—that the true genius of living is to carry the spirit of the child into old age. And what is the spirit of the child, but that of wide-eyed open wonder, excitement and zest; the optimistic attitude that nothing is too good to be true, that the world is literally a wonderful place?

In Montreux, Switzerland, I met Mr. and Mrs. William P. Daggett, school teachers from Long Beach, California, and their children, Lucy, Cathy and Larry. Mrs. Daggett mentioned a quotation from Thoreau which hangs on her kitchen wall at home. "None are so old as those who have outlived enthusiasm." Well, believe me, that is an auspicious saying that could well be engraved on the wall of the mind. It is a fact that the oldest, saddest people are those who have outlived the enthusiasm of their youth.

That quotation from Thoreau set me thinking. I am writing these lines on a balcony of the famous Montreux Palace Hotel of which my friend Paul Rossier is general manager. My balcony looks out on an incomparable vista across the blue waters of Lac Leman (Lake Geneva) to the misty heights of the Alps towering above. Nearby and downlake at the water's edge stand the grim gray walls of the ancient Castle of Chillon, immortalized by Lord Byron.

I well recall my first visit to this old world city and hotel forty years ago. I was very young and enthusiastic and wanted to travel to Europe and see the places I had read about in history books. Having scarcely two nickels to rub together I organized a tour party for which I earned the cost of the trip and a couple of hundred dollars besides. It was the experience of a lifetime. My mind was full of the romantic future, and I lived in perpetual excitement. Like "The Youth, who daily farther from the east must travel, and by the vision splendid is on his way attended," so I was fascinated by sights and sounds. The Montreux Palace Hotel, to my wondering eyes, was the most elegant hostelry imaginable. And I was actually looking for the first time at the Alps and Lac Leman. I just could not believe it. It was all so incredible and wonderful.

Well, four decades have passed since that first enthralling visit. The question now is: How about those youthful dreams? What has happened to that glorious excitement? What is the state of that ardent enthusiasm?

What would be your own honest answer to such reflections?

Ponder well those words from Thoreau: "None are so old as those who have outlived enthusiasm." And just what have we got, you or I, if we have outlived enthusiasm? The Bible has a graphic picture of such persons, "When they shall be afraid of that which is high, and fears shall be in the way . . ." On that basis, one can be old at twenty, and some are. It is the rejuvenation of the mind that keeps enthusiasm alive and, as a matter of fact, restrains aging in spirit and mind, perhaps even in body too.

Well, what is your answer? Want to know mine? I can honestly report that the excitement and enthusiasm of forty years ago are still very much alive, only deeper and more satisfying. So I know from personal experience that enthusiasm can be perpetual; that it need never run down. And that is a fact too, a great big wonderful fact.

KEEP THE FIRES OF ENTHUSIASM BURNING UNDER YOUR GOALS

What an ingredient it is, this vital thing called enthusiasm! And a factor that keeps it perking is an irresistible goal, a fascinating objective, a consuming purpose that dominates, motivates and will not let go of you. Set yourself a goal that you've just got to reach. Then build under it the fire of anticipation and keep it burning—you will acquire enthusiasm and never lose it. That goal will keep beckoning, saying: "Come on after me." And when you reach your goal still new goals will succeed one another as each is attained. New goals, fresh objectives—these are the self-perpetuating motivators of enthusiasm.

Take my friend Paul Chow as an example. I first met Paul in Hong Kong. He had literally walked out of Red China with his family. His astonishing enthusiasm is reflected in a glorious smile and a radiant face. Paul had a dream, a goal, to come to America to raise his family. He was very poor and one of the thousands of refugees crowding into Hong Kong. But Paul had something of much more value than money. He had faith, purpose, enthusiasm.

It is a long story, but one Sunday I looked from my pulpit, in New York City halfway around the world from Hong Kong, and there amidst that huge congregation, right in the front pew, sat Paul Chow and his family. And he was smiling up at me as if to say, "We made it to New York."

Mrs. Peale and I visited his new home in a section of New York where crowding, noise and filth brought back memories of their ordeal in Hong Kong. "Not another day shall they live in this hell-hole," we agreed. We helped them move to Pawling, New York, where Paul has become a valued worker in our publishing plant at the Foundation for Christian Living, and where his family has made a real place for themselves in the community life.

Stephen Chow has become a top honor student in high school, and Ruth and Martha Chow are leaders in their classes. The family has made a second move to a better house. They work hard; indeed they work like Americans worked in the old days. Stephen cannot understand why some young people fail to realize the tremendous privilege and opportunity they have in schools in America.

One vivid picture I carry in mind. Mrs. Peale and I were leaving our farm at Pawling on a beautiful July Saturday afternoon for a vacation in Europe. Paul and Stephen were painting a long white fence. They are always working. They have a goal, so they work. The road runs below a high bank atop which Paul, spattered with paint, was making that fence white and beautiful as his sense of perfection dictated. As we drove away he stood there paint brush in hand, etched against a blue sky and a field of waist-high corn, his face alive with a happy smile, waving farewell to us.

As we drove down the road to the airport I marveled at how far that Chinese refugee family had come from such unpropitious beginnings with so many obstacles ahead. What can possibly explain it? That's easy. It was a goal, an objective, a purpose. It was aspiration for a better way of life. It was enthusiasm that never weakened because it was subject to constant renewal.

Dwayne Orton expressed a solid truth when he said: "Every business organization should have a vice-president in charge of constant renewal." If it is good for an industry constantly to renew itself, then surely it is important for the individual to have an automatic self-motivator that keeps him alive and vibrant, always alert to the dynamic present in which he lives. In the absence of constant renewal he may fail to keep pace with changing times. Then life races ahead of him. He becomes not a living, vital man, but a relic who fades each day further into the dead past. Possessed of enthusiasm one is a citizen of the present regardless of how many years he has dwelt upon earth. Such a vitalized person cannot possibly become a *has-been*. He is perpetually the *is-now* type.

Happy expectations make the ultimate difference in any person. "Every man is enthusiastic at times. One man has enthusiasm for thirty minutes—another has it for thirty days—but it is the man who has it for thirty years who makes a success in life." So says *The Catholic Layman*.

ENTHUSIASM THAT NEVER RUNS DOWN

Colonel Harland Sanders was sitting on his porch in Shelbyville, Kentucky, on his sixty-fifth birthday when the mailman came up the walk and handed him an envelope. It contained his first social security check. While grateful to the government for this tangible expression of concern for its older citizens, Colonel Sanders had no mind to settle down to a nonparticipation status in business. With boundless confidence despite his limited financial position, he turned his thoughts toward using that modest check to begin a new career. What an exciting experience it would be to launch a new career at an age when one is expected to start playing shuffleboard.

Sitting on his porch that day, do you know what he did? He started thinking—and ideas came to his mind. Ideas change things. He remembered the delicious fried chicken his mother used to make, crispy brown and tender. The very aroma seemed to be wafted across the years, filling him with nostalgia. The recipe for that fried chicken was imprinted indelibly in his taste buds and on his memory.

Then came the creative idea that was to change his life. Why not sell the recipe for his mother's fried chicken on a royalty basis to restaurant owners? Immediately he took action on the thought. Getting in to his battered car he set out calling on restaurant owners everywhere, enthusiastically telling them of his out-of-this-world fried chicken. But no one would go for his idea. Across the country from Kentucky to Utah restaurant men maintained that their own recipes for fried chicken were good enough for them and their patrons. In Salt Lake City a restaurant owner who doubted that his northern clientele would respond to Kentucky-type fried chicken was swayed by the Colonel's enthusiasm, and finally agreed to give it a trial.

The result—people crowded his restaurant clamoring for those golden brown chicken pieces for which the positive-thinking colonel had coined the graphic selling phrase: "It's finger lickin' good."

Colonel Sanders, a striking figure in immaculate white suit and black string tie, finally sold out his interests for two million dollars, and then was hired by the new owners as good-will ambassador at an annual salary of $40,000. His ruddy face is full of humor and intelligence; he is now over eighty years old but he still reaches out enthusiastically toward a future that calls for fresh thinking. And what is the motivation of this man and others like him? It's enthusiasm, the kind of enthusiasm that believes there is always something new and better ahead. It is creative conviction that never runs down.

Finally there is a prime factor in the maintenance of continuing enthusiasm, one that brings all other ingredients together into powerful focus. And that is a profound spiritual feeling, a faith in God, that activates a sharp awareness of life and a consuming interest in living. Age does not dull it. Pain and problems do not take the edge off of it. The blows of time and circumstance do not affect it. With this faith, a sense of confidence in life itself continues, unaffected by all the difficulties of human existence. A deep personal and vitalized faith in God is the basic factor in developing enthusiasm that never weakens. And it is vividly expressed in a statement from the Bible: "Be renewed in the spirit of your mind." (Ephesians 4:23)

I tried making a list of the most enthusiastic men I have ever known and discovered that this fundamental statement explained the enthusiasm of them all. One man on my list is an old friend, Bryson F. Kalt. One of New York's top salesmen with a phenomenal selling record, Bryson has the ability to maintain enthusiasm (without which no man can succeed as a salesman) with the help of the principle stated in those words "be renewed in the spirit of your mind."

Asked the secret of his continuing and undiminished vitality over many years, Bryson replied, "Well, it's like this. You taught me to love God and people and life and to keep my mind and spirit renewed and at a high level. I followed your positive teaching and the result has been happiness and enthusiasm that never runs down."

There you have, I believe, the basic answer to the problem of undiminished enthusiasm. Simply "be renewed in the spirit of your mind." Keep the mind perpetually renewed and you're in.

CHAPTER SEVEN

Success-Oriented Personality

Perhaps you have felt yourself geared for failure. You can change that poor self image by consciously constructing a new more success-oriented you.

Dr. Maxwell Maltz, an eminent plastic surgeon, received his degree in science from Columbia University and his doctorate in medicine from Columbia's College of Physicians and Surgeons. In addition to his ten books and eight plays, Dr. Maltz has made numerous contributions to professional medical journals worldwide. He has lectured widely and was a Professor of Plastic Surgery at the University of Nicaragua and the University of El Salvador.

Very early in his career as a plastic surgeon, Dr. Maltz realized that even though the typical reaction of a patient after cosmetic surgery was to "blossom out," there were some patients unable to see any change in themselves. Dr. Maltz finally came to the conclusion that these patients required a "face-lift" of the personality as well of of the body, and so psycho-cybernetics was created; he maintains that one's self-image must be changed in order to effectuate a positive change in the personality and behavior . . . and that this change can be programed into the consciousness of a human brain in the same manner as one programs a computer.

The dictionary definition of "cybernetics" is "the science of communication and control theory that is especially concerned with the comparative study of automatic control systems." (Example: comparing the nervous system and the brain to electrical communicating systems); goal striving and the goal-oriented behavior of mechanical systems" . . . in other words, the science of cybernetics" explains "what happens" and "what is necessary" in the purposeful behavior of machines (an idea that has given birth to myriads science fiction stories). It is also derived from the Greek word "kybernetes" meaning "helmsman" or "leader."

"Psycho" is from the Greek word, "breath" or more broadly . . . "life" or "mind." Dr. Maltz coined the word "psycho-cybernetics" to mean "to steer one's mind to a productive useful goal" in the very literal sense. In the broad sense, it relates to the analogy between the brain and a computer. Almost from the inception of computer technology, these parallels have been drawn. If the "brain" of the computer works thus and so, mimicking the functions of the human brain, then why can't the human brain be programed like a computer; if it could be done, it was postulated, then self-improvement could be programed on a pragmatic mathematical basis, resulting in little guess work to achieve the results we desire. . . . success could finally be guaranteed. This is the premise of *psycho-cybernetics,* and Dr. Maltz uses case histories to document how this is accomplished.

Identifying yourself as a success-oriented personality is a must when you start assemblying your gear. Unless you believe you can change for the better . . . that you can attain the seemingly unattainable, you are defeated before you begin. If you are having trouble finding this particular commodity to put in with your gear, call on your guides . . . they will steer you in the right direction or lend you some from their own supply. This is one item where it would be better to be overloaded. You can always pass on your excess baggage of confidence to those you meet on the trail who may be in short supply.

We Are Programed to Remember Only Our Successes

When I find an idea or concept which appeals to me, I reduce it to a short sentence of a few words and then store it away for instant retrieval in moments of need. They are also used as slogans in my advertising campaign to sell me on myself, to remind myself to keep on track. One idea from *Psycho-Cybernetics* which I have stored away in my mental filing cabinet is the idea that our "body" forgets its failures, but remembers its successes. If this were not the case, no one would become proficient in anything, including such mundane things as walking and talking. We progress by applying this process of repetition wherein we only remember our successes. Many times during my apprentice climbing sessions, I had to bring that mind-jogger out and brush it off.

This process confirms that one can, and does, program his brain, as he would program a computer . . . in my opinion, this on-going act demonstrates that the brain is the only true "P.C." (personal computer).

If "remembering only our successes" is a built-in mechanism of our body, it would seem then to be a rather basic principle, one which should perhaps be incorporated into our way of thinking and acting. It is impossible to think clearly and concisely if we are continually berating ourselves for our failures and mistakes and refusing to forgive ourselves for them.

How Well Do You Do What You Are Programed To Do?

The "science of cybernetics" and its reference to "goal-oriented machines" has always intrigued me. What makes a machine goal-oriented, and do they become disoriented if they don't reach their goals? What makes a machine a failure or a success? The answer would have to be . . . how well does it do what it was designed to do? That is an excellent criterion for our personal "success." How well do we do what we are programed to do? This, of course, takes us back to "who does the programing" . . . or to the big one . . . "why are we here in the first place"?

The last question is a philosophical one that can never be completely answered, though we all have our own theories. Let us consider instead, the mechanics of living since we are here. We know we are equipped with strength and intelligence for survival, to feed, and shelter ourselves, but beyond that . . . what? Have the advance skills evolved by our race only been developed so that we might feed and shelter ourselves better? My intuition tells me that we are intended to use our most advanced skills to meet and solve problems of every nature and description. By doing this we achieve a feeling of well-being which we interpret as happiness.

The other two questions then become the important ones. Who does the programing? . . . who decides how we will react to a situation, or how we will map out our road to success and a richer, fuller, more actualized life? We do! Its as simple as that.

And the final question . . . how well do we do what we are programed and designed to do? How well do we utilize the mechanics of living? Our ability to choose and then accomplish is part of the evolved skills of our race. We are designed to succeed, but we must be programed.

Are you a smooth-running machine, capable of following

through on the date you program for yourself, or do you run into short circuits along the way? Even though we program only the best for ourselves (as we understand it), we sometimes have trouble in getting all the parts to fit together, and sometimes the data is insufficient . . . and so the original question . . . How well do you do what you are programed to do? Only you can answer.

Determine Your Birthskills

People will often ask, "Why are my attempts to reach my goals so often frustrated?" . . . or why do you "short-circuit?" Frustration usually results when we try to perform above our present skill-levels. Pursuing a goal beyond your capabilities is foolhardy. I would like to climb Mt. Everest . . . by myself . . . with no oxygen . . . as was done by Rienhold Messner and a few others. Why can't I? Simply because its beyond my birthskills.

We are all born with certain skills and talents which we should try to identify as early as possible and then accept them for what they are. Develop them as far as possible then accept that there are certain areas blocked to us. Admitting this will enable us to focus on our legitimate abilities. By doing this you will be able to look at the diversions and set-backs inevitably encountered on the way to your performance peaks, in a realistic manner. You will be much better equipped to meet the achievable challenges.

Much frustration can be relieved by eliminating unrealistic expectations of yourself and of others. Don't however, sell yourself short and settle for less than you can be. We are all so much more than we think we are. Develop a success-oriented personality and you will find that your birthskills will surface for what they are. When you've accomplished that, you are well on your way up the mountain . . . and you will become a person others will want to climb with. Developing a success-type personality is the first real stride one makes before becoming a winner . . . a leader if you will; with that behind you, you'll find others looking at you as if you are the guide for their climb.

A success personality, then, is one which uses its skills to the best of one's ability; in a realistic manner, generates a state of well-being induced by accomplishment (which we interpret as happiness) . . . and of critical importance, refuses to settle for less.

Book Title: Psyco-Cybernetics
Author: Maxwell Maltz, M.D.F.I.C.S.
Publisher: Prentice-Hall, Inc.
Chapter: Ingredients of The "Success Type" Personality
              and How to Acquire Them.

Ingredients of The "Success-Type" Personality and How to Acquire Them

JUST as a doctor learns to diagnose disease from certain symptoms, failure and success can also be diagnosed. The reason is that a man does not simply "find" success or "come to" failure. He carries their seeds around in his personality and character.

I have found one of the most effective means of helping people achieve an adequate or "successful" personality is to first of all give them a graphic picture of what the successful personality looks like. Remember, the creative guidance

From the book PSYCHO-CYBERNETICS By Maxwell Maltz, M.D., F.I.C.S. © 1960 By Prentice-Hall, Inc., Englewood Cliffs, NJ 07632 Published by Prentice-Hall, Inc.

mechanism within you is a goal-striving mechanism, and the first requisite for using it is to have a clear-cut goal or target to shoot for. A great many people want to "improve" themselves, and long for a "better personality," who have no clear-cut idea of the direction in which improvement lies, nor what constitutes a "good personality." A good personality is one which enables you to deal effectively and appropriately with environment and reality, and to gain satisfaction from reaching goals which are important to you.

Time and again, I have seen confused and unhappy people "straighten themselves out," when they were given a goal to shoot for and a straight course to follow. There was the advertising man in his early forties, for example, who felt strangely insecure and dissatisfied with himself just after receiving an important promotion.

New Roles Require New Self-Images

"It doesn't make sense," he said. "I've worked for this, and dreamed about it. It's just what I've always wanted. I know I can do the work. And yet, for some reason my self-confidence is shaken. I suddenly wake up, as if from a dream, and ask myself—'what in the world is a small potatoes like me doing in a job like this?'" He had become super-sensitive to his appearance, and thought perhaps that his "weak chin" might be the cause of his discomfort. "I don't *look like* a business executive," he said. He felt plastic surgery might be the answer to his problem.

There was the housewife, whose children were "running her crazy" and whose husband irritated her so much that she "teed off on him" at least once a week for no cause. "What is the matter with me?" she asked. "My children are really nice kids I should be proud of. My husband is really a nice guy, and I'm always ashamed of myself afterwards." She felt that a "face lift" might give her more confidence, and cause her family to "appreciate her more."

The trouble with these people, and many more like them, is not their physical appearance but their self-image. They find themselves in a new role, and are not sure what kind of a person they are supposed to "be" in order to live up to that role. Or, they have never developed a clear-cut self-image of themselves in any role.

The Picture of Success

In this chapter I am going to give you the same "prescription" that I would give you should you come to my office.

I have found that an easy-to-remember picture of the successful personality is contained in the letters of the word "Success" itself:

The "Success-type" personality is composed of:

S-ense of direction
U-nderstanding
C-ourage
C-harity
E-steem
S-elf Confidence
S-elf Acceptance.

(1) SENSE OF DIRECTION:

The advertising executive "straightened himself out" and regained his confidence within a short time, once he saw clearly that for several years he had been motivated by strong personal goals which *he wanted* to attain, including securing his present position. These goals, which were important *to him,* kept him on the track. However, once he got the promotion, he ceased to think in terms of what he wanted, but in terms of what others expected of him, or whether he was living up to other people's goals and standards. He was like the skipper of a ship who had relinquished his hold upon the wheel, and hoped that he would drift in the right direction. He was like a mountain climber, who as long as he looked upward to the peak he wished to scale, felt and acted courageously and boldly. But when he got to the top, he felt there was nowhere else to go, and began to look down, and became afraid. He was now on the defensive, defending his present position, rather than acting like a goal-striver and going on the offensive to attain his goal. He regained control when he set himself new goals and began to think in terms of, "What do I want out of this job? What do I want to achieve? Where do I want to go?"

"Functionally, a man is somewhat like a bicycle," I told him. "A bicycle maintains its poise and equilibrium only so long as it is going forward towards something. You have a good bicycle. Your trouble is you are trying to maintain your balance sitting still, with no place to go. Its no wonder you feel shaky."

We are engineered as goal-seeking mechanisms. We are built that way. When we have no personal goal which we are interested in and which "means something" to us, we are apt to "go around in circles," feel "lost" and find life itself "aimless," and "purposeless." We are built to conquer environment, solve problems, achieve goals, and we find no real satisfaction or happiness in life without obstacles to conquer and goals to achieve. People who say that life is not worthwhile are really saying that they themselves have no personal goals which are worthwhile.

Prescription: Get yourself a goal worth working for. Better still, get yourself a project. Decide what *you want* out of a situation. Always have something ahead of you to "look forward to"—to work for and hope for. Look forward, not backward. Develop what one of the automobile manufacturers calls "the forward look." Develop a "nostalgia for the future" instead of for the past. The "forward look" and a "nostalgia for the future" can keep you youthful. Even your body doesn't function well when you stop being a goal-striver and "have nothing to look forward to." This is the reason that very often when a man retires, he dies shortly thereafter. When you're not goal-striving, not looking forward, you're not really "living." In addition to your purely personal goals, have at least one impersonal goal—or "cause" which you can identify yourself with. Get interested in some project to help your fellow man—not out of a sense of duty, but because you *want to.*

(2) Understanding:

Understanding depends upon good communication. Communication is vital to any guidance system or computer. You cannot react appropriately if the information you act upon is faulty or misunderstood. Many doctors believe that "confusion" is the basic element in neurosis. To deal effectively with a problem, you must have some understanding of its true nature. Most of our failures in human relations are due to "misunderstandings."

We expect other people to react and respond and come to the same conclusions as we do from a given set of "facts" or "circumstances." We should remember what we said in an earlier chapter—no one reacts to "things as they are," but to his own mental images. Most of the time the other person's reaction or position is not taken in order to make us suffer, nor to be hardheaded, nor malicious, but because he "understands" and interprets the situation differently from us. He is merely responding appropriately to what—*to him*—seems to be the truth about the situation. To give the other person credit for being sincere, if mistaken, rather than willful and malicious, can do much to smooth out human relations and bring about better understanding between people. Ask yourself, "How does this appear—to him?" "How does he interpret this situation?" "How does he *feel* about it?" Try to understand *why* he might "act the way he does."

Fact vs. Opinion

Many times, we create confusion, when we add our own opinion to facts and come up with the wrong conclusion. FACT: a husband cracks his knuckles. OPINION: The wife concludes, "He does that because he thinks it will annoy me." FACT: the husband sucks his teeth after eating. OPINION: The wife concludes, "If he had any regard for me, he would improve his manners." FACT: Two friends are whispering when you walk up. Suddenly they stop talking and look somewhat embarrassed. OPINION: They must have been gossiping about me.

The housewife, mentioned earlier, was able to understand that her husband's annoying mannerisms were not deliberate and willful acts on his part for the purpose of annoying her. When she stopped reacting *just as if* she had been personally insulted, she was able to pause, analyze the situation, and select an appropriate response.

Be Willing to See the Truth

Oftentimes, we color incoming sensory data by our own fears, anxieties, or desires. But to deal effectively with environment we must be willing to acknowledge the truth about it. Only when we understand what it is can we respond appropriately. We must be able to see the truth, and to accept the truth, good or bad. Bertrand Russell said one reason Hitler lost World War II was that he did not fully understand the situation.

Bearers of bad news were punished. Soon no one dared tell him the truth. Not knowing the truth, he could not act appropriately.

Many of us are individually guilty of the same error. We do not like to admit to ourselves our errors, mistakes, shortcomings, or ever admit we have been in the wrong. We do not like to acknowledge that a situation is other than we would like it to be. So we kid ourselves. And because we will not see the truth, we cannot act appropriately. Someone has said that it is a good exercise to daily admit one painful fact about ourselves to ourselves. The Success-type personality not only does not cheat and lie to other people, he learns to be honest with himself. What we call "sincerity" is itself based upon self-understanding and self-honesty. For no man can be sincere who lies to himself by "rationalizing," or telling himself "rational-lies."

Prescription: Look for and seek out true information concerning yourself, your problems, other people, or the situation, whether it is good news or bad news. Adopt the motto—"It doesn't matter who's right, but what's right." An automatic guidance system corrects its course from negative feed-back data. It acknowledges errors in order to correct them and stay on course. So must you. Admit your mistakes and errors but don't cry over them. Correct them and go forward. In dealing with other people try to see the situation from their point of view as well as your own.

(3) COURAGE:

Having a goal and understanding the situation are not enough. You must have the courage to act, for only by actions can goals, desires and beliefs be translated into realities.

Admiral William F. Halsey's personal motto was a quotation from Nelson, "No Captain can do very wrong if he places his

Ship alongside that of an Enemy." "The best defense is a strong offense,' is a military principle," said Halsey, "but its application is wider than war. All problems, personal, national, or combat, become smaller if you don't dodge them, but confront them. Touch a thistle timidly, and it pricks you; grasp it boldly and its spines crumble." (William Nichols, *Words to Live By,* Simon and Schuster, New York.)

Someone has said that FAITH is not believing something in spite of the evidence. It is the COURAGE to do something regardless of the consequences.

Why Not Bet on Yourself?

Nothing in this world is ever absolutely certain or guaranteed. Often the difference between a successful man and a failure is not one's better abilities nor ideas, but the courage that one has to bet on his ideas, to take a calculated risk—and to act.

We often think of courage in terms of heroic deeds on the battle field, in a shipwreck, or similar crisis. But everyday living requires courage, too, if it is to be effective.

Standing still, failure to act, causes people who are faced with a problem to become nervous, feel "stymied," "trapped," and can bring on a host of physical symptoms.

I tell such people: "Study the situation thoroughly, go over in your imagination the various courses of action possible to you and the consequences which can and may follow from each course. Pick out the course which gives the most promise —and go ahead. If we wait until we are absolutely certain and sure before we act we will never do anything. Any time you act you can be wrong. Any decision you make can turn out to be the wrong one. But we must not let this deter us from going after the goal we want. You must daily have the courage to risk making mistakes, risk failure, risk being humiliated. A step in the wrong direction is better than staying "on the spot" all your life. Once you're moving forward you can correct your course as you go. Your automatic guidance system cannot guide you when you're stalled, standing still."

Faith and Courage Are "Natural Instincts"

Have you ever wondered why the "urge" or desire to gamble seems to be instinctive in human nature? My own theory is that this universal "urge" is an instinct, which, when used correctly, urges us to bet on ourselves, to take a change on our own creative potentialities. When we have faith and act with courage—that is exactly what we're doing—gambling on, and taking a chance on, our own creative God-given talents. It is also my theory that people who frustrate this natural instinct, by refusing to live creatively and act with courage, are the people who develop "gambling fever" and become addicts of gambling tables. A man who will not take a chance on himself must be on something. And the man who will not act with courage sometimes seeks the feeling of courage from a bottle. Faith and courage are natural human instincts and we feel a need to express them—in one way or another.

Prescription: Be willing to make a few mistakes, to suffer a little pain to get what you want. Don't sell yourself short. "Most people," says General R. E. Chambers, Chief of the Army's Psychiatry and Neurology Consultant Division, "don't know how brave they really are. In fact, many potential heroes, both men and women, live out their lives in self-doubt. If they only knew they had these deep resources, it would help give them the self-reliance to meet most problems, even a big crisis." You've got the resources. But you never know you've got them until you act—and give them a chance to work for you.

Another helpful suggestion is to practice acting boldly and

with courage in regard to "little things." Do not wait until you can be a big hero in some dire crisis. Daily living also requires courage—and by practicing courage in little things, we develop the power and talent to act courageously in more important matters.

(4) CHARITY:

Successful personalities have some interest in and regard for other people. They have a respect for others' problems and needs. They respect the dignity of human personality and deal with other people as if they were human beings, rather than as pawns in their own game. They recognize that every person is a child of God and is a unique individuality which deserves some dignity and respect.

It is a psychologic fact that our feelings about ourselves tend to correspond to our feelings about other people. When a person begins to feel more charitably about others, he invariably begins to feel more charitably toward himself. The person who feels that "people are not very important" cannot have very much deep-down self-respect and self-regard—for he himself is "people" and with what judgment he considers others, he himself is unwittingly judged in his own mind. One of the best known methods of getting over a feeling of guilt is to stop condemning other people in your own mind—stop judging them—stop blaming them and hating them for their mistakes. You will develop a better and more adequate self-image when you begin to feel that other people are more worthy.

Another reason that Charity toward other people is symptomatic of the successful personality is because it means that the person is dealing with reality. People *are* important. People cannot for long be treated like animals or machines, or as pawns to secure personal ends. Hitler found this out. So will other tyrants wherever they may be found—in the home, in business, or in individual relationships.

Prescription: The prescription for charity is three-fold: (1) Try to develop a genuine appreciation for people by realizing the truth about them; they are children of God, unique personalities, creative beings. (2) Take the trouble to stop and think of the other person's feelings, his viewpoints, his desires and needs. Think more of what the other fellow wants, and how he must feel. A friend of mine kids his wife by telling her, whenever she asks him, "Do you love me?"—"Yes, whenever I stop and think about it." There is a lot of truth in this. We cannot feel anything about other people unless we "stop and think" about them. (3) Act as if other people are important and treat them accordingly. In your treatment of other people have regard for their feelings. We tend to feel about objects in accordance with the way we treat them.

(5) ESTEEM:

Several years ago I wrote a contribution to the "Words to Live By" feature of *This Week Magazine* on the words of Carlyle, "Alas! the fearful Unbelief is unbelief in yourself." At that time I said:

"Of all the traps and pitfalls in life, self-*dis*esteem is the deadliest, and the hardest to overcome; for it is a pit designed and dug by our own hands, summed up in the phrase, 'It's no use—I can't do it.'

"The penalty of succumbing to it is heavy—both for the individual in terms of material rewards lost, and for society in gains and progress unachieved.

"As a doctor I might also point out that defeatism has still another aspect, a curious one, which is seldom recognized. It is more than possible that the words quoted above are Carlyle's own confession of the secret that lay behind his own craggy assertiveness, his thunderous temper and waspish voice and his appalling domestic tyranny.

"Carlyle, of course, was an extreme case. But isn't it on those days when we are most subject to the 'fearful Unbelief,' when we most doubt ourselves and feel inadequate to our task —isn't it precisely then that we are most difficult to get along with?"

We simply must get it through our heads that holding a low opinion of ourselves is not a virtue, but a vice. Jealousy, for example, which is the scourge of many a marriage, is nearly always caused by self-doubt. The person with adequate self-esteem doesn't feel hostile toward others, he isn't out to prove anything, he can see facts more clearly, isn't as demanding in his claims on other people.

The housewife who felt that a face lift might cause her husband and children to appreciate her more, really needed to appreciate herself more. Middle-age, plus a few wrinkles and a few grey hairs had caused her to lose self-esteem. She then became super-sensitive to innocent remarks and actions of her family.

Prescription: Stop carrying around a mental picture of yourself as a defeated, worthless person. Stop dramatizing yourself as an object of pity and injustice. Use the practice exercises in this book to build an adequate self image.

The word "esteem" literally means to appreciate the worth of. Why do men stand in awe of the stars, and the moon, the immensity of the sea, the beauty of a flower or a sunset, and at the same time downgrade themselves? Did not the same Creator make man? Is not man himself the most marvelous creation of all? This appreciation of your own worth is not egotism unless you assume that you made yourself and should take some of the credit. Do not downgrade the product merely because you haven't used it correctly. Don't childishly blame the product for your own errors like the schoolboy who said, "This typewriter can't spell."

But the biggest secret of self-esteem is this: Begin to appreciate other people more; show respect for *any* human being merely because he is a child of God and therefore a "thing of value." Stop and think when you're dealing with people. You're dealing with a unique, individual creation of the Creator of all. Practice treating *other* people as if they had some value —and surprisingly enough your own self-esteem will go up. For real self-esteem is not derived from the great things you've done, the things you own, the mark you've made—but an appreciation of yourself for what you *are*—a child of God. When you come to this realization, however, you must necessarily conclude that all other people are to be appreciated for the same reason.

(6) SELF-CONFIDENCE:

Confidence is built upon an experience of success. When we first begin any undertaking, we are likely to have little confidence, because we have not learned from experience that we can succeed. This is true of learning to ride a bicycle, speak in public, or perform surgery. It is literally true that success breeds success. Even a small success can be used as a stepping stone to a greater one. Managers of boxers are very careful to match them carefully so they can have a graduated series of successful experiences. We can use the same technique, starting gradually, and experiencing success at first on a small scale.

Another important technique is to form the habit of remembering past successes, and forgetting failures. This is the way both an electronic computer and the human brain are supposed to operate. Practice improves skill and success in basketball, golf, horseshoe pitching, or salesmanship, not because "repetition" has any value in itself. If it did we would "learn" our errors instead of our "hits." A person learning to pitch horseshoes, for example, will miss the stake many more times than he will hit it. If mere repetition were the answer to improved skill, his practice should make him more expert at missing since that is what he has practiced most. However, although his misses may outnumber hits ten to one, through practice his misses gradually diminish and his hits come more and more frequently. This is because the computer in his brain remembers and reinforces his successful attempts, and forgets the misses.

This is the way that both an electronic computer and our own success mechanisms learn to succeed.

Yet, what do most of us do? We destroy our self-confidence by remembering past failures and forgetting all about past successes. We not only remember failures, we impress them on our minds with emotion. We condemn ourselves. We flay ourselves with shame and remorse (both are highly egotistical, self-centered emotions). And self-confidence disappears.

It doesn't matter how many times you have failed in the past. What matters is the successful attempt, which should be remembered, reinforced, and dwelt upon. Charles Kettering has said that any young man who wants to be a scientist must be willing to fail 99 times before he succeeds once, and suffer no ego damage because of it.

Prescription: Use errors and mistakes as a way to learning —then dismiss them from your mind. Deliberately remember and picture to yourself past successes. Everyone has succeeded *sometime* at *something.* Especially, when beginning a new task, call up the *feelings* you experienced in some past success, however small it might have been.

Dr. Winfred Overholser, Superintendent of St. Elizabeth's Hospital has said that recalling brave moments is a very sound way to restore belief in yourself; that too many people are prone to let one or two failures blot out all good memories. If we will systematically relive our brave moments in memory, he says, we will be surprised to see we had more courage than we thought. Dr. Overholser recommends the practice of vividly remembering our past successes and brave moments as an invaluable aid whenever self-confidence is shaken.

(7) SELF-ACCEPTANCE:

No real success or genuine happiness is possible until a person gains some degree of self-acceptance. The most miserable and tortured people in the world are those who are continually straining and striving to convince themselves and others that they are something other than what they basically are. And there is no relief and satisfaction like that that comes when one finally gives up the shams and pretenses and is willing to be himself. Success, which comes from self-expression, often eludes those who strive and strain to "be somebody," and often comes, almost of its own accord, when a person becomes willing to relax and—"Be Himself."

Changing your self-image does not mean changing your *self,* or improving your self, but changing your own *mental picture,* your own *estimation,* conception, and realization of that self. The amazing results which follow from developing an adequate and realistic self-image, come about, not as a result of self-transformation, but from self-realization, and self-revelation. Your "self," right now, is what it has always been, and all that it can ever be. You did not create it. You cannot change it. You can, however, realize it, and make the most of *what already is* by gaining a true mental picture of your actual self. There is no use straining to "be somebody." You are what you are—now. You *are* somebody, not because you've made a million dollars, or drive the biggest car in your block, or win at bridge—but because God created you in His own image.

Most of us are better, wiser, stronger, more competent—*now,* than we realize. Creating a better self-image does not *create* new abilities, talents, powers—it releases and utilizes them.

We can change our personality, but not our basic self. Personality is a tool, an outlet, a focal point of the "self" that we use in dealing with the world. It is the sum total of our habits, attitudes, learned skills, which we use as a *method* of expressing ourselves.

"You" Are Not Your Mistakes

Self-acceptance means accepting and coming to terms with ourselves now, just as we are, with all our faults, weaknesses, shortcomings, errors, as well as our assets and strengths. Self-acceptance is easier, however, if we realize that these negatives *belong* to us—they *are* not us. Many people shy away from healthy self-acceptance because they insist upon identifying themselves with their mistakes. You may have made a mistake, but this does not mean that you *are* a mistake. You may not be expressing yourself properly and fully, but this does not mean you yourself are "no good."

We must recognize our mistakes and shortcomings before we can correct them.

The first step toward acquiring knowledge is the recognition of those areas where you are ignorant. The first step toward becoming stronger is the recognition that you are weak. And all religions teach that the first step toward salvation is the self-confession that you are a sinner. In the journey toward the goal of ideal self-expression, we must use negative feed-back data to correct course, as in any other goal-striving situation.

This requires admitting to ourselves—*and accepting the fact,* that our personality, our "expressed self," or what some psychologists call our "actual self," is always imperfect and short of the mark.

No one ever succeeds during a life time in fully expressing

or bringing into actuality all the potentialities of the Real Self. In our Actual, expressed Self, we never exhaust all the possibilities and powers of the Real Self. We can always learn more, perform better, behave better. The Actual Self is necessarily imperfect. Throughout life it is always *moving toward* an ideal goal, but never arriving. The Actual Self is not a static but a dynamic thing. It is never completed and final, but always in a state of growth.

It is important that we learn to accept this Actual Self, with all its imperfections, because it is the only vehicle we have. The neurotic rejects his Actual Self and hates it because it is imperfect. In its place he tries to create a fictitious ideal self which is already perfect, has already "arrived." Trying to maintain the sham and fiction is not only a terrific mental strain, but he continually invites disappointment and frustration when he tries to operate in a real world with a fictititous self. A stage coach may not be the most desirable transportation in the world, but a real stage coach will still take you coast to coast more satisfactorily than will a fictitious jet airliner.

Prescription: Accept yourself as you are—and start from there. Learn to emotionally tolerate imperfection in yourself. It is necessary to intellectually recognize our shortcomings, but disastrous to hate ourselves because of them. Differentiate between your "self" and your behavior. "You" are not ruined nor worthless because you made a mistake or got off course, anymore than a typewriter is worthless which makes an error, or a violin which sounds a sour note. Don't hate yourself because you're not perfect. You have a lots of company. No one else is, either, and those who try to pretend they are, kid themselves.

You Are "Somebody"—Now!

Many people hate and reject themselves because they feel and experience perfectly natural biological desires. Others reject themselves because they do not conform to the current fashion or standard for physical proportions. I can remember in the 1920's when many women felt ashamed of themselves because they had breasts. The boyish figure was in vogue and bosoms were taboo. Today, many young girls develop anxieties because they do not have 40 inch busts. In the 1920's women used to come to me and in effect say—"Make me somebody, by reducing the size of my breasts." Today, the plea is, "Make me somebody, by increasing the size of my breasts." This seeking for identity—this desire for selfhood—this urge to be "somebody" is universal, but we make a mistake when we seek it in conformity, in the approval of other people, or in material things. It is a gift of God. You *are*— period. Many people say in effect to themselves, "Because I am skinny, fat, short, too tall, etc.—I am nothing." Say to your self instead, "I may not be perfect, I may have faults and weaknesses, I might have gotten off the track, I may have a long way to go—but I *am something* and I will make the most of that something."

"It is the young man of little faith who says, 'I am nothing,' " said Edward W. Bok. "It is the young man of true conception who says, 'I am everything,' and then goes to prove it. That does not spell conceit or egotism, and if people think it does, let them think so. Enough for us to know that it means faith, trust, confidence, the human expression of the God within us. He says, 'Do my work.' Go and do it. No matter what it is. Do it, but do it with a zest; a keenness; a gusto that surmounts obstacles and brushes aside discouragement."

Accept yourself. Be yourself. You cannot realize the potentialities and possibilities inherent in that unique and special something which is "YOU" if you keep turning your back upon it, feeling ashamed of it, hating it, refusing to recognize it.

Points to Remember
(Fill in)

1.
2.
3.
4.
5.
6.
7.

CHAPTER EIGHT

Self-Reliance

One of the elements of self you must learn is faith in your own self, in your power and ability to achieve new heights. Dr. Ari Kiev is a practicing psychiatrist who has achieved worldwide recognition for his research and writings in the fields of anthropology, psychology and psychiatry. He was Clinical Associate Professor of Psychiatry at Cornell University Medical College and director of the Social Psychiatry Research Institute in New York. He is a frequent guest on network television programs and is the author of eight books.

In a *Strategy for Success,* Dr. Kiev expands upon the principles first outlined in his now classic, *A Strategy for Daily Living,* which has been used by millions in comprehending and achieving the phenomenon of success. In his life strategy questionnaire, he forces one to look critically at himself and his attitudes. The following questions are considered:

- Does your most important goal relate to your natural abilities?

- How much time do you spend each day in activity related to your most important goal?

- How do you master such problems as limited time, multiple commitments, and conflicting priorities?

- How do you reconcile your personal objectives with the objectives of others?

- How do you maintain your good humor in the face of adversity and stress?

- What techniques do you use to conserve time, energy and money?

The strategy questionnaire ends with this caveat. . . . "Remember, the few minutes you take to write down the answers to the above questions will repay you many times over and will increase immeasurably the value of this book to you."

There is enough source material for each chapter to fill a book, but this is Dr. Kiev's style of writing. Instead of taking an idea and worrying it to death by examining it from every conceivable (and sometimes inconceivable) angle, as some writers do, he throws a new idea into almost every paragraph for you to examine from all angles. Dr. Kiev expects you to do some of the work, even though it seems to be human nature to look around for a set of rules to follow. Whether this is instinctive, or something that has been instilled in us by our culture (personally, I lean towards this latter explanation), we will never grow by following someone else's set of rules. If we do, and then decide to adopt them, we have then made them our own, and can thus accept responsibility for the results. Dr. Kiev gives you the necessary tools to make up your own set of rules. This is true self-reliance, and a most critical addition to your survival kit.

The first page of Dr. Kiev's book is devoted to a quote from his father, Isaac Edward Kiev. "No one has the right to say to another fellow adventurer; Friend, you have lost the way. But each of us has an obligation to ask ourselves, Have I lost the way? Have I turned my back on what I know to be true and just? Have I betrayed my own finest instincts? Have I misused God's gift of body and mind?" This quote connotes responsibility for self and to me embodies the true essence of self-reliance.

Self-Reliance is Being Totally Responsible for Oneself.

Until recently, education in most countries was mainly the privilege of the wealthy and titled. In 19th Century England, three poor men who wished to better themselves started meeting three times a week to share the little education they did have. Very quickly the group grew to over one-hundred young men contributing to the total group effort. Their self-instruction was soon augmented by participation from leading educators who applauded their enterprise. (Self-Help by Samuel Smiles) This group demonstrated the self-reliance theme. Major companies have spent millions of dollars trying to instill self-reliance in their employees, particularly since self-starters seem to be well on their way to becoming an endangered species. Corporations know that their company's financial success rests on the ability of their engineers to design and create the product, on the ability of the assembly plant worker to manufacture it, on the ability of the executive to program the product, and the ability of the sales force to move the finished merchandise through the pipeline. A break-down in performance anywhere along the line affects the whole chain. Is it small wonder then that the self-reliance of the individual is important to a company?

Responsibility is standing on your own two feet . . . being responsible enough to make sure you have the education and the workskills that will enable you to support yourself under any circumstances . . . and the willingness to do whatever is necessary (legally) to provide for yourself and any minor members of your family. This applies equally to male or female.

One of the most courageous and far-reaching steps a person can take is to assume total responsibility for his or her actions. When we blame others for our misfortunes or attribute our happiness to a source outside of ourselves, we are admitting that others are in control of our destiny. If so, how can you ever hope to win by any effort of your own? How can you possibly choose a way you wish to go? If you use that premise, any attempts to achieve would become rather futile.

Components of Self-Reliance

Self-reliance is creating your own emotional climate. This is easier than it sounds. If you believe that others are also in control of your well-being . . . that some person or circumstance is vital to your happiness, you will be vulnerable to disappointment and hurt when they, or it, "fails" you. Don't bother putting up a wall to avoid hurt, it is an integral part of living; you lose too much of the good in life by trying to avoid the hurt. Feel it, experience it, accept it for what it is and what you can learn from it, then release it, and use the moment to make tomorrow better. When you are in control, you can act instead of react.

Self-Reliance is accepting yourself where you are at any given moment and accepting that you are there as a result of all that has gone before. The great philosophers emphasized the importance of living in the present. You will understand why if you think of the present moment as the "point of contact," that powerful moment where yesterday and tomorrow meet. Today is the result of past "present moments" and tomorrow will be the result of actions taken right now in the only moment that is ours . . . the present. Self-reliance is understanding that you don't grow by diminishing those around you. Give credit where credit is due. If you wish to stand taller, give stature to those around you and you will find yourself reaching and growing.

Self-reliance is being honest with those with whom you have contracts. Give your boss a full-days work. Give your family the necessary support to give children a good foundation, a secure base camp for all.

Self-reliance is being honest with yourself. Don't be a "phony." As the cliche say's, "There's nothing new under the sun," so we can't avoid doing a bit of plagiarism now and then; however, don't do it deliberately. Don't lay claim to knowledge and skills you don't possess. As Abraham Lincoln said, ". . . you can't fool all the people, all the time." You may be able to sleep through class, crib on exams, have someone write your thesis, manage to get a degree, and even survive in the real world, but at some point, you will have to defend what you advocate. I could claim to be the world's champion mountain climber, and as long as I could adroitly waltz around any attempts to get me on a mountain, I could get away with it; however, without actually gaining the skills by dint of hard work and study, my first climb would find me in a heap at the bottom instead of on top. Mountain climbing is a prime example of teaching yourself self-reliance in one of the most incisive programs for growth. I can use help in getting my gear together, making decisions about where to go, where to stay, making reservations, finding the guide, etc., but I'm the only one who can get me up the mountain and back.

I remember one particularly difficult moment on the "Grand" in the Tetons. I was doing a repel. Basically, this entails pushing away from the mountain with your feet as you maneuver down a rope. One hundred twenty feet is one of the longer drops you will ever make at one time. This one was one hundred thirty feet and very tricky. To the left, it was safe

. . . to the right was a drop-off wall where there was no purchase for my feet to assist in the repel. Directly above me were those waiting their turn, watching as I repelled my body into the clouds and mist which shrouded the entire mountain. Below me were the two climbers who had gone before me. Well into the repel, I could hear the guides voices encouraging me to embrace the solid wall in front of me and to avoid the openness and the drop-off just to my right. I started down all right and then somehow I got turned around in the mist, then banged my arm into a cliff so badly that it was paralyzed for a few moments. I hung there with one useless arm, in a cloud layer so thick I couldn't see a thing in any direction. When my aching arm allowed it, I started a swing in the direction I felt I should be going, praying it was the right way. Finally, I could see where I should be getting a toehold, but I couldn't reach it. I made three complete turns and came face to face with the solid side of the mountain. I'm still not sure how I did it . . . I know I just kept the swing going until I could finally touch the ledge with my feet and could continue my repel. I was forced to help myself. There was no room for error. My guide was high above me, obscured by the clouds, and the other climbers were out of sight in the cloud layer below me . . . there I was, with five others, and yet I was truly alone. The message was loud and clear. . . . help yourself.

In your personal climb, don't wait to be confronted by a need for self-reliance. Make it a habit . . . make it a basic premise of your life. With self-reliance in your backpack, you will discover that motivating yourself is a natural act . . . a formidable one perhaps, but the only path to becoming a self-starter. The ability of the individual to reach his or her potential, can be accomplished only through self-motivation and self-reliance.

Book Title: A Strategy For Success
Author: Ari Kiev, M.D.
Publisher: Macmillan Publishing Co., Inc., New York
Chapter: Self-Reliance

Self-Reliance

> If I were to try to read, much less answer all the
> attacks made on me, this shop might as well be closed
> for any other business. I do the very best I know how,
> the very best I can, and I mean to keep on doing so
> until the end. If the end brings me out all right, then
> what is said against me won't matter. If the end brings
> me out wrong, then ten angels swearing I was right
> would make no difference.
>
> —Lincoln

The modern world, with all its opportunity for personal growth, creates much self-doubt, uncertainty, and anxiety. Advances in medical technology, improvements in the standard of living, and greater mastery of the environment have led to greater freedom but not to improvements in the individual's quality of life. What is wrong? Did the ancients have greater insight into the means of achieving happiness? I don't think so. But they were more fortunate in having work which required individual effort. This fostered self-reliance. They depended less than we do on decisions made by others in their daily lives. Today, people prepare for a time when others will be sovereign over them in their work. We have little control over sources of food, electricity, and information, upon all of which we depend. More important, we depend on others in matters where we may be better able to make our own decisions, such as work and residence.

A STRATEGY FOR SUCCESS By Ari Kiev, M.D. Copyright © by Ari Kiev 1977
Reprinted by permission of the author.

The increased population and an apparent scarcity of the jobs, residences, and rewards that everyone wants create anxiety, which initiates a vicious circle of increasing dependence on the opinions of others. Stop accepting the necessity of obtaining the things you feel you must have. The moment you begin to live below your means or at a level where you can maintain control over your life without economic dependency and insecurity, that moment you gain personal freedom.

Don't discuss your decisions to change with anyone who has an inclination to resist change. He will prove insensitive to your desire. Even listening to the "experts" may weaken your courage to act. This would attest only to your suggestibility; it would not mean that your original decision was invalid. Sounding out others for reassurance does not eliminate the anxiety of decision-making. In fact, if you discuss crucial matters with unqualified people, you may create more anxiety and confusion for yourself. You have added their uncertainty to your own.

Many people turn to parents for advice, only to find that they have re-created childhood patterns of relationships which may create conflict, recrimination, and dissatisfaction. You must believe in the validity of your own wishes and desires. Trust yourself, even if all your judgments in the past have proved inaccurate. Through perseverance, you will find the right track.

The magnetism of outstanding performers derives from their total absorption in activity. Their actions relate to their purposes. They do not seem preoccupied with other matters, nor do they approach their tasks grudgingly. Concentration, persistence, and practice characterize their activities, which at times seem effortless. Belief in oneself and willingness to make the effort count more than talent. You inherit talents and develop them through effort. Reliability and trustworthiness constitute the essence of character, which develops in relation to other people. While talent and character can exist apart, it is the person with character who becomes the leader. Character develops through decision and choices; reputation depends on the opinions of others. As Mark Twain wrote: "The miracle or the power that elevates the few is to be found in their industry, application and perseverance under the prompting of a brave, determined spirit."

Selecting a Course of Action

In selecting a course of action, consider what Pythagoras wrote: "Choose always the way that seems best, however rough it may be, and custom will soon render it easy and agreeable." Developing new habits makes it possible to change all kinds of things, since they overcome bad habits.

Intellectual habits will increase self-understanding, which justifies your effort and commitment. Knowledge brings a reduction of distress—not necessarily happiness. Ignorance creates uneasiness and anxiety.

Talk to those representing established beliefs which favor the status quo when you want confirmation of a decision to stay put. But remember, unless people have experience with personal change, possess considerable autonomy, and listen skillfully and sympathetically, don't talk to them about your plans which do not favor the status quo.

People with negative attitudes won't encourage you, and those struggling with similar problems may reinforce your doubts about doing what you want. Conversely, action-oriented people may encourage you without listening because of their zeal for action. Avoid talking to gossips, who may spread rumors about your plans. You will know this has boomeranged when inquisitive busybodies offer uninvited opinions. Only someone who can view your problem sympathetically and objectively will help you without influencing you one way or the other in terms of his own situation.

Your self-concept and your world view determines your overall adjustment. Misconceptions about yourself or the world based on outdated attitudes and knowledge will color your perceptions, encourage illusory thinking, and reduce your effort. And fear of humiliation and exposure will lead to further self-doubt, self-deception, and defensiveness.

Recognition of your characteristic behavior can help you gain control of yourself and your life. Understanding the origins of such behavior will facilitate the development of such insight. Inasmuch as your self-concept influences the outcome of your efforts, and inasmuch as you decide what to think of yourself, you can program yourself for success or failure by virtue of the self-concept you adopt.

Assessing Conflict

At times you may be attracted to something you want to avoid. Or you may have to choose between two undesirable or two desirable possibilities. Such choices create conflict, which may in turn stimulate change. Initiating changes which permit self-expression may put the conflict in abeyance and give you a sense of satisfaction. Deciding to change can lead to an assessment of present circumstances, and further stimulus to change if you discover that your present situation does not fulfill your real needs.

Consider how much you have invested in symbols and myths rather than real things. Successful people focus their concerns on getting a job done rather than on the external trappings of their position.

When you try to change, distinguish between changing symbols and changing the real substratum of your existence. Consider where you feel most creative or satisfied. Is it at work or

at home, away from the daily pressures of committees, supervisors, or subordinates?

We obtain what we expect from situations. You may only
reluctantly stop depending on others to define your identity.
Dependency can be very comforting while it also meets the
dependency needs of those on whom you depend. When you
stop acting in terms of established expectations, you will experience discomfort. This invariably happens when you begin to
take responsibility for yourself. Those on whom you have
depended may begin to show evidence of their dependency.

Obstacles to Self-Reliance

1. Criticizing yourself to avoid anticipated criticism from
others constitutes a major obstacle to self-reliance. Fear of
criticism from others can inhibit efforts to take the initiative.
Checking things out with others before you act will reduce
your sense of responsibility for your actions and your sense of
satisfaction in accomplishment. You must of course weigh this
against the secure feeling that comes from an activity ap-
proved by others.

Discussing the feasibility of your goals with your peers may
divert you from your natural interests or may involve you with
approaches which do not capitalize on your own resources.

If you invite others to predict the outcome of your efforts,
they will do so without accounting for the subtle factors that
make for success, such as your willingness to keep going despite failure. Others may assure you that it is okay to stop
before you reach your objectives. Such "support" can impede
last-ditch efforts to achieve a goal.

Dreams are fragile and ought not to be exposed to either the
unsympathetic responses of others, which can discourage
effort, or the generous enthusiasm of others, which can turn
a challenge into an obligation to perform. Anticipating the

responses of others, you may unwittingly try to meet their objections or obtain their approval in your daily efforts. This will distract you from your objectives. You may begin to play-act, to do "the right thing." You may appear to be busy, attending meetings which lead nowhere or becoming excessively fastidious.

At home, you may keep the house so neat as to make it unsuitable for relaxing, or you may feign positive responses to mask negative ones. Unfortunately, the more you suppress, the more you will experience anxiety and fear of losing control. When consciously suppressed, emotions tend to become magnified, leading to more effort to create a conventional impression. Efforts to become self-reliant are minimized by efforts to be accepted and not criticized.

2. Unwillingness to allow yourself to feel good or to act confidently also impedes self-reliance, and stems from fear that others will reject you unless you accept their pessimism or caution about you and act critically toward yourself. This might be satisfactory if you obtained approval from such self-criticism. More likely, such behavior will invite affirmations from others about your negative view of yourself, which can only confuse you further.

Criticizing yourself because of failure to measure up to someone's expectations does not necessarily cut off their criticism. The same principle applies to efforts to meet internalized parental standards. In fact, the more you try to meet any standards other than your own, the more you will build up resentment toward yourself. The self-reliant individual relies on his own standards to judge his actions. This leads to freedom and creativity.

The same is true of any external standards. The achievement of such goals adds little to your sense of self. Recognizing this, you may feel distressed when others praise someone who has attained these superficial materialistic or conventional goals. You need not criticize others or point to the greater validity of your goals. Such "sour grapes" can only lessen your confidence in yourself.

Feeling good about yourself may require the avoidance of opinions people have of you or of other people, the latter being more personal than you may think. Additionally, realistic self-contained goals can be achieved through the cumulative impact of daily efforts, so that you can gain satisfaction from your work each day.

It makes no sense to suffer because of failure to achieve unrealistic goals which cannot be pursued on a daily basis, or which require you to delay acting until you have met the perfectionistic standards of others.

Define what gives you positive feelings and confidence. It may require considerable effort to test your limits and to discover your real potential.

3. Self-sacrifice, justified by custom, loyalty, and friendship, is also an obstacle to self-reliance. Duty and tradition often serve to justify neglect of self and keep others bound to you through their reciprocal obligation to you. To overcome this obstacle, review the ways in which you sacrifice your own interest or neglect to pursue your own objectives. Self-interest does not require you to be boastful, selfish, overbearing, or controlling, but for you to recognize your talents and interests and the validity of pursuing them without waiting for others to do it for you.

Self-sacrifice may mean doing what you cannot comfortably refuse to do. Unwittingly you may draw anger. Doing something you do not really want to do will generate resentment and the obligation of reciprocity, which reinforces dependency on others.

4. Fear of solitude discourages self-reliance because of the belief that it will perpetuate isolation from others. Extreme

dependency, which depletes the sense of self, constitutes the basis of this fear. Involvement in solitary activities builds self-reliance and increases your ability to respond selectively to the demands of others.

Shyness and a preference for solitude can help you become self-reliant. You may have difficulty in dealing with the dependency needs of others. An inclination to cooperate simply to be agreeable, a willingness to go along with others, reduces personal strength and self-reliance. Even though you may feel comfortable in solitude, you may not know how to prevent the intrusion of others.

You may be afraid to be alone. You may be tied to the demands of others or feel obligated to explain your time to them. When alone, you may fear that it is necessary to explain your thoughts to others—thereby defeating the value of solitude. It takes time to learn to rely upon yourself, time for practical experiences in building up self-confidence.

Practical experiences in being alone can be traveling alone, eating alone in a restaurant, and other activities which ordinarily might be done with others. A valuable by-product of this is an increased awareness of the people around you, and tolerance for others who may also be experiencing discomfort in similar situations.

5. Excessive efforts to be consistent can impede the development of self-reliance. Must you be consistent? At what point does a shift of plans serve as rationalization for neglecting responsibilities or shirking objectives? A good rule is to allow yourself sufficient time at any activity to decide whether you really wish to continue it. Stick to what you decide to do. Don't feel obligated to persist in tasks carried over from the past. Periodically assess what you really wish to do and what your next goals may be, and set aside time for implementing them. You can shift gears at any time, but allow yourself time to ascertain whether you wish to relinquish an activity.

You may not want to change directions because others may be upset by the shift. You can tie yourself to the past and reduce the faith that others have in your ability to do what suits you best. Thus, your adherence to previously successful behavior patterns can create constraints, particularly if you don't wish to give them up.

An undue investment in the symbols and trappings of power can prove burdensome when economic demands require that you relinquish them. The opinions of others weigh heavily here and add to the discomfort. Ideally, you should have functioned from an inner center of drives and dreams in the past and should never have invested too heavily in external symbols.

If you have been mysterious and suddenly open up, you may find that others harbor various misconceptions about yourself and your activities. Do not accept these notions as indications of things to come, but as a reflection of misinformation.

6. Try to overcome the compulsion to do more than one thing at a time. Such overcommitment generates anxiety and a feeling of not having sufficient time. You may overschedule activities in your eagerness to reach your objectives. Ideally, you should plan for periods of rest and solitude, as well as for periodic reassessment of progress and realignment. Consider also the extent of your omnipotent fantasies reinforced by the dependency of others, which give you a feeling of being special and indispensable. Learn to admit your failings and be willing to relinquish the illusory power assigned to you by others. Allow others to do things for themselves and to share in the credit of joint tasks. This will enable you to concentrate on your own most important issues. Begin to establish priorities. If you concentrate on one thing at a time, you will be encouraged to delegate routine tasks to others.

Mastering the present moment will increase your sense of self-reliance as well as your chances of achieving your objectives without feeling harried. You may have multiple objectives, but focus on only one at any given moment. Like many people, you may try to contain the tasks before you by allocating specific amounts of time to them. Once you establish control over many activities and phenomena, you may reach an equilibrium, at which point you may again experience anxiety because the relative calm may make you feel that you are not accomplishing enough or that there is insufficient challenge. This may lead to further overcommitment. Thus you may fluctuate from being overwhelmed to being understimulated. Ideally, you should be able to strike a balance between the two states. If you find yourself fearful of concentrating on what is before you, ignoring other matters, remember that this state will pass, and so will the urgency to do many things.

Thus you will begin to flow with your own feelings, doing more sometimes and less at other times, without self-doubt or guilt.

7. Trying too hard to order your thoughts may inhibit your thinking. You may even become so anxious about being ill-prepared that you will devote excess energy to organizing and scrupulously planning your thoughts, often becoming preoccupied about leaving things out. You may try to make black-and-white distinctions and may be intolerant of ambiguity and uncertainty. Actually, organization of your thinking may lead to reduced spontaneity, inhibition, and uncertainty.

To cope with this, try absorbing activities which require focused but not planned thought. A good example is skiing, for in order to avoid falling while engaged in this activity, you must concentrate. This involves the processing of information through the brain but not thinking about thinking, an activity which can be highly maladaptive.

8. Seeking permission from others to pursue your objectives invites resistance and an excuse to delay beginning. When you act insincerely or contrary to your instincts for the sake of cooperativeness, your self-doubt will increase. Consider how often you agree with others espousing ideas you don't believe in, and how often you willingly share thoughts which you really prefer to keep to yourself. Such efforts to appear to be someone you are not rather than to be who you are create conflict and self-doubt. When you act contrary to your inclinations, you automatically inhibit self-reliance.

On the other hand, self-reliance facilitates concentration and independence of thought, and will enable you to do what you choose to do without having to conform to public opinion. Self-reliance will help you overcome obsessions, self-doubt, and excessive emotionalism.

9. An inclination to follow the crowd impedes independent thought. Concern about the opinions of others results in a reluctance to step forward with your unique view of the world and diminishes the confidence so critical for original thinking. The moment you begin to think for yourself, you may find yourself obsessed with what others think; this may cloud your thought processes producing turmoil and loss of will.

Start acting in some direction. Movement itself will eliminate uncertainty, procrastination, indecision, and anxiety of inertia.

The self-reliant individual focuses on the present, not on the past. He does not overreact to events but awaits their inevitable outcome, focusing only on what he can do at any one time. The key is involvement in activity which draws upon all your resources, letting them flow forth naturally. Such abandonment in constructive activity leads to inspiration. Many seek this feeling of abandonment in alcohol or drugs, which create a semblance of a mystical union with higher powers. War, gambling, and other dangerous pursuits produce similar states of self-abandonment.

Life-Styles Compatible with Self-Actualization

Self-actualization develops best with minimum social activity. Socializing fosters sentiments of affection, tolerance, and understanding which can make you abandon your own realm of thoughts. The less frustration you have in areas unrelated to your objectives, the more you will be able to concentrate on efforts likely to facilitate growth and development.

The absence of cares, however, may prove to be a trap if you concern yourself with the opinions of those who would discourage original activity. The same applies to efforts to find happiness outside yourself. An excessive concern for results, particularly immediate ones, will also stifle creativity and the desire to persevere in the face of obstacles.

A respect for truth increases the ability to withstand adversity. Real strength comes from recognizing that others may supersede you. Let things happen. Don't hold on to the past at your own expense. Avoid identifying yourself in terms of material possessions, position, and the symbols of "success."

Everyone differs in the preference of values which must be pursued. Beware of those who presume to know what is best for you. The risk here is that you may give up what you prize most.

Resist the inclination to justify yourself to others. You should be neither chided for what you do wrong nor overpraised for what works out.

Don't focus excessively on the past to determine what to do. The past can only suggest clues as to what may give you the most excitement and satisfaction. Don't feel that you must keep constant. As Emerson said, "Why should we import rags and relics into the new hour? What you do now ought to hold for now and only now. You need not feel obligated to continue to do it."

Every moment offers the opportunity to begin anew.

You may prefer certainty, but once you recognize the inevitability of change, you will be better able to cope with the present and will not try to fit it into an idealized model of the past. Only by living fully in the moment can you truly learn about yourself and the nature of the world; "so to be is the sole outlet of so to know," said Emerson.

When you read, for example, do so thoughtfully. Know what you are looking for before you start. Avoid the inclination to get caught up with the fascination of words, or to drown yourself in facts without a purpose or a system. By reading with a purpose, you will read more rapidly and retain more of what you read.

Solitude promotes self-actualization by putting you in touch with your innermost thoughts, which differ from the social thoughts produced in company. Take the opportunity to focus on your innermost thoughts next time you find yourself waiting impatiently for a bus or a plane. This will surely reduce your distress. At times you should find a hideaway—with no phones or interruptions—for concentrated thought and effort.

Concentrate on one mental image at a time. To do this, make a conscious effort to avoid talkative, distressed, and conflict-ridden people. When you cannot avoid such individuals, try to be silent until they have expended their thoughts. Do not become captivated or involved with them or even with those whose company you enjoy, for they can distract you when you wish to concentrate. Remember, too, that interest and calmness of mind and body can facilitate concentration. So focus on what interests you and avoid unnecessary movement.

Whenever you resume an intellectual activity, begin with the themes that interested you previously. When your thinking becomes dull and focused on words, conjure up images of real people, events, or situations. This will revitalize your thoughts. Think of examples even if you don't ultimately use them.

Intrusive thoughts may interfere with concentration. These thoughts may be pleasant or negative but often cannot easily be dismissed from consciousness. Close inspection of such obsessive thinking often reveals an underlying fear of failure and an excessive concern for the opinions of others, which interfere with involvement in the task.

These thoughts may also occur in the course of a relationship with others, such as being especially affable to someone you dislike, which generates repressed thoughts and anger. Consider whether this type of circumstance may have preceded your efforts to concentrate.

Writing can help you to focus attention and initiate activity. By writing things down, you reduce vagueness and unwillingness to commit yourself. In writing down your goals, you automatically assume more responsibility.

To improve your focus, record the central theme of your goal on a 3″ × 5″ card and periodically examine it as a reminder to keep on target. Genuine interest increases the incentive to concentrate. Find models for thinking in other areas which may be applicable to your present situation. Consider how well something may be done.

Self-Reliance Checklist

1. List activities you shared with others this past week, dividing the list in two columns: those you wished to do and those you felt obligated to do.

2. List the activities in which you persuaded someone else to do what you wanted to do.

3. List activities that you would have preferred to do alone.

4. List the people you find it easiest to get along with.

5. Which people do you naturally find yourself being friendly with?

6. Do you prefer to keep slightly uninvolved when work-

ing with others, or do you find yourself becoming absorbed by the group and losing your identity?

7. Do you overreact to criticism, or are you able to listen quietly while others criticize or rebuke you, moving on without saying anything about it?

8. Are you uncomfortable when people turn to you for advice?

9. Do you willingly assume responsibility?

10. Do you have trouble delegating tasks to others?

11. Do you like everything to be orderly—for example, do you like to do routine things at the same times each day, and do you become upset if you are off schedule?

12. In doing things you have never done before, do you seek permission or advice from others before proceeding, or are you willing to take small risks on your own?

13. Do you take on jobs which are harder than the routine? Do you try to achieve goals over your head?

14. Do you avoid doing things that you don't understand or that you find complicated? How long does it take you to give up on a task?

15. Does fear of criticism or ridicule prevent you from doing what you want?

16. Are you inclined to criticize others, to be ''helpful,' or do you allow them to fumble so that they may learn more effectively?

17. Do you like to plan everything down to the smallest detail?

18. Do you review past mistakes to try to correct them in the future? How much time do you spend doing this?

19. Do you believe you can determine what is best for you or do you believe others know best?

20. Do you put your interests aside to help others?

21. Do you feel uncomfortable about reaching decisions by yourself?

22. Do you keep at a task even when you become frustrated and feel as though you are getting nowhere?

23. How easily are you distracted by others? What techniques do you use to silently convey to other people that you wish to stop a conversation and get back to what you were doing?

24. Do you have difficulty expressing anger?

25. Do you have difficulty expressing affection?

26. Do you avoid giving advice when asked so as not to make people dependent on you?

27. Do you frequently ask questions of others when you know the answer, or when you should be able to come up with an answer as good as anyone else's?

28. Do you ask advice about decisions before acting on them?

29. Are you afraid of assuming new responsibilities?

30. Are you meticulous, exacting, perfectionistic?

31. Do you enjoy taking risks?

32. Do you like new situations?

33. Do you have trouble saying no?

CHAPTER NINE

Commitment

Not only must you rely on your own power and ability but you must be completely committed to gaining your objective despite obstacles and interference. Merle Shain is a graduate social worker with experience as a case worker in family counseling. She is also a radio and T.V. scriptwriter, story editor, interviewer, hostess and critic, as well as having been a newspaper feature writer and associate editor of Chatelain, a Canadian woman's magazine. She has written one other book, *Some Men Are More Perfect Than Others,* which has also received wide acclaim.

The publishers of Ms. Shain's *When Lovers are Friends,* have described her style of writing as being ". . . like a letter from a compassionate and wise friend." By exploring the question of how to find the right kind of love for ourselves, she subtly points out that self-acceptance is the key not only to successful loving, but succesful living.

If you're looking for "another list" of ten steps to guide you up your mountain, read this chapter later; that is simply not

Ms. Shain's style. What you will find is the clairvoyant insight of a woman who has lived through the modern problems of loving and living, remained loving and objective enough to share them. Though her reflections are personal, they are universal in scope.

When Lovers Are Friends is divided into three sections, which correspond to the basic initial phases of any relationship; they are:

1. Trusting
2. Connecting
3. Touching

You've heard the phrase, "No man is an island" many times, but have you ever really stopped to think about the truth behind the statement? There is nothing you do . . . from taking a solitary walk . . . to leading a nation . . . that doesn't affect someone else in some manner. We are all together in this thing called "life."

The ideal way to approach life is to realize that everyone is doing the best he knows how to do; hold out a hand whenever possible, but when you do, don't offer it as a crutch for a fellow climber; if you do you'll end up pulling him up the mountain. That doesn't help either of you.

By committing ourselves to be part of the interwoven fabric of life, and to the welfare of our fellow climber whenever possible, we are committing ourselves to seeking the highest good of all we come in contact with . . . and that includes yourself. With commitment in our survival kit, we will try just a little harder; that extra effort will be the subtle difference between success and failure.

There are many shades of meaning in the word "commitment," all the way from "imprisonment" and "duty" through "friendship" and understanding to "dedication" and zeal"; its all in the way you look at it. In *Climb Your Own Mountain,* we use commitment in the context of "zeal" and "dedication."

Know Your Traveling Companions

When desire turns into commitment, you automatically begin to use every avenue available to develop a better understanding of all parameters. Since you don't know the trail, or what conditions you will encounter, I urge you to learn all you can about those with whom you are traveling. As much as you are able, know how they will react to you . . . or to any given situation. When you know your climbing companions so well that "trust" is taken for granted, then "connecting" is automatic . . . "touching" will come when trust becomes confidence. It is equally important here to know yourself, for without a genuine understanding of your own motivation, trusting yourself will only happen in no-risk situations and that's not trust, that's betting on a sure thing . . . only a surface bravado.

The value of *When Lovers Are Friends,* and in particular the chapter "If You Can't Commit to Something Big, Commit to Something Small," is that it gives me insight into the relationship between men and women . . . actually broader than that . . . the relationship between people. . . . from a feminine point of view. We all have within us both the masculine and feminine characteristics that make our anima and animus one. In order to have a total and complete personality, these two sides of our androgynous nature must be kept in balance and harmony. Just as there is nothing wrong with the female showing positive aggression, translated into drive, it is alright for a man to let his sensitive and intuitive aspects show . . . in fact, it is recommended. But the important thing to remember is that we all have the same basic drives; we all need to feel successful, creative and fulfilled.

There Is a Place For Women in Business

During the evolution of our species, man's role, because of his superior strength and size, became that of protector and provider. It did not necessarily mean that he was smarter or superior in all ways. The woman's movement of today has very little to do with competition . . . that is to say . . . with the woman trying to prove she is better than a man; it has to do with a woman desiring the opportunity to express in any area of interest . . . and it isn't always housekeeping. If a businessman can understand what is really behind the seeming aggressiveness of the woman's movement, he will feel less threatened by it and less reluctant to accept the increasing role of women in business. Years of conditioning has made it difficult for men to accept that some women may be better at his job than he is; this is especially difficult when some men's egos will not even let them compete with other men who may outdo them.

I've had to come to terms with women in the business world at a very personal level. When I was first granted the rights to the Solar Pool Blanket by Sealed Air Corporation, the only staff I had was my secretary of four years, Edith Nielsen. Her professional business experience was nil, and her business skills borderline, but she was forced back into the workplace when her husband became disabled. In assessing her skills, I had overlooked the fact that during twenty years of marriage to a very successful, highly intelligent physicist, she had served on the board of directors of several community theaters, had produced and directed productions, been a P.T.A. president, etc., all as an unpaid volunteer; essentially using the same skills and common-sense required from a so-called professional. She had proven to me during those past two years, that even though her mechanical skills were not the best, she was a very intelligent person who had offered invaluable support and loyalty.

I had planned to build the success of the product with a team of young lions, right out of college. Sealed Air, however, as the supplier of goods and money, had other ideas. (Sealed Air Corporation is the company we discussed in Chapter Two.) In the beginning, very few of the company's top personnel took the Solar Blanket seriously (there were times when even I had my doubts). Within weeks of initiating the program, one of Sealed Air's secretaries, Sue Pope, was assigned to us.

Very apprehensively, I took to the road selling, leaving my destiny in the hands of my new base-camp team. . . . comprised of two secretaries. . . . Edith, who was considered by the plant personnel as a stranger (even intruder), who had been left there to answer the telephone for John Zaccaro (whoever he was), and Sue, who didn't even know me and vice-versa, but who had been assigned to see that I had product to sell. I knew I could sell, but had doubts that she had the strength to make sure I had product to back up my sales. I was certain we were very low on the list of company product priorities. (I was wrong, indeed).

Why so apprehensive? . . . because I've always had women working for me . . . not with me. I had met only one or two women whom I felt were functioning effectively in the world of business. I had met others who were trying, but they all seemed to me to be pushy and brassy (traits abhorrent to me in men, as well as in women). As a student of history and business, I was aware of the Rubensteins and the Mary Kays of the cosmetic industry; however, admittedly, I felt that women had little place in the world of business, other than that of secretaries or the like. In light of what happened the next few years, I ended up having to eat quite a few of my words and changing many pre-conceived beliefs.

My two "secretaries" both turned out to be the best "men" I could have gotten for the job. Under very difficult conditions, Edith and Sue learned to work together, learned how to fight for machine time and get orders out, giving me all the back-up support I needed, and even learned to let their femininity stay in control. It seems they had both been hiding the depth of their intelligence (no one had ever really asked them to use it), and they both possessed capabilities even they weren't aware of, which, as it turned out, complemented each other. Within a year, my selling efforts, combined with their special abilities, and the commitment of all three of us, turned into a team which produced sales of over a million dollars a month with the company now taking the solar pool blanket quite seriously. Quite a record in anyone's book.

As a team, we developed the "trust" in each other that was needed, we definitely "connected" with each other as we learned to work together smoothly, almost reading each other's minds, and even the "touching," as we celebrated an accomplishment with a hug born of the real affection that develops when things are right. During this hectic period, Sue was raising two small children and keeping a working husband happy, while Edith was involved with her two teen-age children and a handicapped husband. Sue subsequently went on to become a distribution manager for a large distributing company, while Edith is now the Vice-President of my present company,

I have told this story for two reasons; first, to get the message across that gender has nothing to do with capabilities or success; everyone should be given an opportunity and a fair chance . . . by themselves . . . as well as by others. Men and women can work together, can be friends, can form a master-mind alliance, and can maintain their respective femininity and masculinity, realizing that it can make for a well-balanced business relationship, since both points of view will be covered; secondly, to illustrate an example of commitment that paid off for all concerned. Commitment is the backbone of the preparations that will take you up the trail to the "summit feeling" so important to any one of us.

Book Title: When Lovers are Friends
Author: Merle Shain
Publisher: Lippincott
Chapter/Title: If You Can't Commit to Something Big,
                Commit to Something Small.

If You Can't Commit to Something Big, Commit to Something Small

I know a man who has searched for fulfillment all his life. In the beginning, perhaps because he was born poor, he thought it had to do with having the things that money seems to carry in its wake. And after he'd become an engineer and then a developer and a millionaire, he discovered that money was not it. He tried women, and fancy cars, and even a dog and a yacht, but they failed him too. So he tried traveling, and not working, and ultimately dropping out. But nothing seemed to work.

By the time I'd met him he'd searched everywhere anyone could suggest he look, searched and searched, trying to find he knew not what. He tried guitar lessons, taking three a day, one in classical guitar, one in flamenco, and one from a hippie folksinger who taught him also about grass. He tried figure skating, practicing every afternoon between four and six, working his figures out with his slide rule in a three-ring binder

WHEN LOVERS ARE FRIENDS By Merle Shain (J.B. Lippincott) Copyright © 1978 by Merle Shain Reprinted by permission of Harper & Row, Publishers, Inc.

every night. He tried antique collecting, filling his apartment up with so many grandfather clocks and Persian rugs he had to open a store. He alternately tried eating and dieting and getting married and getting divorced, and finally he tried fasting and celibacy and giving up his worldly goods.

He'd been a Buddhist monk for several years when I saw him next. His hair was gray, he wore a robe, but he still looked the same. And when I asked him if he'd found fulfillment yet, he answered, "No, it's out there still."

No one knows much about fulfillment except that it's hard to find, and maybe doesn't exist, and a lot of people who believe in it when they are twenty stop believing in it later on. You can look too hard for fulfillment, and you can not look hard enough. And although you're guaranteed the right to pursue it, it isn't a money-back guarantee, so there is no one to complain to if you blow it and spend your life barking up the wrong tree.

Fulfillment is always something the other guy's got, something just over the hill. It's an immensely agile boxer who lets us get him in a clinch a hundred times a day but then somehow slips away. It's the pot of gold at the end of the rainbow, and catching the brass ring. It's true love, becoming rich, and even staying thin. But whatever it is, it always eludes you and keeps you on the run like the carrot on the stick, and even when it bites your line a million times you rarely reel it in.

All of us feel there must be more, but wonder what the more really is, and often the more we yearned for last year isn't enough today. So we wait in vain for something else, something just a little better than what we've got, and often we trade in the thing we have for something we think we should want.

We are the "Is this all there is?" generation, waiting for the perfect thing to commit to—the perfect job, the perfect love —and we feel miserable all the while we wait, somehow failing to understand that loneliness lies in the suspended state.

Some feel the lack of fulfillment our generation feels stems from our unwillingness to commit. We live at a time when modern communications make us aware of so many things we can do nothing about, and tell us of the suffering of countless people we have no choice but to try and shut out. So a lot of us have stopped caring or, caring so much that we feel impotent and frail, have had to reduce our pain by pretending the suffering of people we don't know is somehow not quite real.

And there is another problem modern communications bring—the dream of perfection fostered by a host of adman dreams. We live ringed around by sugar-plum fairies, dancing at us from every page and every screen, and real life when we meet it never seems somehow as good. We are encouraged to expect perfection, and perfection doesn't exist, so we are always a little disappointed and hold back again, hoping the next round will really be it.

It's nice to have choices, and flexibility makes life more interesting, it's true, but you can get lost on the sea of infinite possibilities, and there is nothing liberating about that. And people who are always trying to make the perfect choice, rejecting what they have for what they hope to find, but the present on the future and end up missing both.

The Greeks had a legend about a man named Sisyphus who was banished by Zeus to a desert island, an island which had nothing on it to keep him occupied. And after a while Sisyphus started losing his mind. Then one day he took it into his head to push a big rock up the mountain on the island, and all day long he labored with the big rock, pushing it and pushing it in the hot sun, until at night, with the top of the hill almost in sight, he finally gave up and let the rock roll down the hill again. He did this again the next day, and the next, and for many months to come, and though he never reached the top of the mountain with his rock, when they finally found him he was sane, just as sane as he'd ever been.

I've always liked this story because it made me conscious of something which I'd only half guessed before—the fact that it's our commitment to life which saves us, and what we commit to is not what's important at all. I know it's not easy to rid yourself of the notion that you need something important to commit to, or to learn to find pleasure in what is, rather than displeasure in what you wish there'd be, but the trick of life is to stop worrying about finding the perfect something to commit to and commit to something, anything at all. And if you can't commit to something big, then commit to something small.

CHAPTER TEN

Role Models

One of the best incentives is a role-model, someone who you can admire and look up to as having won his or her dream.

Anyone who listened to the radio or read a major newspaper in the early 1950's, will be familiar with the five-minute "This I Believe" vignettes.

This program originated in 1949 at a business luncheon, when four friends were decrying the seeming decline of spiritual values in favor of materialistic ones (sound familiar?). As a result of that conversation, the idea arose of having a chosen number of successful men and women spend five minutes telling about their personal philosophy and the rules by which they run their lives. One of the men at that lunch was Edward R. Murrow, a prominent television newscaster and personality, who agreed to introduce the series.

These four men were well aware that the motivating and deciding factor in any person's life, is what he truly believes . . . about himself and about the world . . . his "core beliefs" if you will; thus any action taken will be one to reinforce or justify those beliefs . . . the only things he will notice or respond to will be those things which correspond to or are in harmony with his core beliefs. The purpose of the series was to urge the listener to examine his own beliefs when he listened to those who had achieved their summit and were willing to share their success by relating their deepest convictions. This I Believe contains interviews with famous people from many diverse fields, such as General Lewis B. Hershey, Aldous Huxley, Helen Keller, Andre Kostelanetz, Margaret Mead, Lauritz Melchoir, Jackie Robinson, Eleanor Roosevelt, etc . . . all are inspiring and any one would be a worthwhile role model. "Your" personality is made up of bits and pieces you take from everyone you meet; hence, the importance of making sure you have the right guides as you begin to prepare for your climb.

The role model we've chosen to include is an article by Lionel Barrymore, who was born into a theatrical family. A native of Philadelphia, he was the son of Maurice and Georgianna (Drew) Barrymore. His theatrical career began when he was a child, and his formal stage debut came in 1893 when he was seen in the *The Rivals,* with his grandmother, Mrs. John Drew. After appearing in other productions, he became associated with the the great D.W. Griffith and the old Biograph film studio. Returning to Broadway, he acted in such plays as The *Copperhead, The Jest* (with Brother John), and *MacBeth.* Again attracted to the movies, he established a new reputation in the "talkies," winning an Acadamy Award in 1931.

Handicapped later in his life, he captivated a new generation by his playing of "patriarchal invalid roles." His annual broadcast of *"A Christmas Carol"* in which he played Scrooge, became an American tradition. Successful also as a composer and a writer (with a novel to his credit), he spent his last years on a quiet farm in California.

Recognize and Develop Your Birthskills

The great Frank Capra movie, *"It's A Wonderful Life,"* has become almost as much a part of the Christmas Season as Santa Claus. Jimmy Stewart, one of our most beloved actors, who starred in it, considers it to be his greatest part. Most critics agree, but also point out, that the supporting cast, was, by any standards, monumental, and will be remembered for as long as there is one person left who has viewed this classic movie.

But there is one actor in that memorable supporting cast who stands out from all of the others, (including perhaps Stewart himself) . . . the one who portrayed that dastardly, miserable villian of villains, Mr. Potter . . . our next featured author, Lionel Barrymore. It is impossible to separate the character from the actor or the actor from the character because when Lionel Barrymore believed in something, you believed it along with him. Audiences left the theater after every showing hating Mr. Potter. Barrymore once said that if he had wanted Potter to have a single sympathetic bone in his body, he would have played him that way. Since he couldn't find a single redeeming quality in Potter's make-up, he decided that his "own mother" would leave the theater hating Mr. Potter. Who is to say that the scion of the Barrymore family was John or Lionel or Ethel, or their parents, or grandparents? In my opinion, even John Barrymore's *"Hamlet"* must take a back seat to the complete conviction and believability that Lionel brought to all of his roles from the kindly doctor in the Kildare series, the stubborn "Gramps" who kept "death" up the apple tree in *"On Borrowed Time,"* to the contemptible Mr. Potter. Lionel Barrymore was the consumate actor/philosopher of stage and motion pictures.

I had a chance encounter with Lionel Barrymore. His personality was so over-powering, that it took me a few moments to realize that the man was actually confined to a wheelchair and that it wasn't just a prop he had adopted for a role. Barrymore never considered himself handicapped. Being confined to the wheelchair was not detrimental in any way to the achievement of the goals he had set for himself. He was a true exponent of knowing one's birthskills and developing them to the fullest.

We come by our birthskills, of course, by heredity, but seldom is it so clear-cut as to just what you have inherited as it has been in the Drew-Barrymore family. The "Royal Family" of the theater has been supplying accomplished and renown actors and actresses to the stage for at least five generations. The newest member to carry on the tradition is an eight-year-old girl. Those who have worked with her insist that it is impossible to know as much about acting as she does at her age, without it being in the genes. There is still the age-old controversy of heritage versus environment. Genes are important, but who can discount the influence of a role model in the shaping of a future? Lucky is the child, who because of the role model influence in his environment; can early discover his birthskills and is given the freedom to develop them at his own pace. The sooner we are able to discover our birthskills, and then determine their use in our life plan, the more we will be able to accomplish because of this head start.

I was one of the lucky ones. Without even thinking about it, I began doing voice impressions at a very early age. The laughs I received gave me the positive feedback I needed to decide it would be worthwhile to develop this particular birthskill and use it. My father had a wonderful sense of humor which made laughter and fun a part of our family life. If I had been told to "stop showing off" or that "children should be seen and not heard," no doubt I would have let it go. As it turned out, that particular talent was my entree into the Hollywood scene, and I continue to use it today in my business career. I have a "stock company" of characters who travel with me to my seminars, the most famous of whom is Dr. Gregor Forensky . . . Chairman of the Russian Solar Energy Institute; oddly enough, Gregor started life as an actor himself. He was *born* as the result of a lecture I had been asked to give to an advance acting class on the "Stanislavski Method" of acting. A very simplistic explanation of this "method" is that you put yourself so thoroughly into the role you are playing that it is no longer a role . . . you become the person or thing. If you are supposed to be an apple tree, you become that tree . . . you feel the leaves change and drop off . . . you feel the seeds. . . . you become the fruit . . . you are the very soul of the apple tree.

I felt that the best way to "teach" and "motivate" the class would be to give an "entertaining" demonstration. Per the advance publicity, the class of some 250 graduate students in Theater Arts came prepared to hear a lecture by John Zaccaro, professional actor, stuntman and successful businessman; however at the beginning of the meeting, the instructor announced to the assembled students that Mr. Zaccaro had been taken ill and would not be lecturing. Sitting on the stand, wearing a heavy black top coat and Russian fur cap, I was gratified to hear some evidence of disappointment, which immediately changed to murmers of anticipation when it was announced that Mr. Zaccaro had sent a replacement, a friend of his whom he had met while in Leningrad studying the 'method" In fact, it seems that Dr. Forensky had been an instructor at the school.

I took my place at the podium . . . or rather Gregor Forensky did. I explained, in a heavy Russian accent, that I was "just visiting in this country, and that it was a pure stroke of luck that I was . . . how do you say it? . . . available. . . . and I welcomed this opportunity to meet with my fellow actors." I then proceeded to deliver a ten minute monologue in my Russian accent. I told them my specialty in Russia was my ability to do American accents . . . and demonstrated by starting with a scene from a classic American play, "Death of A Salesman," utilizing a somewhat New York accent. I then did an imitation of the great voice of the late actor, Ronald Coleman. At first, there was a dead silence, then an astounded class applauded generously. I thanked them and then casually mentioned that the most difficult and challenging accent for me was the American western or cowboy accent. I told the class I had learned one in particular by watching American Westerns, but didn't feel I did it well enough to do it for them. After allowing myself to be persuaded, I did an imitation of Walter Brennen (recipient of three supporting Oscars). There was, once again, silence . . . then thunderous applause. I felt it was time to confess, so I introduced myself as John Zaccaro, in my own voice. "You have just had a demonstration of the method." I told them. Amid more applause and much laughter, I continued my talk. My greatest compliment and testimony to my success came at the end when I opened the lecture to questions. One lady in the back of the room held up her hand and very indignantly asked me. . . . "Now who are you really, John Zaccaro or Gregor Forensky." Gregor has been one of my constant companions ever since . . . a lot of fun to have along.

Don't Measure Yourself By Another Person's Standards.
In the marketing field, the different characters such as Gregor Forensky and Pierre Pavillion, have become my "gimmick." my stock-in-trade which I use to liven up a seminar. The characters have become a tool I use to sell myself, and thus my product. It is my thing, and unique in my chosen field. Other successful marketing men have their own tools which they have developed. I don't use theirs and they don't use mine.

Ninety-eight percent of the time when you lack confidence it is because you are measuring yourself by standards unrealistic to yourself. In selecting a role model, we tend to conjure up a picture of an outstandingly successful person . . . a superman in our field, then try to pattern ourselves after him or her. Imitation may be the sincerest form of flattery, but it is not personally creative. For example, a salesman has an idea of the perfect salesman . . . clever, debonair, witty, dynamic, attractive, quick with a joke, never fails, is never discouraged, knows how to ask for an order and get it. His charisma causes everyone to fall all over himself to push business the salesman's way. The truth of the matter is that such a paragon doesn't exist in the sales field. Even Joe Gerrard, who is mentioned in the Guinness Book of Records as the "world's greatest salesman," blows an occasional sale.

You Can Be Your Own Role Model

There is no perfect "role model." The best one is a projected self-image, put together like a puzzle from bits and pieces of those you meet and things you've read or experienced. Take the time to assess yourself. If there are still pieces missing, determine the total person you would like to become, then project that image in front of you and work towards that person. This projected image is the analog your success regulation mechanism uses to measure the progress of your current image. Realize that the image cannot remain static. As you grow and change, your projected image will also change. You determine the set point and create the image. That is the perfect role model.

Book Title: This I Believe
Author: Edited By Edward P. Morgan
Publisher: American Book. . . . Stratford Press, Inc., New
              York
Chapter: Does Anyone Believe an Actor . . . by Lionel
              Barrymore

Does Anybody Believe an Actor?

By Lionel Barrymore

First off, I think the world has come a mighty long way toward believing that what a man does to make a living can't rob him of his integrity as a human being, when it will listen to an actor talk about what he believes. I can remember when nobody believed an actor didn't care what he believed. Why, the very fact that he was an actor made almost everything he said open to question, because acting was thought to be a vocation embraced exclusively by scatterbrains, show-offs, wastrels and scamps. I don't believe that's true today and I don't think it ever was. I don't think there were ever any more ne'er-do-wells, rogues, poseurs and villains in the acting profession than in any other line of work. At least I hope that's the case. If it isn't, it's too late tochange my mind and much too late to change my profession.

The fact is, I think, every successful man today has prepared

THIS I BELIEVE By Edward P. Morgan, Editor Copyright © 1952 by Help, Inc. Renewed © 1980 by Edward P. Morgan Reprinted by permission of SIMON & SCHUSTER, Inc.

for his success by planning and living his life in much the same way that an actor plans and creates a part. We don't make anything up out of whole cloth when we decide the way we want to play a role, any more than the author, who wrote it, made it up out of thin air. The author has one or two or perhaps a great many models in mind from which he takes a little here and a little there until he's built up a new character out of substantial material. The actor who must play this part now has to dig back into his life and recall one or two or more people who are, in some way, similar to the person the author put on paper. What I'm saying is, everybody connected with the actor's work had a model and copied this model, more or less exactly, adding to it here and there, until something new emerged. I think this is the way a person must plan his life. Adopting, borrowing and adapting a little here and a little there from his predecessors and his contemporaries, then adding a few touches until he's created himself.

I believe the difference between an eminently successful person and one whose life is just mediocre is the difference between a person who had an aim, a focus, a model upon which he superimposed his own life and one who didn't. To put it bluntly, you can't get anywhere unless you know where to start from and where to go.

The thing to be careful of in choosing a model is: don't aim too high for your capacity. It's necessary, it's true, to believe in the Almighty, but don't make Him your model. Have faith in Him but try for something you're more apt to make. Shoot a little closer to home. If you keep aiming at an attainable target, you can always raise your sights on another and more difficult one. But if you start off for the impossible, you're foredoomed to eternal failure.

I believe if a man remembers that, sets an attainable goal for himself and works to attain it, conscious that when he does so he will then set another goal for himself, he will have a full, busy and for this reason a happy life.

CHAPTER ELEVEN

Finding Love

In both the New Thought and the Think Positive movements there are two approaches to motivational thinking. One is the religious approach, characterized by Philosophies such as that of Dr. Norman Vincent Peale. This Credo incorporates the concept of God, or a Universal Mind as a partner in your success. The second approach is secular, characterized by theories such as the one revealed in *Psycho-Cybernetics,* which maintain that everything needed for success is to be found in the body/mind complex. In this book, I have presented both ideologies; in my opinion they are most valid when blended rather than divided.

One of the most important items to be included in your backpack is love. In my opinion, whether your approach to life is religious or secular, love is an indispensable element. When you possess the secret of love you won't climb mountains, you will move them. It will be the most powerful and compulsory addition to your climbing gear.

Love Is One of the Most Important Items to be Included in Your Backpack.

Love is the emotion that is most evoked, sworn by, even died for . . . and yet the one least understood. Just as "thoughts are things," so is love a very real and powerful building block. Under no conditions, start your climb without formulating a theory as to the role love will play in your move from the safety of the base camp to the summit. It is not necessary to fathom the mysteries of what love really is . . . or to label it; whatever your need for love is, pack it right at the top . . . where you can see it . . . where it will be a continual reminder that you could not have come this far, nor can you reach the summit, without it.

For many years, my own inability to give more than surface affection, rather than closeness, had won me the label of "private person." It has taken me a good portion of my life (as it should if it is to be meaningful) to achieve a glimmer of the real purpose and power of love.

Like the other qualities we've included in our survival kit, love is something we must first find within ourselves. We make a mistake in thinking that love must always be objectified to be present in our lives. In reality, love can be a power that flows through us, filling every fiber of our being, then radiating out in all directions. When we can experience that form of unconditional, and pervasive love, then it can be objectified.

Self Love Is Most Important

The most important person to love is yourself. Until that happens, you can't really love anyone or anything else. This is not to be done in a narcissistic way, but rather in the sense of the most universally-accepted definition of the word (as used in an objectified relationship) . . . "Love is a commitment to the well-being of the other person . . . a desire to help the other reach his highest potential." This definition is equally valid when applied to self-love.

Self-love is respecting our own uniqueness, acknowledging our good qualities, caring for our bodies, surrounding ourselves with beauty, trusting ourselves, seeing ourselves as equal to anyone, forgiving ourselves, knowing we deserve the best, and most important of all, letting ourselves win. If you don't think you deserve to have success, you will find yourself unconsciously engaging in self-defeating behavior at the most inappropriate times. If you don't think you deserve to be loved, you will alienate those who offer any degree of affection. These can, of course, be seen as simplistic black and white suppositions. Human relations and motivations are more complex, but if the basics are agreed upon then one can work out the challenges and opportunities engendered by the intricate interplay of diverse personalities.

Love can be an energizer stronger than the most potent pep-pill on the market. It is such an exhilerating emotion that we often make the mistake of falling in love with love. When we do, it becomes a narcotic we cannot live without. If it reaches that point, you are giving another person control over your life and this imitation of love becomes one of the most damaging and self-defeating of actions.

Love in the impersonal sense, can help smooth many a thorny path. Catherine Ponder, in her book *The Dynamic Laws of Prosperity*, states that "It has been estimated that only 15 percent of a person's financial success is due to his technical ability, while 85 percent is due to his ability to get along with people. Personnel managers agree that more than two-thirds of the people who lose their jobs do so not because of incompetence, but because they cannot get along with others." Love means non-judgment and acceptance, whether in the personal or impersonal sense. By realizing that everyone is doing the best he or she knows how to do, you can approach a situation with tolerance and understanding and others will respond proportionately. Anger begets anger; the human tendency seems to be to react rather than act. Someone must break the cycle. The person who is acting from a position of love is better able to take the initiative and act from a position of strength.

There may be times in your life when you will not be able to enjoy a loving intimate relationship. This is the time it becomes the hardest to love . . . and yet the time when is the most important to continue loving. If you carry love inside you, sharing as much as you are able to with all whom you meet, it will illuminate your thoughts and manifest itself in every physical action. When you love . . . "You". . . . and not the recipient . . . are the one enriched. If you find yourself in that situation, there is a spiritual fountainhead you can return to for the rejuvenation that is usually associated with a personal intimate love relationship. Learn to listen to your inner light and you will intuitively know the best strategy for recouping the power, energy and joy of loving which may become dim in the dark vicissitudes encountered by all who aspire to climb. I can best return to my own source when I'm on the mountain. While I'm completely involved in the climb, I feel an unabashed kinship with the trees, the birds, the sky, the earth itself . . . an integral part of the landscape. At the summit, the emotions within me are part of a universal love.

Look for the Rainbows
The top of the "Grand" in the Tetons is especially gratifying because, unlike some mountain tops, the Grand has a small peak. When you get to the top, you know it. While there is room for a few people on the summit, the highest point is barely comfortable for one person. Not long ago, I stood there alone and felt like I was on top of the world . . . literally . . . and figuratively. To go any higher I would have had to fly.

. . . and I was already soaring. There on the peak, I surveyed the vista spread before me; as I watched, a rainbow appeared . . . a perfect circle . . . directly below me.

With some coaxing on my part, my guide set up a rope and lowered me safely into what seemed the center of the rainbow. I could swear I saw the yellows and greens on my hands and arms as I was bathed in the glow of the rainbow's spectrum. I shall carry the glow of that rainbow with me for the rest of my life. It was one of my most profound summit feelings.

While I'm still working for a better understanding of the meanings and shadings of love (its a life-time occupation), I know that as long as I retain the feeling of elation which I brought down the mountain that day, and incorporate it into my life, I will carry with me a vibrant power to be the lodestar of my search. Whatever your "lodestar" . . . you too must first find it within yourself and then follow it. If you aim for the stars, you may . . . at the least . . . reach the top of the mountain.

Book Title: *Love*
Author: Emmett Fox
Publisher: DeVorss & Company
Chapter: "Love is Important"

Love Is Important

By Emmett Fox

Love is by far the most important thing of all. It is the Golden Gate of Paradise. Pray for the understanding of love, and meditate upon it daily. It casts out fear. It is the fulfilling of the Law. It covers a multitude of sins. Love is absolutely invincible.

There is no difficulty that enough love will not conquer; no disease that enough love will not heal; no door that enough love will not open; no gulf that enough love will not bridge; no wall that enough love will not throw down; no sin that enough love will not redeem.

It makes no difference how deeply-seated may be the trouble, how hopeless the outlook, how muddled the tangle, how great the mistake; a sufficient realization of love will dissolve it all. If only you could love enough you would be the happiest and most powerful being in the world.

LOVE By Emmet Fox Reprinted by permission of DeVorss & Company, Marina del Rey, California.

SECTION III
How To Climb

CHAPTER TWELVE

Awareness

Start where you are! Don't look at someone else's climb. Climb your own mountain but first learn the techniques needed to succeed.

My mountains are special, and your mountains, though different from mine, are special. We all have it in our make up to shape and define the mountain we wish to climb. The top of the mountain is often obscured, but its our mountain and we climb it . . . or we don't . . . and those who have a clear picture of their self worth and a positive outlook for their goals, are the ones who see the peak as reachable; they are the winners who make it to the top. To accomplish this, you must change the way you see things . . . the way you think and feel, the way you see yourself. As you elevate yourself, you will become equal to the tasks you have set for yourself.

There are always two ways of looking at anything . . . a productive way and a non productive way. If your attitudes and viewpoints are not productive, throw them out. If a mountain climber has scaled certain peaks and now wants to go higher, he must alter his thinking toward himself, not towards the higher peak. He must strengthen his muscles, gather additional supplies, throw out the pre-conceived garbage and replace the inadequate tools with the right tools before he starts up the mountain. If the attempt is made to climb the higher peak while using lower-peak equipment, defeat and frustration are certain. Its too easy to blame the peak, or the goal, instead of examining your peak-scaling capabilities. When you speak about the "potentials" you never achieved, then you are guilty of carrying your "garbage" with you, littering the truth and beauty of the mountain.

Get to know yourself and identify your attainable levels as early in your life as possible. Don't sell yourself short, but do realize that setting unrealistic goals is as sure-fire a way to failure as setting none at all. Reach for your potential and not someone else's. Look at your self-image. People accept you at your face value. Whatever your opinion of yourself is, that is what you will see reflected back to you from the people you meet.

There are ways to climb a mountain that are more successful than others; in some instances, there is only one way to climb and attempting any other method would prove fatal. This section will present some of the methods that others have found to be successful. If any particular chapter strikes a responsive chord in you, please find and read the entire book. It will help you to find the best "pitch" by which to ascend.

Once your goal has been established and the proper gear assembled, it is time to apply yourself to the mechanics of the climb itself. How does one go about reaching the highest potential possible? In this section, we will demonstrate how to use your "birthskills" and your acquired knowledge (education) to best advantage in the challenges you've chosen for yourself, by presenting some of the methods others have used successfully.

The First Step Seems the Hardest
Starting always seems the hardest, but if a climber is following our suggested plan of action, he has already made two good starts; the decision to climb and the examination of the necessary gear. All is now in readiness to carry the analogy to its third step . . . the mechanics for the actual climb. This section will show you how to motivate yourself to make the first move towards the summit; there is no way to get from the bottom to the top without touching the bases and ledges between. Pull out your map and chart a tentative route, knowing full well that it will change along the way.

Choose a path commensurate with your abilities; one which forces you to "stretch" into it without defeating you. Since a great deal of learning is by trial and error, don't select a terrain or "pitch," if you will, where your errors will be terminal. As you start up the mountain, develop a technique or rhythm that fits you, then perfect it in the easy early stages of your climb. As the ascent becomes more difficult you can forget about concentrating on technique, and direct your attention to listening to your intuition and exercising the deftness brought into being by the synergism of your birthskills and education. Birthskills are those qualities you are equipped with at birth; education is obtaining the power to get what you want, when you want it, without violating the rights of others. Birthskills and education must be used in tandem. Any successful person in any field, develops a sixth sense about his profession, by combining intuition, birthskills and education, which even they cannot explain. Don't ask them "how" or "Why?" . . . they will only be able to tell you . . . "It felt right!" In other words . . . do the thing and you will have the power.

In this section, we've chosen to use selections from the following books: *Success Through a Positive Mental Attitude,* by Napoleon Hill and Clement Stone, *The Peter Prescription* by Lawrence J. Peter, *Act Your Way to Successful Living* by

Neil and Margaret Rau and *The Magic of Believing* by Claude Bristol. All of the articles will give you a basic methodology to help you unlock the hidden depths of your creativity and productivity, thereby increasing your chances of achieving those things you most desire . . . those things which you consider to be success.

In summary then, this section suggests the following as the next step in the sequential plan to climb your own mountain.

1. Make a start.
2. Chart your route
3. Know your birthskills
4. Develop a climbing technique
5. Do the thing and you will have the power.

CHAPTER THIRTEEN

Chart Your Route

Without a concrete plan you are destining yourself for defeat. Therefore chart a productive course one which will lead you to your desired goal and not to a dead end or wrong destination.

The "Peter Principle" was defined and expanded upon in a book of the same name. After publication of this book, which has now become a modern-day classic, Dr. Laurence Peter was inundated with letters exclaiming . . . "how right you are! Now what do we do about it?" The *Peter Prescription* (The Peter Principle: *"In a hierarchy every employee tends to rise to this level of incompetency."*) tries to answer the questions raised by Dr. Peter's first book, *The Peter Principle,* (The Peter Prescription: *"Forward to a better life."*) by giving an understanding as to why conventional attempts to solve the problems only make them worse. Dr. Peter then gives guidelines which will generate the confidence needed to live your life in a creative and competent manner which will enable you to increase your efficiency in managing your own life.

His format is extremely clever. Each point he makes is highlighted by a bon mot excerpted from the most illustrious names of our civilization . . . all of the sayings are extremely apropos. Even though he has chosen some pretty high-class collaborators, and some very amusing ones, my favorite homily is his that says "Make three correct guesses consecutively and you will establish a reputation as an expert."

I've sat through seminars with some of these so-called "experts" who are so unknowledgeable and so dull they cheer up a room by leaving it, and more often than not, I simply cannot restrain myself from interrupting the presentation by giving facts and figures he left at home, or embellishing his lackluster approach with anecdotes, etc. This technique, though disconcerting to the speaker, more often than not, had added interest and rescued what could have been a disaster to the "expert" who has gone beyond his level of competency; however, I'm careful to do it in such a way so that the person is never made to look foolish.

When Dr. Peter's first brush with national prominence was at its peak, his book was in thousands of attache cases in offices and airports all over the world, a primer to seek support from in moments when executives, salesmen, doctors, lawyers, housewives, etc., sought the humorous analogy that would crystalize an otherwise cloudy situation.

Additional humor is achieved by his use of sub-titles. For example, chapter one, with a title of "Onward and Upward," is sub-titled, "Up, Up and Oop!" . . . a subtle way of advancing the book's theme of moving forward to greater creativity, as opposed to moving upward to incompetency; one of the touches I find to be most original and hilarious, is the use of cartoons (most of them from *Punch* magazine issues of the last century) supplied with new imaginative captions to underscore the points he wishes to make. I enjoyed also the droll and whimsical pseudonyms of the characters in his case histories, such as Ike O. Noklast or N. Ventive.

Laugh and The World Laughs With You

Dr. Peter proves with his book, *The Peter Prescription,* that serious topics need not be treated reverently in order to get a message across. My father was a strict disciplinarian, but he could hardly resist putting a humorous twist to almost everything he did, only the twinkle in his eye gave him away. With four boys around the house, his tools were always being misplaced, which exasperated him no end. He would come storming up out of his basement workshop bellowing "Where is my screwdriver? I used to have six of them!" . . . this with a broad Italian gesture holding up five fingers. The offender would run for the screwdriver, while all the rest of us stifled a laugh. (He always had "six" of everything, emphasized by his outstretched hand).

Humor has saved many a situation from becoming intolerable, but the most important thing is being able to laugh at ourselves. When we can laugh at ourselves, it means we can forgive ourselves. Be quick to laugh at yourself, and slow to laugh at others. A misplaced or mocking laugh can do untold damage. Laugh with a person freely, but not at him.

Salesmen, like professional comics, are forced to smile and tell a joke many times when they don't feel like laughing at anything. It goes with the territory; funny, though, the times I have been forced into that position, I cheer myself on; this is a graphic example of "Act as if you were and you will be."

Learn to Recognize Your Strengths

I've chosen this article, "Know Your Direction . . . or Peep Before You Leap." because the content so aptly portrays the necessity of recognizing your strengths and weaknesses in order to know where you are going and to chart a proper route. The combination of your birthskills and acquired learning becomes the framework on which you build your life. Within this framework, you can accomplish miracles, but an attempt to venture beyond your understanding and birthskills can only bring frustration. This may sound like a contradiction to the theme of this book, but it isn't. Much leeway is accorded within this window created by experience gained, opportunities presented and talents inherited. The message in *the Peter Prescription* is to go forward to greater achievement rather than up to incompentency.

A Look At Alternative Routes to Your Goals

It is imperative to have goals, but what direction do you take to reach them? If a rigid vertical approach is taken, step-by-step, there is only one correct action to take in most cases, which becomes very limited; it calls for analytical thinking and perhaps a great deal of manipulation, which is tricky at best and self-defeating at worst. A more sensible, creative and satisfying approach is to be laterally oriented. For example, in trying to reach a solution to a problem, the tendency is to organize your thinking in sequential order . . . if I do this then such and such will happen, which will lead to the next step . . . and on to the solution; functioning in this way leaves little room for error. Make a wrong step or leave one out and there is no answer. In vertical thinking the solution to the problem is the goal, however, if you approach a problem creatively or laterally, you will allow your thoughts to roam at will, creating a stream of consciousness to aid in seeking an alternative. Even when a solution is reached, more solutions will present themselves if you indulge your imagination a little further with more "what if's"?

Use this "what if" approach as you set your goals at each plateau along the way, and you may be rewarded with a new goal . . . with a resultant "summit feeling" far exceeding that which your original goal would have provided. There are alternatives to any goal and in actuality, there is no "one" correct solution. Each time you are faced with a decision, you will find there are several choices, each with many things to recommend it. How then, can you decide which is the right one? Frankly, if they all have correct components, what does it matter which one you choose? The only important things to take into consideration are, first. . . . that you do make a choice, or decision, and then not vacillate in carrying out the necessary action to implement the strategy; second, that the choice harms no one including yourself; if your motives are right, and actions taken with a sense of good-will, nothing more than a few feelings may be hurt, BUT . . . be honest about your motives; third, be sure it is what you really want to do (we will even wish to do distasteful things at times, because we will know it is correct to do so).

These are ideas you need to play with . . . to consider the ramifications of, especially as they apply to yourself. When you understand these things about decision making, you will realize that intuition is the tie-breaker in making the final decision.

In 1977, a manufacturer of swimming pool products was facing bankruptcy; its products, in the main, were the "me-toos" of filters and pumps that scores of its competitors were better able to promote, produce and sell. One of the company products was an automatic pool cleaner; what made it different from the then Number One product, was that in addition to "sweeping" the pool, it also "vacuumed" it. True, the product was a winner, but without the "intuition" which led to a dogged resolve on the part of one of the owners, the product would have, in my opinion, died along with the other products doomed to bankruptcy.

I choose to include the story of the Polaris Vac-Sweep, and its intrepid leader, Jim Edmiston, because no one in my recent memory charted a route so specifically and followed it so religiously; never once failing to see the humor in the occasional set-back in his way up his personal mountain. Today, he and Polaris are the recognized leaders in their field. . . . . a clean sweep . . . if you will.

In the final analysis, intuition is the most important quality. In my estimation you can get along passably well with "wit" alone, but without the considerable use of your intuition, you will accomplish very little. By heeding your intuition, you take command of your life's direction. By relying on your wits alone, at best you get along with life, but not ahead of it.

Mountain Climbing Requires Wit, Intuition and Risk

In the world of mountain climbing, you absolutely must rely on both your wits and your intuition; use one without the other and you relegate the safety of the climb to "luck," a tool which has no place in your backpack. "Luck" is merely the correct use of all your faculties. A successful endeavor, whether it be on the mountain, or in your personal or business life, should rely on the total knowledge you have of the terrain or your chosen field. The more knowledge you have, the more sure your chance of success will be. Coupled with knowledge and intuition, must be a willingness to act, to take a risk if necessary. Risk is always present, but can be minimized by knowing the direction you wish to go, by being honest with yourself, and by being aware enough to know your capabilities . . . *without selling yourself short*. . . . then strive to put as much richness as possible in to the framework you have built for your life. You will find the challenges you need and go forward to success.

Book Title: The Peter Prescription
Author: Dr. Laurence Peter
Publisher: William Morrow & Co., New York
Chapter   Know The Direction . . . or . . . peep before you
              leap.

Know The Direction or Peep Before You Leap

The heaven of each is but what each desires.
—T. MOORE

THE ultimate purpose of the Peter Prescription is to help you chart a course toward a more rewarding life. Careful consideration of the priorities for your life will help you keep moving forward while you focus on some of the relevant factors that influence your direction in life.

> My interest is in the future because I'm going
> to spend the rest of my life there.
> —C. KETTERING

PETER PRESCRIPTION 14
*The Peter Persona: Develop a concept of
the person you would like to be*

Your self-concept has many facets, including how you per-

"Know Thy Direction or Peep Before You Leap" from THE PETER PRESCRIPTION by Dr. Laurence J. Peter Copyright © 1972 by Laurence J. Peter By permission of William Morrow & Company.

ceive your body and physical abilities, how you see yourself in social situations, how you visualize yourself sexually,
and how you view your mental abilities. Although all of
these are relevant to your direction in life, for purposes of
the Peter Persona, focus your attention on your *Humanite
self-concept.*

Do you feel that the establishment hierarchy has shaped you
into something less than a fulfilled human being? Do you understand the influence the hierarchy has had on your development and how you have been molded by the educational and
advertising establishment? If your answers to these questions
are in the affirmative, then you are ready to formulate your
ideal self-concept.

> For they can conquer who
> believe they can.
> —VIRGIL

You live in a world filled with destructive influences that
impinge upon you. A self-concept that is consistent with the
Humanite vision provides a defense against these influences
and contributes to peace of mind and life on your own terms.

Unfortunately, in Western civilization a positive self-concept has too often been equated with aggressiveness, upward
mobility, wealth, and material acquisition. These are the very
characteristics that when excessively escalated destroy the
individual and threaten survival of the human race.

> Golden shackles are far worse than
> iron ones.
> —M. GANDHI

To strengthen your self-concept, begin by visualizing yourself as a Humanite. Use constructive thought to create an

image of yourself as an individual able to determine your own purposes in life. See yourself as living your life free from the escalatory pressures of advertisers, commercial interests, and other manipulators. As your self-concept is translated into action, you become your real self and your constructive thoughts are a beacon to a life in tune with nature.

> Our problems are man-made, therefore they can be solved by man. And man can be as big as he wants.
>
> —J. F. KENNEDY

Real, constructive mental power lies in the creative thought that shapes your destiny, and your hour-by-hour mental conduct produces power for positive change in life. Develop a train of thought on which to ride. The nobility of your life as well as your happiness depends upon the direction in which that train of thought is going.

> He who persists in genuineness will increase in adequacy.
>
> —T. LYNCH

PETER PRESCRIPTION 15
The Peter Proficiency: *Focus your efforts within your area of competence*

At every level of any hierarchy there are opportunities for fulfillment. You do not have to be president of the mousetrap company to build a better mouse trap. As a matter of fact, as president you would be too busy to give much thought to designing a better mouse trap. Look to your experience and concentrate your efforts within your area of competence.

If you are a university student involved in current social problems, you should apply your proficiency for maximum effectiveness. As a science major you can contribute to improvement of environmental quality by using your scientific skill and the laboratory facilities available for testing environmental samples. You can then turn your findings over to mass communicators, conservationists, and political-action groups. As an English major you can contribute to peace by using your writing skill to describe eloquently the beauty of peace, the horrors of war, and the constructive actions that can be taken to build a peaceful world. As a psychology major you can contribute to social justice through your knowledge of behavior modification and through reinforcing every move made by civic leaders in the direction of social justice. As an engineering, law, education, or medical student you can use your area of competence to contribute to solutions of the problems of your concern.

Escalation might remove you from your area of competence and place you in activities that are counterproductive. This does not mean that you should not participate in political action. It does mean that each student can make an effective contribution through utilization of the skill he is acquiring in the professions, sciences, humanities, or the arts.

> Consider well what your strength is equal to,
> and what exceeds your ability.
>
> —HORACE

Most real improvement in the quality of life is the result of dedicated individuals performing their jobs with art and skill. Much individual discontent, as well as the defects in products and services, is the result of eyes turned upward to higher-level jobs rather than forward to the task at hand.

If the Peter Proficiency were universally applied, it is highly probable that there would be sufficient competence for every position. Society could then value every individual's unique contribution.

> We both exist and know that we exist, and re-
> joice in this existence and this knowledge.
> —S. BUTLER

PETER PRESCRIPTION 16
The Peter Preferment: *Choose the
enduring pleasures*

Improvement in the quality of life consists of abiding competence and contentment derived from your life style.

> Enjoy your present pleasures so as not to in-
> jure those that are to follow.
> —SENECA

Nat Churrell spent much leisure time in the garden of his Northern California home. His patio, swimming pool, and garden provided him with healthful exercise, fresh flowers, fruit, vegetables, and a place of quiet beauty in which to relax and read. He gave all of this up to accept a promotion to the head office in Manhattan. Now with the shorter season for outdoor living and the increased commuting time, Nat Churrell's life provides little contentment.

> Unhappiness is not knowing what we want, and
> killing ourselves to get it.
> —D. HEROLD

When you stop to consider that you may have the enduring pleasures within reach, you will not deny the present for some long-delayed reward.

Performing a job that is not in conflict with your values, sharing with loved ones, and discovering your individuality will produce contentment and lead to a greater sense of personal fulfillment.

> I take him to be the only rich man that lives upon what he has, owes nothing, and is contended.
>
> —S. Howe

PETER PRESCRIPTION 17
The Peter Potential: *Find a realistic alternate route*

The established hierarchies will not provide satisfaction for everyone. Hierarchal Regression has reached such an advanced stage that many people advocate destruction of the establishment. An alternative with greater potential is to encourage the growth of organizations that will eventually replace the established bureauracy.

> Act well at the moment, and you have performed a good action to all eternity.
>
> —J. Lavater

Ike O. Noklast, a young lawyer, was concerned about the violation of consumer rights by government, business, industry, and agriculture. No people's lobby existed to hire him to protect them against unsafe automobiles, contaminated foods, or outrageous prices. Although Ike O. Noklast had to work outside the establishment, he was soon joined by supporters and now heads an effective agency protecting consumer rights.

A heart unspotted is not easily
daunted.

—W. SHAKESPEARE

N. Ventive was employed as a counselor at M. T. Employment Agency. When he observed that his employer made no special effort to place black applicants, he conducted his own survey of employment opportunities in the black community. This resulted in his establishing a successful employment agency for black citizens.

SATTINGER'S LAW: It works better if you plug
it in.

In spite of the entrenched incompetence within the establishment hierarchies, it is still possible to develop effective organizations that are responsive to human needs. With reality as a foundation, some people have left the establishment and formed successful organizations. Others dropped out and failed because they did not assess their potential realistically.

Real joy comes not from ease or riches or from
the praise of men, but from doing something
worthwhile.

—W. GRENFELL

Breaking away from the establishment to open your own competing business, political, or social organization can earn you alienation, distrust, and repression from bureaucrats who stand to lose by your actions. This, along with your competence, is the reality you must assess in determining your potential for success outside of the establishment bureaucracy.

There are two things to aim at in life: first, to get what you want; and, after that, to enjoy it. Only the wisest of mankind achieve the second.

—L. SMITH

PETER PRESCRIPTION 18
The Peter Predictor: *Foretell your level of competence*

When you are offered a promotion, or at any other decision point in life, do not lose sight of the direction you have chosen. The unwillingness to turn down a challenge has caused many men to change their life goal with each change of job. This results in loss of self, mindless escalation, and the feelings of futility so common in Western man. Greed enables a person to buy things money can buy while losing the things money cannot buy.

When a man has not a good reason for doing a thing, he has one good reason for letting it alone.

—SIR W. SCOTT

To achieve your maximum potential, move *forward* toward progressively greater fulfillment. You need never be incompetent through becoming the best human being that your potential, your creative mind, and circumstances will allow.

There's more credit and satisfaction in being a first-rate truck-driver than a tenth-rate executive.

—B. C. FORBES

To use escalation to find your maximum potential, you must climb past your level of competence and then, when you realize you are incompetent, move back down to your level of competence. Although this is theoretically possible, in practice it is extremely difficult and meets with uncommon resistance on the part of everyone with an ever-onward-and-upward philosophy.

To find the optimum position of a worker is like operating a radio receiver. You wish to tune in a station very precisely. You have a meter that indicates signal strength and as you near the optimum point the needle begins to move across tthe dial. It is not until the needle passes the maximum and starts to fall back that you can be certain that it has reached the maximum.

—J. GOLDSTON

PETER PRESCRIPTION 19
The Peter Prognosis: *Anticipate the consequences*

Now that you are aware of the pitfalls and pleasures the establishment has to offer, you will understand that nothing fails like success.

At one time a ship was loaded by men running up a plank with sacks on their backs. But sack carriers, hod carriers, barrow pushers, and the like have been replaced by conveyor belts, forklifts, elevators, and mobile cranes. As rungs are removed from the ladder of human employees you will be nearer Final Placement than you think. Awareness of the inevitable consequences of escalation will help you answer the question, How high is high enough for me?

By working faithfully eight hours a day, you
may eventually get to be a boss and work twelve
hours a day.

—R. Frost   .

PETER PRESCRIPTION 20
The Peter Possibility: *Try another occupation*

The rate of men leaving establishment jobs to find contentment
in new occupations is accelerating. The medical doctor who
recently decided to quit his practice and become a writer was
not chasing after more money. Like many men today he was
bored and wanted to try another occupation.

Men with imagination or a strong creative urge tend to get
bored in routine jobs. Change of occupation for the individual
with a spirit of adventure is healthy and desirable.

> Since I left university I have spent ten years
> as a doctor, two years as a merchant seaman,
> seven years as a businessman, eight as a jour-
> nalist and fifteen as a novelist.
>
> —J. Wilson

PETER PRESCRIPTION 21
The Peter Pathway: *Let conscience*
be your guide

Much mental torment is created through employment that is
in conflict with your basic values.

Hiam Atteez enjoyed his work as photographer for the Irvin
Blight Advertising Agency. Some of his best pictures were
natural landscapes used in the advertisements for Hawk Ciga-

rettes. After the release of the Surgeon General's Report linking cigarette smoking with lung cancer, circulatory disease, and emphysema, Hiam became concerned that his work was contributing to the sale of disease-producing cigarettes. Atteez was now ill at ease.

Hiam submitted a folio of his best scenes of natural beauty to a conservation group, Friends of the Land, who published the pictures along with Hiam's own descriptive passages. No longer with Irvin Blight, Hiam is now a professional photographer for Friends of the Land. His pictures and writing have awakened thousands to the beauty of their environment and to the need to preserve it. Hiam Atteez now regularly experiences the joy of accomplishment and inner peace.

> Labour to keep alive in your breast that little spark of celestial fire, conscience.
> —G. WASHINGTON

CHAPTER FOURTEEN

Getting Started

Once you have formulated the plan, don't procrastinate, get started. In 1908, Napoleon Hill, a young newspaperman, was employed by the then Governor of Tennessee to write a series of success stories. Hill was twenty-five years old. His first interview, with Andrew Carnegie, lasted for three days and nights. Mr. Carnegie was so impressed with the young man that he commissioned him to undertake a project which had always fascinated him . . . and that was to discover why successful men became successful. The task took Hill twenty years to complete. During that period, he interviewed over five hundred of the most successful men of his day, including Henry Ford, William Wrigley, John Wanamaker, George Eastman, John D. Rockefeller, J.P. Morgan, Harvey Firestone, Thomas Edison, and Luther Burbank. One cannot help but envy the illustrious company Mr. Hill kept; keep in mind however, that a lesser mind than his would have missed much of the insight poured out by these giants in their sometimes week-long interviews. Hill's Edison interview was a classic, lasting over a month. I get chills when I think of the opportunities presented to Napoleon Hill and experience delight and satisfaction to see the influence of the great minds he met in his life time reflected in his own written word.

His personal interpretation of the "philosophy of success" was first published in 1928, in a set of seven books, entitled *The Laws of Success,* which were eventually condensed into the book which has become one of the most widely-read books of the 20th Century, *Think and Grow Rich.* Napoleon Hill was an advisor to three presidents, as well as being a lecturer and teacher; he wrote his last book at the age of eighty.

Use the Mastermind Alliance Principle

One would be hard-pressed not to classify Hill's concept of the *Mastermind Alliance* as a gimmick . . . if it were not for the exciting examples of the alliance in action. The *Mastermind Alliance,* when reduced to its simpliest definition, is a "device" or "relationship" of two or more people who ally themselves for the purpose of accomplishing any given task; the resultant relationship is the Mastermind, a third mind which may be used by all of those involved in the alliance, a practical and literal application of the Biblical statement, "Where two or more are gathered together in my name, there will I also be." Some good examples of a *Mastermind Alliance* are: a loving, compatible husband and wife working together in harmony to create a beautiful home environment; or an employee and employer working in harmony. Hill placed great emphasis on the word "harmony." Out of the harmonious blending of minds, comes the "mastermind," which dissolves the moment the harmony is broken. One of the most successful Mastermind *Alliances* in history included Henry Ford, Thomas A. Edison and Harvey S. Firestone. They were friends who met frequently during all of their creative and productive years. Napoleon Hill formed a creative alliance with Clement Stone, whom he met in 1953. Mr. Stone was president of *Combined Insurance Company of America,* which he started with $100 and a copy of Hill's *Think and Grow Rich,* from this meager financial start, and buoyed by the wisdom of Napoleon Hills' words, he built his company into a $24 million concern, at which point he solicited the personal help of Mr. Hill to teach his philosophy of personal achievement to the insurance personnel of Mr. Stone's company. It was a ten-year Mastermind Alliance, but Mr. Hill felt it proved conclusively that his twenty year search had given birth to a valid way of achieving success.

Success Through a Positive Mental Attitude was one of the tools developed to educate and motivate Stone's personnel; it is dedicated to "The Most Important Living Person . . . You!" It is designed to help you change your attitude towards life and yourself. The book emphasizes that you must begin with yourself if you wish to achieve success. It encourages the reader to believe that he or she can change their particular world and make it what he or she wishes it to be by unlocking the potential within a person in order that goals might be set and reached; further, it challenges the reader to put the principles into action and gives a list of books for further reading, along with an admonition to study each day.

As I write this, I've just returned from a meeting with Mr. Stone at the Los Angeles airport. He had been the guest speaker at a special service in the famous "Glass Cathedral" in Garden Grove, California, and very graciously agreed to meet with us before boarding his plane for Chicago. The short time we had was richly filled with the wisdom and charisma of Mr. Stone. I was particularly impressed with his story of reading an article in his youth written by a man who had met President Lincoln. The author had said "I've met many of the great political figures of our nation and what I remember most about Lincoln is the fact that he read less, but "thought more" than any of the others."

Its important to read, but more important to do your own thinking, for only then is it yours., but the most salient point of the conversation was Mr. Stone's conviction that the philosophy expounded by *Success Through a Positive Mental Attitude* had withstood the test of time. We are living in an era of rapid and chaotic change; day after day we see new attempts made by groups and individuals to develop new philosophies to bring order from the chaos of new mores and standards. As these new methods of behavior and belief are tried, and found wanting, more and more are turning again to the tried truths of yesterday. Mr. Stone says that the climate of receptivity for the "PMA" approach to living and success is much greater now than it was at its inception. There has of course, been further evolution of the process and philosophy since the book was published in 1960, as Mr. Stone is a man with his finger on the pulse of today. We are truly indebted to Napoleon Hill and W. Clement Stone for the Master Mind Alliance which made *Success Through a Positive Mental Attitude* possible.

Start Where You Are

How does one get started up the mountain? Very simple . . . *just start!* No, I'm not being facetious, I'm merely suggesting that you stop procrastinating. Get your bearings, know where you are . . . and start from there. "Putting things off" for the moment, or "doing things tomorrow" that should have been done today, is . . . in my opinion . . . one of the ills of our society. "Catching up," once a luxury the decision maker could ill afford, is now, all too often, a commonplace act, aggravated by an increasing dependency upon mechanical tools such as copiers, calculators, computers, etc. Since the "machine" can do the job so quickly, many use that as an excuse for procrastination.

In the early days of television, everything was done "live." The pictures that went out over the channels were as perfect as painstaking care and early know-how could make them. Each director, announcer, talent, ad agency personnel and technical crewman knew it was a "live" one-chance-only production. No one will ever forget the zany antics of Ernie Kovacs, Milton Berle, Sid Caesar and Imogene Coca, some of which has been captured on film. *Studio One and Playhouse 90* gave us original productions such as *Twelve Angry Men* by Reginald Rose and *Requiem For a Heavyweight* by Rod Serling, which have become theater classics.

The *Kraft Company* commercials demonstrating how to use company products, were works of art. Around 1960, video tape was perfected and welcomed with open arms by the industry as a tool to improve the quality of television; now a commercial or a scene from a series could be taped, looked at immediately, then reshot if it wasn't quite right. It didn't work out quite that way at first. Quality went down. Attitudes became relaxed and complacent, knowing it could be done again if something wasn't right; but then time would run out and a commercial that "wasn't too bad" had to be used. My diagnosis. . . . too many people procrastinating. The industry finally learned how to use video tape to best advantage, but during its infancy, it was an example of the "tool" running the show.

I'm not suggesting you should toss out automation, but I'm suggesting you not rely solely on electronic wizardry. The 1970's and 1980's have spawned a generation dependent upon "machines" to do its work, and to some extent, its "thinking." Many children cannot do simple math without the aid of a calculator.

Because of this type of dependency, independence is often

a lost art. I recently asked the officer of a moderate-size company about one person in a specific division of his company. The officer had worked side-by-side with the person in question, but because his computer was "down" the information he gave to me was spotty at best. No other files were available. When the computer was back in operation, the file revealed the pertinent information about his Social Security number and his years in service, but not a hint of his work habits, or real capability, as assessed by his fellow workers or supervisors. There must be a balance between the mechanical and humanistic. We can't allow ourselves to be robbed of our ability to think and make decisions.

Consider the size of the human brain, then compare it to today's most sophisticated main frame computers and you will still find a striking superiority in the human brain cell. Every thought you jot down, every idea you register in long hand or on a typewriter, each sentiment you speak, are all the sole property of the files in your brain where you have the concepts filed. These are the files you draw upon for decision making; they can never be replaced by a "machine" but they can be rusted shut through non-use. Continue to use your mind actively, then making correct decisions at the correct time will become rote for you. . . . . you will automatically DO IT NOW!

I Decided to Become a Mountain Climber . . . Three Years Too Late

The first year we vacationed at the ranch in the Tetons, several times a week I drove by a sign that shouted at me. . . . CLIMBING SCHOOL. I was quite curious about it, but there always seemed to be too many other things to see and do, so I put it out of my mind.

One day, while on a day-long horseback ride to Lake Solitude, we stopped to water our horses. Our horseback group was at eight thousand feet enroute to eleven thousand feet, when we sighted the minisicule figures of a group of climbers on the sheer side of a mountain wall. The view of those three men courageously battling the mountain was awesome. As we remounted our horses, I thought how free they seemed . . . at one with the beautiful earth. I made up my mind at that very instant that the next day I would enroll in the climbers school that I so long had resisted.

In retrospect, I guess it was a good thing I made the decision at that point and then stuck to it. On the way back down from the lake, in one of the sheerest and narrowest portions of the trail, a storm arose out of nowhere, as they so often do in Wyoming. This storm rivaled anything I have ever seen. In less than a minute the blue clear sky turned black and we found ourselves battling hailstones, wind and rain, as well as our horses. I was one rider from the rear when the horses began to "spook" and break into a run down the winding path which had been made even more treacherous because of the mud and rocks washed down by the storm. I looked back over my shoulder at my friend who was the last rider and saw that he was in trouble. His horse had slipped partially off the trail . . . right front and right rear legs were now straddling the path, virtually hanging off of the embankment. I jumped from my horse and ran back to him. We managed to steady his horse, getting her back up on all four legs, then started working to calm her down.

She was terrified . . . shaking and bucking. I put my slicker over the horse's head to shield her from the hail, but more importantly, to keep her from seeing where she was. Every instinct in the horse was shouting "danger" and she was reacting to the terror. We finally managed to calm her down and to ride back down the mountain in safety, only to discover that the rest of the group had not only managed to descend safely, but had, for the most part, enjoyed the bout with Mother Nature. None of them, including my wife, knew that we had been in danger. They all thought we were still right behind them.

As we unsaddled back at the barn, I thought of the climbers. What did they do in that kind of weather? I was forty-six years old, and many would say I was too old to take up any serious mountain climbing. Some days, I would agree with them wholeheartedly; however, the significant thing is that I finally got started. I had already spent too much time at the bottom thinking about how to begin my climb. You too, should begin your climb today, despite what you think may be your weaknesses and infirmities.

Book Title: Success Through a Positive Mental Attitude
Author: Napoleon Hill/W. Clement Stone
Publisher: Prentice-Hall, Inc., Englewood Cliffs, N.J.
Chapter: The Secret of Getting Things Done.

The Secret of Getting Things Done

In this chapter you will find the secret of getting things done. You will also receive a self-motivator so powerful that it will subconsciously force you to desirable action, for it is in reality a *self-starter.* Yet you can use it at will. When you do, you overcome procrastination and inertia.

If you do the things you don't want to do, or if you don't do the things that you do want to do, then this chapter is for you.

Those who achieve greatness employ this secret of getting things done. Take for example the Rev. James Keller, a Maryknoll father of the Jesuit order. Father Keller had been developing an idea for quite some time. He hoped to motivate "little people to do big things by encouraging each to reach beyond his or her own little circle to the outside world." The Biblical command, "go ye forth into all the world" was to him the

From the book SUCCESS THROUGH A POSITIVE MENTAL ATTITUDE By Napoleon Hill and W. Clement Stone © 1960 By Prentice-Hall, Inc., Englewood Cliffs, NJ 07632 Published by Prentice-Hall, Inc.

symbol of an idea where by the mission he had in mind could be fulfilled.

When he responded to this command, he employed the secret of getting things done. And when he did, he went into action. This happened in 1945. It was then that he organized the Christophers—an organization most unusual.

It has no chapters, no committees, no meetings, no dues. It doesn't even have a membership in the usual sense of the word. It simply consists of people—no one can say how many —dedicated to an ideal. The Christophers operate on the concept that it is better for people to "do something and pay nothing" than to "pay dues and do nothing."

What is the ideal to which each is dedicated?

Each Christopher is dedicated to carry his religion with him wherever he goes throughout the day—into the dust and heat of the market place, into the highways and byways, into the home. And thus he brings the major truths of his faith to others.

The thrilling story is told by the Rev. James Keller in *You Can Change the World.* It came about because he conceived and believed in an ideal. But he did little or nothing about it until he responded to the secret of getting things done.

You get the feel of this secret from the statement of E. E. Bauermeister, supervisor of education at California Institution for Men, Chino, California, who told the authors:

"I always tell the men in our self-adjustment class that too often what we read and profess becomes a part of our libraries and our vocabularies, instead of becoming a part of our lives."

Remember the Biblical statement: *For the good that I would, I do not; but the evil which I would not, that I do.* Now how can you train yourself to get into action immediately when it is desirable?

And then we told Mr. Bauermeister how the good things we read and profess can become a part of our lives. We gave him the self-starter for getting things done.

How do you make the secret of getting things done a part of your life? By habit. And you develop habit through repetition. "Sow an action and you reap a habit; sow a habit and you reap a character; sow a character and you reap a destiny," said the great psychologist and philosopher William James. He was saying that you are what your habits make you. And you can choose your habits. You can develop any habit you wish when you use the self-starter.

Now what is the secret of getting things done and what is the self-starter that forces you to use this great secret?

The secret of getting things done is to act. The self-starter is the self-motivator DO IT NOW!

As long as you live, never say to yourself, "DO IT NOW!" unless you follow through with desirable action. Whenever action is desirable and the symbol DO IT NOW! flashes from your subconscious mind to your conscious mind, immediately act.

Make it a practice to respond to the self-starter DO IT NOW! in little things. You will quickly develop the habit of a reflex response so powerful thatin times of emergency or when opportunity presents itself, you will *act*.

Say you have a phone call that you should make but you have a tendency to procrastinate. And you have put off making that phone call. When the self-starter DO IT NOW! flashes from your subconscious to your conscious mind: *Act*. Make that phone call immediately.

Or suppose, for example, that you set your alarm clock for 6:00 A.M. Yet when the alarm goes off, you feel sleepy, get up, turn off the alarm, and go back to bed. You will have a tendency to develop a habit to do the same thing in the future. But if your subconscious mind flashes to the conscious DO IT NOW! then come what may—DO IT NOW! Stay up! Why? You want to develop the habit of responding to the self-starter DO IT NOW!

In Chapter Thirteen you will read how one of the authors bought a company with one million six hundred thousand dollars in net liquid assets with the seller's own money. This became a reality because at the proper time the buyer responded to the self-starter DO IT NOW!

Now H. G. Wells learned the secret of getting things done. And H. G. Wells was a prolific writer because he did. He tried never to let a good idea slip away from him. While an idea was fresh, he immediately wrote down the thought that occurred to him. This would sometimes happen in the middle of the night. No matter. Wells would switch on the light, reach for the pencil and paper that were always beside his bed and scribble away. And then he would drop off to sleep again.

Ideas that might have been forgotten were recalled when he refreshed his memory by looking at the flashes of inspiration that had been written down immediately when they occurred. This habit of Wells' was as natural and effortless to him as smiling is to you when a happy thought occurs.

Many persons have the habit of procrastination. Because of it, they may miss a tain, be late for work, or even more imporant—miss an opportunity that could change the course of their lives for the better. History has recorded how battles have been lost because someone put off taking desirable action.

New students in our PMA Science of Success course sometimes state that the procrastination habit is the one they would like to eliminate. And then we reveal to them the secret of getting things done. We give them the self-starter. We may motivate them by telling them the true story.

What the self-starter meant to a war prisoner. Kenneth Erwin Harmon was a civilian employee for the Navy at Manila when the Japanese landed there. He was captured and held in a hotel for two days before he was sent to a prison camp.

On the first day, Kenneth saw that his roommate had a book under his pillow. "May I borrow it?" he asked. The book was

Think and Grow Rich. Kenneth began to read. As he read, he met the most important living person with the invisible talisman imprinted with PMA on one side and NMA on the reverse.

Before he started to read it, he had the feeling of despair. He fearfully looked ahead to possible torture—even death—in the prison camp. But now as he read his attitude became one inspired by hope. He had a craving to own the book. He wanted it with him during the dread days ahead. In discussing *Think and Grow Rich* with his fellow prisoner, he realized that the book meant a great deal to the owner.

"Let me copy it," he said.

"Sure, go ahead," was the response.

Kenneth Harmon employed the secret of getting things done. He swung into immediate action. In a fury of activity he began typing away. Word by word, page by page, chapter by chapter. Because he was obsessed with the possibility that it would be taken away at any moment, he was motivated to work night and day.

It was a good thing that he did for within an hour after the last page was completed, his captors led him away to the notorious Santo Thomas prison camp. He had finished in time because he started in time. Kenneth Harmon kept the manuscript with him during the three years and one month he was a prisoner. He read it again and again. And it gave him food for thought. It inspired him to: develop courage, make plans for the future, and retain his mental and physical health. Many prisoners at Santo Thomas were permanently injured physically and mentally by malnutrition and fear—fear of the present and fear of the future. "But is better when I left Santo Tomas than when I was interned—better prepared for life— more mentally alert," Kenneth Harmon told us. You get the *feel* of his thinking in his statement: "Success must be continually practiced, or it will take wings and fly away."

Now is the time to act.

For the secret of getting things done can change a person's attitude from negative to positive. A day that might have been ruined can become a pleasant day.

The day that might have been wasted. Jorgen Juhldahl, a student at the University of Copenhagen, worked one summer as a tourist guide. Because he cheerfully did much more than he was paid to do, some visitors from Chicago made arrangements for him to tour America. The itinerary included a day of sightseeing in Washington, D.C., while he was en route to Chicago.

On arriving in Washington, Jorgen checked in at the Willard Hotel, where his bill had been pre-paid. He was sitting on top of the world. In his coat pocket was his plane ticket to Chicago; in his hip pocket was his wallet with his passport and money. Then the young man was dealt a shocking blow!

While getting ready for bed, he found that his wallet was missing. He ran downstairs to the hotel desk.

"We'll do everything we can," said the manager.

But the next morning the wallet had still not been located. Jorgen Juhldahl had less than two dollars change in his pockets. Alone in a foreign country, he wondered what he should do. Wire his friends in Chicago and tell them what had happened? Go to the Danish embassy and report the lost passport? Sit at police headquarters until they had some news?

Then, all of a sudden, he said: "No! I won't do any of these things! I'll see Washington. I may never be here again. I have one precious day in this great capital. After all, I still have my ticket to get me to Chicago tonight, and there'll be plenty of time then to solve the problem of the money and the passport. But if I don't see Washington *now* I may never see it. I've walked miles at home, I'll enjoy walking here.

"Now is the time to be happy.

"I am the same man that I was yesterday before I lost my

wallet. I was happy then. I should be happy now—just to be in America—just to have the privilege of enjoying a holiday in this great city.

"I won't waste my time in futile unhappiness over my loss."

And so he headed off, on foot. He saw the White House and the Capitol, he visited the great museums, he climbed to the top of the Washington Monument. He wasn't able to take the tour of Arlington and some other places he'd wanted to see. But what he did see, he saw more thoroughly. He bought peanuts and candy and nibbled on them to keep from getting too hungry.

And when he got back to Denmark, the part of his American trip he remembered best was that day on foot in Washington —a day that might have gotten away from Jorgen Juhldahl if he had not employed the secret of getting things done. For he knew the truth in the statement. *NOW* is the time. He knew that *NOW* must be seized before it becomes: yesterday-I-could-have . . .

Incidentally, to round off his story, five days after that eventful day Washington police found both wallet and passport and sent them to him.

Are you scared of your own best ideas? One of the things that often prevents us from seizing the *NOW* is a certain timidity in the face of our own inspirations. We're a little bit afraid of our ideas when they first occur to us. They may seem novel or far-fetched. There's no doubt about it: It takes a certain boldness to step out on an untested idea. Yet it's exactly this kind of boldness that often produces the most spectacular results. The well-known writer, Elsie Lee, tells about Ruth Butler and her sister Eleanor, the daughters of a nationally-known New York furrier.

"My father was a frustrated painter," says Ruth. "He had talent, but the need to earn a living left him no time to build a reputation as an artist. So he collected paintings. Later, he started buying paintings for Eleanor and me." Thus, the girls developed a knowledge and appreciation of fine art, along with an impeccable sense of taste. As they grew older, friends would consult them on what types of paintings they should buy for their homes. Often they would loan pieces from their collection for brief periods.

One day Eleanor woke Ruth up at 3 A.M. "Don't start arguing, but I have a *terrific* idea! We're going to form a Master Mind alliance."

"Now what in the world is a Master Mind alliance?" Ruth asked.

"*A Master Mind alliance is coordination of knowledge and effort, in a spirit of harmony, between two or more people, for the attainment of a definite purpose.* And that's just what we're going to do. We're going into the business of renting paintings!"

And Ruth agreed. It *was* a terrific idea. They set to work the same day—although friends tried to warn them of dangers: Their valued paintings might be lost or stolen; and there might be law suits and insurance problems. But they went right on working—accumulating $300 in capital and talking their father into loaning them the basement of his fur shop, rent free.

"We hauled 1,800 paintings from our own collections in among the coat forms," Ruth recalls, "and ignored father's sad and disapproving eyes. The first year was grim—a real struggle."

But the novel idea paid off. Their company, known as the New York Circulating Library of Paintings, became a success —with about 500 paintings constantly on rental to business firms, doctors, lawyers and for use in homes. One valued client was an inmate of the Massachusetts Penitentiary for eight years. He wrote humbly that perhaps the Library wouldn't rent to him, considering his address. The paintings went to him rent free except for transportation costs. In return

Ruth and Eleanor received a letter from prison authorities. telling how the paintings were used in an art appreciation course that benefited many hundreds of prisoners. Ruth and Eleanor started their business with an idea. And then they backed their idea up with immediate action. The results were a profit to themselves and increased pleasure and happiness for many others.

Are you ready to double your income? In 1955, W. Clement Stone was one of seven executives who made a tour of the Asiatic and Pacific areas as representatives of the National Sales Executives International. On a Tuesday in mid-November, he gave a talk on motivation to a group of businessmen at Melbourne, Australia. The following Thursday evening, he received a phone call. It was from Edwin H. East, manager of a firm that sold metal cabinets. Mr. East was excited: "Something wonderful has happened! You'll be as enthusiastic as I am when I tell you about it!"

"Tell me about it. What did happen?"

"An amazing thing! You gave your talk on motivation Tuesday. In your talk you recommended ten inspirational books. I bought *Think and Grow Rich* and started to read it that evening. I read for hours. The next morning I started reading it again and then I wrote on a piece of paper:

"My major definite aim is to double last year's sales this year. The amazing thing is: I did it in forty-eight hours."

"How did you do it?" Mr. Stone asked East. "How did you double your income?"

East responded: "In your speech on motivation, you told how Al Allen, one of your Wisconsin salesmen, tried to sell cold-canvass in a certain block. You said that Al was lucky because he worked all day and didn't make a sale.

"That evening, you said, Al Allen developed *inspirational dissatisfaction.* He determined that the following day he would again call on exactly the same prospects and sell more insurance policies that day than any of the other representatives in his group would sell all week.

"You told how Al Allen completely canvassed the same city block. He called on the same people and sold 66 new accident contracts. I remembered your statement: 'It can't be done some may think, but—Al did it.' I believed you. I was ready.

"I remembered the self-starter you gave us: *DO IT NOW!*

"I went to my card records and analyzed ten 'dead' accounts. I prepared what might previously have seemed to be an enormous program to present to each. I repeated the self-starter *DO IT NOW!* several times. And then I called on the ten accounts with a positive mental attitude and made eight large sales. It is amazing truly amazing—what PMA will do for the salesmen who use its power!"

Now Edwin H. East was ready when he heard the talk on motivation. He listened to the message that was applicable to him. He was searching for something. And he found what he was looking for. Our purpose in relating this particular story is that you, too, have read about Al Allen. But you may not have seen how you could apply the principle to your own experience. Edwin H. East did. And you can, too. You can apply the principles in each of the stories you read in *Success Through a Positive Mental Attitude.*

Now, however, we want you to learn the self-starter, *DO IT NOW!*

Sometimes a decision to immediately can make your wildest dreams come true. It worked that way for Manley Sweazey.

You can mix business and pleasure. Manley loved hunting and fishing. His idea of the good life was to hike fifty miles into the woods with his pole and his rifle, and hike back a couple of days later exhausted, muddy, and very happy.

The only trouble with this hobby was that it took too much t' ie out from his work as an insurance salesman. Then one day as he reluctantly left a favorite bass lake and headed back to his desk, Manley had a wild idea. Suppose, somewhere, there were people living in a wilderness—people who needed insurance. Then he could work and be out-of-doors at the same time! And indeed, Manley discovered, there was such a group of people. The men who worked for the Alaska Railroad. They lived in scattered section-houses strung out along the 500-mile length of the track. What if he were to sell insurance to these railroad men, and to the trappers and gold miners along the route?

The same day that the idea came to him, Sweazey began making positive plans. He consulted a travel agent and began packing. He didn't pause to let doubts creep in and frighten him into believing that his idea might be scatterbrained . . . that it might fail. Instead of picking the idea apart for its flaws, he took a boat to Seward, Alaska.

He walked the length of the railroad many, many times. "Walking Sweazey," as he was called, became a welcome sight to these isolated families, not only because he sold insurance when no one else had thought them worth bothering with, but because he represented the outside world. He went the extra mile. For he taught himself how to cut hair, and did it free of charge. He taught himself how to cook, too. Since the single men ate mostly canned foods and bacon, Manley, with his culinary skills, was a welcome guest. And all the while he was doing what came naturally. He was doing what he wanted to do: tramping the hills, hunting, fishing and—as he puts it, "living the life of Sweazey!"

In the life insurance business there is a special place of honor reserved for men who sell over a million dollars worth of business in one year. It is called the Million Dollar Round Table. Now the remarkable and almost unbelievable part of Manley Sweazey's story is that: having acted on his impulse, having taken off for the wilds of Alaska, having walked the railroad where no one else had bothered to go, he did his million dollars of business, and more, in a single year, to take his place at the Round Table.

And none of it would have happened if he had hesitated to employ the secret of getting things done when his "wild" idea came to him.

Memorize the self-starter *DO IT NOW!*

DO IT NOW! can affect every phase of your life. It can help you do the things you should do, but don't feel like doing. It can keep you from procrastinating when an unpleasant duty faces you. But it can also help you as it did Manley Sweazey, to do those things that you *want* to do. It helps you seize those precious moments which, if lost, may never be retrieved. The endearing word to a friend, for example. The telephone call to an associate, just telling him that you admire him. All in response to self-starter *DO IT NOW!*

Write yourself a letter. Here is an idea to help you get started. Sit down and write yourself a letter, telling the things you always intended to do as though they had already been accomplished—some personal, some charitable, and others community projects. Write the letter as if a biographer were writing about the wonderful person you really are when you come under the influence of PMA. But don't stop there. Use the secret of getting things done. Respond to the self-starter *DO IT NOW!*

Remember, regardless of what you have been or what you are, you can be what you want to be if you *act* with PMA.

The self-starter *DO IT NOW!* is an important self-motivator. It is the important step towards understanding and applying the principles of the next chapter entitled, "How to Motivate Yourself."

Thoughts to Steer By

1. It is better for people to do something and pay nothing, than to pay dues and do nothing.
2. "Too often what we read and profess becomes a part of

our libraries and our vocabularies, instead of becoming a part of our lives."

3. "Sow an action and you reap a habit; sow a habit and you reap a character; sow a character and you reap a destiny."
4. The secret of getting things done is: *DO IT NOW!*
5. As long as you live, never say to yourself *"DO IT NOW!"* unless you immediately follow through with desirable action.
6. *Now* is the time to act.
7. *Now* is the time to be happy.

DO IT NOW!

CHAPTER FIFTEEN

Know Your Capabilities

Only the very innocent feel immortal and perfect. Maturity means understanding yourself—your assets and liabilities. This self knowledge is a great asset in reaching your aim.

Act Your Way To Successful Living was written by Neil and Margaret Rau, who have had a thirty-year association with the theater community. During this period they saw case after case where timid and unsophisticated talent was changed into polished award-winning entertainers, by using certain techniques. They feel that if these techniques work so dramatically in the entertainment industry they must be based on a universal principle available to all who can understand and embody them. Even though these are things we all know instinctively, the secret is finding a formula that best allows you to utilize your instincts. All of us recognize truth when we hear or see it . . . the only difference (and it is this very difference which give such a kaleidoscopic joy to this wonderful business of living) is in the way we choose to apply it. What we must understand and realize is that we are indeed free to apply it in any way we wish. This book is just one more proof that the basic principles of life apply regardless of "where" they are applied. In *Peel Your Own Onion,* David Prosser showed that a person's life could be managed quite easily and successfully by using the same approach one would use in running a business. Maxwell Maltz, due to his familiarity with the field of medicine, was able to see the significance of correct thinking in the healing process, and thus was able to show the correlation between what you think you are and the subsequent events in your life.

Napoleon Hill spent twenty years in finding out first hand what went into the making of a successful person, and was then astute enough to condense the results into a format that anyone could follow. If the principles work for one person, they can work for all.

Basically, all of the authors within this book have stayed within their fields of expertise to make the discovery that a truth is a truth, no matter where you find it, then astutely applied the lessons learned in their respective disciplines to the other aspects of their existence.

Act Your Way to Successful Living first points out that we are all actors involved in dramas of our own making. Since we are responsible for our own scenarios, we should create our lives with the same child-like exhuberance and sense of fun we had as children. It stresses the importance of observing ourselves and our fellow climbers in order to arrive at correct conclusions; it postures that being at one with your environment enhances your intuition and helps you become aware of your own strengths, allowing you to be, above all else, yourself. By being aware of yourself, you will be aware of the image you present to others; learn to radiate your feelings from inside you so as to project the positive emotions which attract the good things of life to us. Imagination, the Rau's feel, is the magic key that creates for us. Anything that can be imagined, can be achieved, good or bad, especially with the addition of enthusiasm.

Another theory of Mr. and Mrs. Rau is that the sub-conscious is your submerged treasure house and should be used to achieve goals. Along with every other person whose life plan we have looked at, the Raus stress the importance of goals. Just as in a stage play there must be a super objective, or the end toward which each play must move (without which it is merely a series of loosely-connected acts like a vaudeville show), so we too must have goals in our personal dramas. Some would argue that life is one "slapstick" scene after another, with the Almighty acting as director, producer, props, etc . . . with the inevitable role of pulling the curtain on each performance as one's act comes to an end; personally, I'd use the "hook" to remove those "players" who take life as slapstick. As Shakespeare said "The whole world's a stage," so we might as well try for an Academy Award performance while we're here.

How Do You Know What You Are Capable Of?

This is a touchy one. The important thing to keep in mind is that we are all so much better than we think we are . . . no matter how successful we are, we can improve upon it. We always have a challenge in front of us if we care to accept it.

It has been estimated that we use only one-tenth of our brain cells. For years, scientists have been so intrigued by the "unknown quality" of the human brain that they consider it sacrilege to even suggest we are using our total brain. When we consider what a marvelously complex instrument the brain is (acknowledging that we cannot fully comprehend it), and when we work with the proven attributes of our mind to make our lives richer . . . we realize the question is not germane to our expression of life at this moment. Just think, however, if the scientists are only half-right, what wonderful surprises are in store for humanity as we learn to utilize our total brain. In the eons to come, what will our progeny become? (Wish I could stick around to see it).

I think that one of the things that makes for discontent is feeling this potential within us, yet not knowing how to unlock it . . . its pure frustration . . . like an itch that can't be scratched; but it can be relieved by the search for expression. I highly recommend setting aside a few minutes every day for some sort of inspirational activity, such as reading and absorbing books similar to those presented here . . . or just a quiet period of listening to and touching your inner self . . . all this will help you develop a better understanding of yourself and your capabilities.

Keep a Youthful Exuberance With Your Mature Judgment

When we are young, we are aware that there is a big, wide, wonderful world out there for our taking . . . we know that life is a clean page on which we can inscribe anything we wish . . . we can be anything we want to be. We know we are special . . . that we are going to write the Great American Novel when we grow up . . . or be the most famous Movie Star of all time. . . . the first one to land on Mars. . . . or solo-climb Mt. Everest.

I decided to start my climbing career with the Triboro Bridge, spanning Manhattan's East River (this is the first my mother has heard about this). Even though the chance of plummeting to the concrete road bed or river below was a very real possibility, I decided the risk was worth the exhilaration; besides, at thirteen, we all consider ourselves immortal . . . "risk" is a word with little meaning to us. Much more important than the risk, was looking good to my friends, after all, my "Sherpas" were with me, that is to say . . . my gang . . . harmless kids in love with the Yankees, Giants and Dodgers (take your pick); with that audience, there was no way I could not complete the climb; after all, we were now teenagers and there was no mountain we couldn't climb.

I started up . . . I had no ropes, pitons or carabiners. Where would I have found them among paraphernalia which consisted of dried out hand-me-down baseball gloves, cracked bats and our one heavily-taped baseball. Getting to the top was easy enough, since I did not have to look down, but descending was a different story. My descent became more harrowing by the second. Below me, the river, complete with tossing whitecaps, was racing along in one direction; the zig-zagging head-long rush of multi-colored traffic streaming in the other direction blended with the river to create a dizzy whirl of chaos which gave me an instant case of motion sickness . . . every parameter by which I could gauge my descent was moving its own independent way.

At that instant, I contracted Amnesia . . . I simply could not remember what the hell I was doing there . . . nor even how I managed to make it the rest of the way down. It seems as though my birthskills were adequate for the deed, but my maturity was grossly inadequate to handle the consequences which followed.

At some point, we all come in contact with challenges, obstacles if you like, which are Herculean at first inspection. Early on, you undertake them blithely, with little or no concern for the big picture or the bottom line. In most cases, we get away with these unthinking acts as youthful indulgences . . . later on, we hesitate to even try; I'm not sure which is worse. The hard-core reality of the real world is that there will be no compassion offered for scaling peaks which we have no business being on in the first place. With maturity, we learn discretion; we also learn more is involved than just deciding to do something and blundering ahead.

Everyone Is Special

If we could retain that childlike feeling of our "specialness," and the unquestioning confidence in our abilities, we might be more motivated to succeed; unfortunately, as we grow older, very few make the effort to realize "that specialness," or to become more than just average. In spite of this, we expect "others" to do the best they are capable of, particularly when it affects us personally. When you're sick, you don't want to be attended by an "average" doctor. We often go to great lengths to find the "best." In a legal matter, you don't go to an attorney who was at the bottom of his class; you seek out the specialist, the one who is knowledgeable, bright and persuasive. We have the unmitigated gall to expect a high degree of excellence in others with no willingness to expect, or offer, the same excellence from ourselves.

The phrase . . . "The best in me for the world . . . the best in the world for me," clearly states that you get out of life exactly what you put into it; however, we should also recognize that our egos are so protective of us, that it is quite often difficult to be honest with ourselves about our actions, motives and feelings; we may be so into our roles that it is quite easy to delude ourselves; we may be giving such a good performance that others are taken in . . . but you can't "con" the universe. What you truly believe will be shown by your experiences and your environment.

I've chosen the chapter "Yourself" from *Act Your Way to Successful Living,* because Neil and Margaret Rau ask some very penetrating and pertinent questions about the person you are most intimate with. . . . Yourself! If you honestly try to appraise yourself by taking inventory of your birthskills, your education, your core beliefs, your goals, your self-image, etc., you will be able to gauge quite accurately your reactions to the challenges of the climb, and assess where your strengths and weaknesses lie. It will also help you appreciate just how special you really are. One word of caution . . . do not spend your whole life assessing your qualifications; those who do, spend all their discretionary time on the porch swing, never risking a hike, to say nothing of a climb.

Others Accept Your "Real" Evaluation of Yourself

The image you present is a reflection of what you think about yourself. We each have a certain style and when you attempt to be something you aren't, it backfires. You may picture yourself as being the "Renaissance Man," even acting the part on the surface, but if you don't feel the part and can't back it up with "truth," you will end up looking more like a "flim-flam" man. If you see yourself as Sir Galahad, but the image you portray is that of the Black Knight . . . don't hold your breath waiting to sit at the Round Table. If your image reflects the personality of a dial tone, then you must do something about the "out of order" sign around your neck. No one wants to be in the company of a loser (except another loser). People react to your style with equal style. Don't expect to be the hit of the party or the first one on the summit, if you cheer up a room by leaving it.

Get to know yourself and identify your attainable levels as early in life as possible. Don't sell yourself short, but do realize that setting unrealistic goals is as sure fire a way to failure as is setting no goals at all. Recognize what you are . . . don't always be comparing yourself to someone else. . . . that is not realistic . . . no one can possibly be all things to all people. I flatter myself that I have a wide range of interests, birthskills, and knowledge . . . I get along well with company presidents, maitre d's and mailmen . . . I'm glib . . . and see myself as a raconteur. . . . I'm quick on my feet . . . take care of my body. . . . but just when I start feeling like I'm "King of the Hill" I meet someone who is an ultra-qualified expert in a field I've only been able to dabble in. Due to my competitive nature, my first reaction is usually one of pique, then my good sense and sense of humor come to the rescue; I remember that I'm not five hundred years old, which I would have to be in order to become an expert in just a few of the areas which interest me. With this in mind, I try to take what will be of benefit to me out of the exchange; this is a most valuable learning tool. In one personal contact, you are expected to be the "Master," in another a Journeyman," and still in others (providing our ego is in check), we must settle for "apprentice."

Knowing Yourself Is Not Easy, But Possible To All

Knowing one's self is easier for some than it is for others. The more complex our life, the more facets of our personality there are to crowd up our self-image. Cave dwellers spent the majority of their time in pursuit of life survival. Modern man's quest for survival is not nearly so straightforward. I would hazard a guess that one present-day vocation not in vogue in prehistoric times, was the psychiatrist (head-shrinkers were commonplace, but they plied the trade in the very literal sense of the word). What, pray tell, would his clients have to report beyond the fact that he had made it back to his cave, or perhaps they could consider together whether the killing of the mastodon was an act of hostility, necessity, or both.

Self-image and self-motivation are enhanced by each summit you reach, no matter how easy or difficult the climb. One person's boulder may be another's Everest. You cannot clone someone else's mountain, and for that we should be thankful. As the old Indian proverb says, "Don't judge another until you have walked in his moccasins." Whenever I come in contact with a climb beyond my skill, I am reminded of something my father used to say . . . "God gives hard bread to people with no teeth." Translation: The good things in life are God-given to us, but we have to figure out how to utilize them . . . in other words, Everest is open to all, but to venture up its peaks without knowing yourself, is wishful thinking.

You Are Who You Are . . . Appreciate Yourself

Accept yourself as you are, and where you are, and start from there. Remember, this is your mountain. As you read through this anthology, you may find yourself saying, "Boy, if my friend, John or Mary, would only read this book! . . . it is just what he/she needs to cure all of his/her bad habits and problems." Well, my friend, you would not even be able to recognize a problem in someone else, unless you were aware of it in yourself. This is your life . . . live it for yourself . . . let others find their own way . . . for the sake of their growth. My mountains are special to me . . . and your mountains, though different from mine, are special to you. We all have it in our make-up to shape and define the mountain we wish to climb. The top of the mountain is often obscured, but it is our mountain and we either climb it . . . or we don't. Those who have a clear picture of their self-worth and their capabilities, plus a positive outlook for their goals, are the ones who see the peak as reachable. . . . they are the winners who make it to the top.

Book Title: Act Your Way to Successful Living
Author: Neil & Margaret Rau
Publisher: Prentice-Hall Inc.
Chapter: Yourself

Yourself

LET'S TALK ABOUT YOU

Now we come to the most important subject of all—yourself.

WHAT DO YOU THINK OF YOURSELF?

Perhaps you haven't really given yourself genuine thought. Or perhaps you have been looking at yourself in a deprecatory manner. We are apt to feel guilty thinking about ourselves. And when we do think about ourselves we tend to accept the image the world throws back at us.

In this way we lose the depth of individuality that would make our role in life such an exciting and worthwhile adventure. To remedy such a state of affairs, this chapter will deal

From the book. . .ACT YOUR WAY TO SUCCESSFUL LIVING By Neil and Margaret Rau © 1966 By Prentice-Hall, Inc. Published by Prentice-Hall, Inc., Englewood Cliffs, NJ 07632.

with you specifically, offering suggestions to bring out the truly great actor that lives within you.

YOU AND YOUR INFERIORITY COMPLEX

Perhaps you feel there's no hope for you. Your inferiority complex is so bad that you couldn't change if you tried. So we use this excuse for explaining our failures and our fears—in short, our background acting!

However, an inferiority complex is the most normal thing in the world. This is because it's based on actuality. We are all really inferior, in some degree, to every other person in the world.

Take your looks, for instance! Do you secretly feel that with a more attractive front the world would be yours? Has it ever occurred to you that some people have inferiority complexes just because of their good looks?

It took Jeff Hunter a long while to reach the point where he'd accept leading roles. He had been in the habit of choosing supporting parts. He was afraid that people hired him for his looks and that he'd let them down when he started to act.

Many of the screen's glamor girls have such inferiority complexes about their acting abilities that they place an inordinate emphasis on appearance to carry them through. One of the screen's most beautiful actresses, Gina Lollobrigida, was so terrified of destroying her image as an irresistible siren that she insisted on wearing glamorous makeup even in the role of a street gamin.

In contrast, Sophia Loren found early in her career that looks have little to do with playing a role effectively. She learned to appear homely whenever the part called for it. Such a role, that of Cesira in *Two Women,* won Sophia her Academy Award as the best actress of 1964.

THE SELF *IS* SUPERIOR

All outstanding actors and actresses come to the final realization that great acting springs from the revelation of the intrinsic self. They know that in that self lies their claim to genuine superiority, for being unique, it cannot be duplicated. No matter how inadequately these people may handle their private lives, the real self they display in their professional work guarantees an outstanding performance.

To prove that the commanding presence of a screen personality is due solely to exposing the unique self to the public eye, the late actress Carole Lombard liked to play this trick. She would go down a crowded city street acting like a simple member of the crowd around her. No one would take the least notice. Then all at once she would "transform" herself into Carole Lombard and be almost instantly recognized.

Recently Rock Hudson rented a car and drove through the Deep South from Miami to Atlanta. His only disguise was a pair of hornrimmed glasses, which he actually wears in off-screen life. He mixed freely with people. Yet despite his arresting figure and familiar face he was recognized less than ten times during that long drive.

Because he wanted anonymity he had deliberately retreated into background acting to give himself this change of pace.

PUT FORWARD A BETTER SELF

Perhaps you may feel this is all well for film and stage personalities who are born with latent magnetic personalities. You yourself are so dull that nothing possibly can help.

Then you'll be interested in the story Tony Barr told us of the young poultry expert who called himself a chicken doctor.

He had come to Hollywood from the Midwest on a vacation and for the fun of it registered for one of Barr's beginners courses for aspiring actors. He was an awkward, self-conscious fellow, so tongue-tied he could scarcely get out two words in sequence. Barr didn't think the fellow would find the courage to continue those classes, where he would have to put himself on public display.

But the young man did and finally his self broke through. From then on he had a lark. By the time he was ready to go back home he had become a self-assured out-going person with a new zest for living.

"This acting is a piece of cake," he told Barr. "It's changed my whole life."

You can change your personality, just as he did, by putting in some effort. So why not take the first step?

RECOGNIZE YOUR MASK

Sit down alone; with your magic projection machine throw onto your imaginary screen the image of yourself as you have been presenting it to the world.

What do you see there? A failure? A mere cog in a machine? A person without individuality or character—just one more cipher in a multitude of ciphers? A forlorn, ugly, rejected human being?

If this is what you see, it means you are on the outside looking in. All you see is the mask you present to the world, which you have come to accept as the real you. It is no more the real you than the clothes you wear.

Unfortunately, we construct these ugly masks out of a conglomeration of minor events stretching back over the years. And we even accept them without question from the hands of others.

THE MASK OF REJECTION

Bob Gist told us of one of his students whose beautiful spirit was crammed behind the dull mask she had accepted as her own personality when her husband deserted her.

"I'm not only ugly. I'm the ugliest person alive," her mask mourned for the whole world to hear.

But the girl was sincere about wanting to be an actress. She came to classes regularly. She conscientiously performed the dramatic exercises. These included improvisations and dramatic renditions of situations in which she was theoretically placed by her teacher.

At first she reacted only to the promptings of the mask and consequently her acting was wooden and unconvincing. But she was encouraged to search below her mask and call up organic responses from her inner self.

The girl cooperated fully. Conquering her apathy she reached down into her real self for material for her portrayals. As she came into closer contact with that self, her acting became more vibrant. But of greater importance was the complete change in her everyday personality.

She began to dress smartly. She started wearing lipstick again. Her sullen mask-like face began to glow with a natural radiance. Presently no one would have recognized the beautiful young woman as the ugly duckling who had first come to study with Gist.

THE MASK OF IMPORTANCE

Perhaps, on the other hand, you're wearing a mask of "importance." This mask insists on going after every material possession Mr. Jones owns simply for the sake of keeping up.

"We spend our lives accumulating status symbols for only one reason," Jack Lemmon told us, "approval and the applause it brings. What we should realize is that applause means something only when we earn it by being more truly ourselves instead of trying to please and impress everyone."

YOU ARE NOT YOUR MASK

Once you have taken a good look at the image presented to the world, tell yourself firmly that it is not the real you. The real you does not feel rejected because somebody deserts it, or insecure without carloads of material possessions. It does not accept a few failings as an indication of failure, nor will it tolerate being relegated to the role of a background actor. It will fight back with conflict.

The real you is a great and wonderful being in which all the creative forces of nature and spirit have combined to fashion something wholly unique. There is no one like you in the whole world. There is no one in the whole world who can play your role as you yourself can play it, for you were created to that end.

As James Cagney used to say to the extras who worked with him, "My railroad may be longer than yours, but yours is just as wide."

So whether you think your role is big or small, don't underestimate its importance. Remember: It's up to you to make it important.

GETTING DOWN TO PARTICULARS

As a first step make a list of the qualities, not earthly possessions, you would display as a new personality. We all possess fine qualities because they are part of the heritage of the human race. In some people they are scarcely developed; in others they are repressed. But with effort we can all waken them in ourselves.

HOW GEORGE HAMILTON DID IT

After you list your qualities, select the one most important to you and begin to work on it. Once you see results, you will be eager to experiment with other qualities.

Here are techniques used by actors to bring out the qualities they needed to portray a character adequately.

George Hamilton is a sophisticated, intellectual young modern. He had to transform himself into the ingenuous Fabrizio, the Italian boy in *Light in the Piazza,* before he could attempt the role. Following Zina Provendie's advice he forgot his usual self. Instead, he filled his mind with the love, warmth and generosity that were attributes of the Italian boy. He made them shine in his eyes and he demonstrated them in his gestures.

As a result George played to perfection a role that was diametrically opposed to the personality people associated with him.

You yourself can *think* into being the qualities you want if you concentrate on them wholeheartedly enough. Practice radiating them in the color which expresses the quality most vitally to you. Walk in its rhythm. Relax and let this rhythm take complete possession of you.

SUPPOSE YOU STILL CAN'T GET INTO THE FEEL

If you still can't get into the feel of the quality, take out your easel and paint a picture to express it. Even though you are no artist, the effort you make to put this special quality into pictorial form will help to rouse it.

Or try singing it. Singing is a great medium for releasing hidden qualities and bringing the self to the fore. Any kind of music is great therapy.

Dean Martin told us that when he first arrived in Hollywood he was so shy he used to sit mute and miserable in a corner. He came from a background of gambling casinos and night clubs, and his way of talking murdered the English language. Because he was so handsome, his aloofness was misinterpreted as snobbishness.

Dean decided to *sing* his way into self-confidence. He began to sing at gatherings where previously he had been too tongue-tied to open his mouth. He made a pleasing impression on others which increased self-confidence. Today Dean is one of the screen's most self-assured actors.

Perhaps you haven't enough voice to expose in public. But if you like to sing, try it, anyway—at home, in the shower. Let yourself go! Choose the melodies that express qualities you are trying to develop. The warm vital emotion which singing rouses brings these feelings to the surface. Then you can capture them to carry with you through the day.

THE MAGIC "AS IF"

The magic "as if" is another method many actors and actresses use to vitalize the qualities they need for their roles. It was devised by Stanislavski for his pupils. Here is how it works.

When Jeff Corey wanted to create the personality of the wino in *Lady in a Cage* he behaved *as if* he were afraid of all art objects and shied away from them. Only Corey knew what his character feared. The audience was only aware of the eccentric arrhythmic patterns of the character he was playing. But those erratic movements conveyed more vividly than words the impression of insanity.

Similarly, the late Roman Bohnen, in the memorable part of

Candy in *Of Mice and Men,* acted *as if* he were behind a plaster wall with one eye set against a chink, watching the world but never participating in it. Again, though the audience had no knowledge of the image in Bohnen's mind, they were deeply stirred by the poignant little man he created.

We play this magic "as if" game all the time without being aware of it. Unfortunately, too often we select negative "as if" formulas to reflect to the world. Then we can't understand why we're the victims of ill will.

If you have unconsciously projected a negative "as if" picture, deliberately change it to a positive "as if" and you will discover how quickly the attitude of others toward you follows suit.

Here are some brief trial exercises by which you can familiarize yourself with the formula. You may think of other exercises yourself.

Try walking *as if* on cloud nine. Or start behaving *as if* you're a king wearing a golden crown, or a beautiful woman who has the world at your feet.

Of course, people won't see the image you are evoking, but you'll be amazed at how quickly they pick up the quality which it represents.

WHEN THE MAGIC "AS IF" WON'T WORK

There may be moments when you find some desired quality so alien to your conscious mind that even with a magic "as if" you cannot call it into being. If so, solve the problem by putting your powers of observation to work.

Select a person in whom you recognize the quality you wish for yourself. Check his gestures, his mannerisms, his tone of voice, his body stance. Then start aping him—in private at first —but with feeling. Throw yourself wholeheartedly into the role.

At first you will depend almost entirely on the gestures and mannerisms of the person you are copying. Then, gradually, as you step into his shoes, you will get the *feeling* which animates him. Once this happens, you can begin to express it in your own way.

Use of his methods should be only the booster that sends your space ship into orbit. To be effective you *must* develop your own style.

A WAY FOR EVERYONE

You have a particular style, just as everyone on stage, screen, and television has. To ignore that style is to "step out of character" and a poor performance will invariably result.

Compare the acting style of Richard Boone and the late Gary Cooper. Boone has an earthy forthright manner. Cooper had a more easygoing, quiet quality. Yet both styles are symbols of manliness.

If you're the quiet type like "big Coop," you needn't throw your weight around to get your due. It won't impress anyone, because your rhythm will be wrong. There are other effective ways of getting what you want. Cooper knew them all—and used them, off stage as well as on.

Once on location he found his dressing room at an inconvenient distance from the camera. Instead of creating a scene he just grinned pleasantly and began ambling back and forth between the set and his room to get various things he "needed." He wasted a great deal of everyone's time that first day with his good-natured ambling.

The following day, without a comment from anyone, he found his dressing room moved closer to the camera.

Use your imagination to solve your problems in your own style. You'll be far more effective, and what's more, you won't end the day with a headache caused by the tensions of playing your part out of character.

MAYBE YOU'RE AN EXTROVERT

If you are an extrovert don't feel obliged to conceal your expansiveness under a false cloak of modesty. Don't be afraid to take your bows openly.

Writer Walter Reisch told us how one great actor who craved attention solved his problem. He was the late Emil Jannings, who had spent most of his life on the European stage and was accustomed to many nightly curtain calls.

In Hollywood he missed those bows. So whenever there was a touring company in town he went to the theater to look up some actor friend in the troupe. He always managed to arrive backstage about 10:45.

Shortly after his arrival the curtain would come down and the actors would go out for their bows. Jannings, unnoticed, would join the cast and take a bow with them. In this whimsical and harmless way he was able to satisfy his need for attention.

Even those who recognized Jannings never resented his presence. As a great artist he had earned the right to all the bows and applause he could get. Remember: You have as much right as Jannings to take bows if you have earned them. Accept the praise with genuine and outgoing pleasure. It's as much yours as the suit or dress you're wearing.

Jackie Gleason put it to us this way, "You see a person in a large organization who proudly displays a watch or some other memento he has received from the boss in appreciation of his outstanding performance. The talent you possess, for every one of us possesses a talent of some sort, is a similar gift of appreciation from your Creator. Surely, then, you will gladly and proudly show it off."

ARE YOU SEEKING APPLAUSE?

Many people think applause is due only for the big accomplishments of the business, political, artistic or social worlds. And they engage in a cutthroat competition for the sole sake of being important. The person who seeks applause for this sort of surface deed will never be satisfied.

The only way to bring applause that is truly satisfying is to play our role in its richest capacity.

Many actors and actresses realize the need to express themselves in ways beyond their acting. This is a side of Hollywood that has never really been explored. In the field of painting alone there are many notable artists among film personalities —Kim Novak, Claudette Colbert, Red Skelton, Edward G. Robinson, Richard Whorf, Hedy Lamarr and Richard Conte, to name just a few.

Jack Lemmon plays the piano and composes music in his spare time. Bob Mitchum writes poetry, Yvette Mimieux short stories. William Holden and Dame Flora Robson study languages.

The list of avocations among stars is almost endless. Vincent Price has made practically a full-time career for himself lecturing on art, and he is considered an authority. Mickey Rooney always had a desire to teach, particularly in the performing arts, and the desire led him finally to set up a national chain of schools called Mickey Rooney's Actor's Workshops. He told us his next move will be the founding of The University of Imagination, which will embrace all the arts.

YOU, TOO, CAN CREATE

Lajos Egri points out that we are equipped with several talents which should be developed not for the sake of monetary gain but for the sheer pleasure of creativity.

So ask yourself if there's something you've always wanted to do but have lacked the courage to start. Perhaps painting, writing, gardening, decorating, or something so far out there's not a name for it. Cultivate it! Attend classes where you'll meet others interested in the same subject.

Don't concern yourself about the world's reaction. Work for the sheer joy of it. Perhaps you will turn out to be another Grandma Moses and your paintings will bring you fame. And you may discover then that all the acclaim in the world can't equal the pleasure of creating something for its own sake.

THE SOCIAL SERVICES

Perhaps instead of creative work your interest lies in helping others. This kind of service is therapeutic for physical and mental ailments. Dr. Rex Kennamer recommends it to his patients who suffer from a common ailment—loneliness. He advises interest in church or political work, or in volunteer service at hospitals, orphanages or schools for the handicapped.

There are many worthy causes that will repay your efforts with a sense of fulfillment and completion. Just make sure that you look for your reward in the doing and not in expectation of gratitude.

THE REWARDS

As you express your creativity, you will discover how vitally you are enlarging your role in life. Soon, old hesitancies will disappear. New self-confidence will take their place. How the world treats you will no longer carry such traumatic weight. You will no longer feel slighted at apparent snubs and barbs.

Dudley Murphy, former film director and present owner of the famous Holiday House near the Malibu film colony on the

Pacific Coast Highway in California, told us he can pick out the truly important people among his patrons.

"The people who have not yet found themselves and are uncertain of their roles in life," explained Mr. Murphy, "have to assume pompous airs to convince themselves and others they're somebodies. They're the ones who are always deeply hurt when they're not recognized immediately, even though it's only the second time they've been to the restaurant."

In contrast Mr. Murphy likes to remember the man who came in one night with an easy smile, extended his hand and said cheerfully, "Good evening, Mr. Murphy."

"I'd known him for twenty years," Mr. Murphy told us, "but I hadn't seen him for four and I couldn't for the life of me recall him."

The man noticed Mr. Murphy's quizzical look and his smile broadened.

"Cary Grant, sir," he introduced himself.

Cary Grant's ego could afford to go unrecognized because he'd come to recognize his own self. It's an axiom that you *have* to recognize and *have* respect for your self before you can show tolerance for the foibles of others.

"Self-love is not the same thing as selfishness," Dick Van Dyke told us when we pressed him for an analysis of the secret magnetism of his brand of humor. "Self-love is true regard for your self. And the person who possesses this virtue is able to laugh at the world's barbs and even at his own pomposity when it gets the better of him."

THE VALUE OF LAUGHTER

Once you have reached the point of laughing at your mistakes you have brought your true self into focus with the world.

Drama coaches realize the efficacy of self-laughter as a cure for self-consciousness in their beginner students. When Diane

Baker, who today is a self-assured young actress, first arrived at Warner Brothers to study under Estelle Harman, she was a very self-conscious young girl. She walked with her head down, spoke in a quiet voice and couldn't get on stage without clinging to furniture.

Miss Harman knew Diane would never make a good actress as long as she was so desperately concerned about her appearance. So she gave Diane clown assignments. When the actress realized she was going to look silly no matter how she performed those assignments, she loosened up. Thus she learned that poise is not a matter of outer appearance but of vitality of the inner self.

YOU DON'T HAVE TO BE A CLOWN

You don't have to wear a clown costume or a mask to make use of the relaxation that self-laughter will bring you. Remember that often our foolish acts endear us most to others.

Ida Lupino told us the following story to demonstrate how a ludicrous accident can work to your benefit.

Ida and twenty-eight other girls were all auditioning for George Bernard Shaw for a part in his play *Heartbreak House*. It was in the heat of summer and Ida, a frightened young teenager at the time, was the last to be called. She had plenty of opportunity to fret and she kept combing nervously at her blond hair.

Finally she found herself standing before Mr. Shaw. He gave her a long, surprised stare and then said tersely, "Go ahead, read."

Ida got through the part somehow. She knew she wasn't doing well. The other girls were all more professional than she. So she was astonished when, at the end of her reading, Mr. Shaw said, "Any girl who will go to such extremes to get a job deserves it. You have the role."

Ida didn't know what he was talking about. So she thanked him timidly and left.

On the way out she happened to pass a mirror and glanced at her reflection. She couldn't believe her eyes. The heat of the day had melted the lipstick in the bottom of her purse and her comb had become smeared with it. Her blond hair was streaked with bright red.

George Bernard Shaw, thinking she had purposely chosen this eccentric appraoch to land a job, had rewarded her for her "imagination."

Ida sat down and laughed at herself until she cried. Now, whenever she finds herself faced with a difficult situation, she reminds herself of that first audition with Shaw.

Look back at your own life. Haven't there been times when a little unexpected humor, even at your own expense, would have helped you through a difficult situation? Haven't there been times when a little humor on your part might have eased the atmosphere and enabled you to play your role with more self-confidence?

Make a practice of allowing this saving grace of humor to demonstrate itself in all your future relationships. It will not only enable you to display your self more effectively but will also relax tensions among your fellow actors in the play of life.

CHAPTER SIXTEEN

One Step at a Time

Move cautiously and carefully. Plato understood the mean between rashness and cowardess is courage. Apply this maxim to the course you have set for yourself and begin the climb one step at a time.

The major point that has been stressed by each author I've selected is to choose a goal. Keep one thing in mind however; a major goal is composed of a myriad of minor goals. You will not be overwhelmed by the big picture, if, after choosing your major goal, you concentrate on the next immediate handhold or toehold on the cliff. As you gain in confidence by doing this, you will be surprised at the surge of power which will flow into your life. Your very action of starting sets the wheels in motion at all levels . . . conscious and sub-conscious. With this action you will gain access to your creative intelligence.

Mr. R. Kopmeyer simplifies this message for us with the next essay, "Do The Thing and You'll Have the Power."

Book Title: Thoughts to Build On
Author: M. R. Kopmeyer
Publisher: The Success Foundation, Inc., Louisville, Ky
Chapter: Do the Thing and You Will Have the Power

Do The Thing And You Will Have The Power

Fortunately, I learned one of the most useful facts of life at an early age. I don't remember who said it and I wish I did, because I would like to send him a mental message of thanks every morning when I wake up.

What I learned, as a very young man, was this:

("DO the thing and you will have the power!")

That one simple, yet almost incredible, statement has enabled me: (1) to try; and (2) to actually accomplish things—more than any other statement I have ever heard.

If I had not believed, deeply *believed,* that just by the act of *doing*—somehow, from somewhere, I would be given the *power to do it*—I would not have attempted, much less accomplished, half of what I have done (the difficult, rewarding half).

How can this be possible, that the act of *doing* something generates the *power* to do it?

One answer comes from the psychologists. The most conservative psychologists say that a person never uses more than *half* of his actual capability. Others say that we are operating only at *one-tenth* of our capacity. Thus, depending on which psychologist is right the very *least* you can accomplish is *twice* as much, and it may amount to *ten times* as much. So, since everybody normally operates at only a fraction of his potential, each of us can accomplish much more just by *trying* . . . just by *doing*.

DO the thing and you will have the power!

Henry Ford, who must have made some sort of record for doing things, put it simply, "Whether you *believe* you can *do* a thing or *not*—you are right."

Perhaps that's an over-simplification of a very profound fact of life. Nevertheless, there is a great reservoir of power ready to be used by anyone who begins to *do* something. *Do* the thing and you will have the power.

Maybe the ego calls on the super ego, which in turn draws the necessary power from an omnipotent ultra ego.

Or to state it in other terms, your conscious mind draws upon your subconscious mind, which, properly used has at its disposal the unlimited power of the universal mind which theologians call the God-Mind, or simply, God. Whatever the terminology, the *fact* is that there is an unlimited *supply* of power, and as you *do* the thing, you will have the power to accomplish it.

In the late years of his idea-filled life, Thomas Edison said, "Ideas come from space. This may seem astonishing and impossible to believe, but it is true. Ideas come from out of space." Edison should have known, because he had more ideas than any man who ever lived.

And if ideas come from "space", there is reason to believe that the power you need will come from "space," too. Certainly, whatever power—no matter how much power—you need to accomplish what you determinedly set out to do, *will be furnished you* from "somewhere". We have not evolved sufficiently to know all the answers. As a philosopher said, "Man's knowledge may be compared to a potato bug in a sack of potatoes in the hold of a great ship—wondering what makes the ship go".

But, because we do not know the *source* of our almost unlimited power for accomplishment, does not prevent our using the *fact* that such power does exist and is readily available for our use to achieve our goals.

So do not hesitate to strive for your goal. Start now—with the sure knowledge that whatever man can conceive and believe, man can achieve. Start now—without hesitation or fear, because the power to do, comes with the doing, and as *you do the thing, you will have the power!*

SECTION FOUR

Overcoming Obstacles

CHAPTER SEVENTEEN

Accepting Challenges

There is no easy way to climb mountains. To do so you must overcome obstacles as you move upward. So it is with life goals. In one exciting incident from my mountain climbing experiences this truth is made clear.

We started our descent from the base camp on Mt. Rainier in the beginnings of a storm. It didn't seem as bad as it would eventually become. We were exhilarated by our success in reaching the summit and could virtually taste the "real" food, cooked and served by someone other than ourselves, that awaited us at sea level. I had a ravenous hunger. Funny, I never get hungry going up the mountain, only coming back down it. Visions of steak and wine danced in my mind (there was no inkling that we were to spend the night in an ice cave). As much as I delight in the finesse of Northern Italian and French sauces, veal and Corton Charlemagne, that type of menu never plays well with me on the mountain. . . . steak and potatoes, beer and red wine . . . yes . . . and lots of it. So you can see why I plodded ahead, carefully placing my boot in the boot track of my guide, increasingly aware that he was becoming invisible before my very eyes, flickering in and out of my sight, there one second and gone the next, finally to disappear all together. We could literally only see each other if we came to a complete halt and faced each other squarely. My guide instinctively knew that the compass was only doing half the job . . . not that it was really mis-functioning, but we could see no landmarks to confirm our direction. The synergy of time in descent, the compass, and visual landmarks were required to successfully reach the original base camp. The time of descent was three hours . . . which indicated. . . . if indeed we were headed in the right direction. . . . that we were approximately five hours from safety. There were no visible landmarks and the com-pass was performing as expected . . . it was the fallibility of man . . . manifesting in a distrust of things mechanical.

I asked one too many questions and my usually placid, self-assured guide blew up. "Shut up! . . . for crying out loud . . . let me think, Damn it!" He told me to stay put, as we were at the top of what looked like a steep incline . . . with the wind now howling and the snow fast becoming a blizzard, I didn't have much choice. The mid-morning light had been playing games with us. For brief seconds, brighter light would open up a window for us and we could see a slope which seemed familiar, only to darken before we could get to it safely. It was now scary as hell. Here we were in the most technologically advanced country in the world . . . at mid-morning . . . and neither of us could descend a foot in safety.

My guide descended quickly out of my sight . . . four, maybe five steps; I couldn't even hear him, let alone see him; then his yells came and his voice falls betrayed his stolid self-confi-dence and his loss of footing brought him to an abrupt stop. He couldn't have been gone from my side over thirty seconds; there was at least a bit of reassurance in that . . . wherever he stopped falling, he wasn't far from me. His voice grew stronger and safer-sounding almost immediately.

He ordered me to follow. I did. . . . only to repeat his acrobatics, but with damn less skill. I bounded past him, coming to rest just out of his sight. Where we were and the safety of our landing spot was, was a complete mystery

My guide decided we had to retrace our steps . . . as accurately as was possible, until we reached our last recognizable landmark. Did I dare question him, I thought? Hell, yes! Did he mean as far back as twenty minutes in this complete white-out, with our boot tracks all but obscured seconds after we impress them in the snow? "Yes," he said, "exactly that. We have to acknowledge our error . . . retrace our steps, find familiar ground . . . or stay here until, and if, this white-out clears."

"Lead the way," I told him. With the threat of avalanches falling off the mountain and crevasses under our feet, we proceeded back up the mountain. I will always be amazed by our finding our last landmark and ultimately, our target. Some of the luck is blind faith . . . of that I'm sure, but more of it was the instinctive urge to try harder . . . to do . . . the power was with us. The first thing that should be done is to remove the stigma attached to the word "obstacle" . . . if not, you stand little chance of making it even as far as the base camp. One can get so totally concerned with the premise of the obstacle, that it can bog down any attempt to get past it. Obstacles are as natural to life as breathing. I don't believe there are any insurmountable obstacles, unless you insist on going over the top by brute force on a very rigid path you have laid our for yourself

If its within the capabilities of your birthskills, you will find the way up the route you've chosen . . . if not, choose another pitch; we can't all climb the north face. Discovering the best pitch for you becomes the challenge, a puzzle to be solved, and nothing more. Start then, by calling an obstacle a challenge with the realization that when you meet one, there is a chance to sharpen the skills that will make the next mountain easier to climb. You will find the way to this by using your intelligence, your intuition, your sensitivity towards other who are on their climb . . . or by using any of the applicable tools we have discussed in previous sections.

Use the Serendipity Principle

One of my favorite words is "Serendipity." Horace Walpole's delightful "Tales of the Serendip" from which the word serendipity is drawn, refers to the finding of unsought agreeably-wonderful or valuable things. By letting the creative process flow through you, without demanding instant gratification of every desire, or that every ego-wish be satisfied, you may be surprised at the results. The Serendipity Principle says, "Start your climb with a sense of excited anticipation, eager to see what will happen next in your life scenario, maintaining a firm belief that right action will always take place."

In other words, goals are important, but should be formulated with the understanding that they may change along the way as you discover hidden talents, unforeseen opportunities, or come to the realization that what you thought you wanted . . . you really don't! Always remain totally open and be alert to opportunities as they present themselves. We spoke earlier of "implacable" personalities as those who find comfort (and strength) in their inflexible nature . . . how sad for them; when the windfalls arrive unexpectedly into their lives, they fail to bend to the curve in the road that is the right path for them.

Some philosophies, especially some Eastern religions, carry the Serendipity Principle to the extreme by saying, "Don't expect anything and you won't be disappointed." (Loose, but basic, translation). I consider that interpretation cynical and negative. Goals must be formed in order to focus energies;

start your journey expecting the best, in terms of what you feel would be best for you, and you will receive the best in a form that is entirely acceptable to you though it may not be exactly what you had in mind. If you end up being happy, what does it matter how you get there?

It is impossible to stand high enough to see the "real big picture," even if you were to stand on the peak of the highest mountain. I'm reminded of the song . . . "on a clear day you can see forever"; a wonderful thought for those who contemplate their metaphorical climb. Though it really is beyond the scope of this book, I would like to digress a moment. There are still millions living in the valleys, in the shadows of the mountains, with little hope for much more than survival. Success is a relative thing, meaning different things to different people, but it is possible at every level, and each accomplishment can bring an equal degree of summit feeling. While your idea of success could be two weeks on the Riviera every month, with chauffeur and maid, another's dream may be to have three hot meals a day. You start where you are and reach as high as you are able, both of you using the same principle. That's success.

Over the centuries, only a few have had access to the degree of literacy we take for granted; even in today's world, those of you reading this book are blessed with more opportunities to take great personal strides than any one, anyplace else in the world, at any time in history. Think about that! To my way of thinking, it is a crime against yourself not to take advantage of your opportunities.

Believe that there is an orderliness to the universe, of which you are an important part, no matter where you are standing on the mountain, you're living aren't you? Any thinking person will know by observation that there *is* a "method" inherent in our universe by which we all can achieve our goals and live a fulfilled happy life. We can achieve our greatest success by working with the method, not by trying to fight it. There is but one basic principle or method in the orderliness of the universe, but it has so many applications that can be used in such a variety of ways, it sometimes seems like a myriad of impossible concepts. Don't get hung up here . . . there is no one right way to do anything. You can find your personal Shangri La by:

1. Making a conscious effort to do so.
2. Listening to your intuition, which is plugged directly into the orderliness of the universe.
3. Being persistent and sincere in your attempts.
4. Learning from your mistakes
5. Going beyond your comfort zone
6. Experimentation. Results will tell you when you are on the right track.

This final section will give you some insights into ways of over-coming pitfalls you may trip into. Realize that every author we have used is saying, though in different ways, "It all starts with you"! If you are the prime mover in your life, then you must also be the stumbling block. Actually, that simplifies it. If you were a victim of outside events, how could you correct it? You are the only one whose actions you can control. Remember, there are no insurmountable obstacles, only challenges to be undertaken and problems to be solved. Above all, remember that you can trust yourself and the universe. You can overcome any obstacle. Use as your role model any one of the great figures of history who have overcome every conceivable form of "obstacle" . . . from physical deformaties to paralyzing diseases and other afflictions. Milton was blind and Beethoven was deaf. What's your excuse?

CHAPTER EIGHTEEN

Be Persistent

Calvin Coolidge said, "nothing in the world takes the place of persistence". This is true if you really desire to scale giant heights, whether they are mountains or ambitions.

James Cash Penney was born in 1875 on a small farm in Missouri, the seventh of twelve children. His father was an "old school" Baptist minister who preached for free on Sunday, then farmed during the week to provide for his family. To teach Jim the value of money and self-reliance, his father told him when he was eight that he must start earning his own money for clothes. His first venture was raising pigs, horses and watermelons, all of which takes a great deal of persistence: he soon began developing skills in trading and marketing. After high school, he learned the fundamentals of storekeeping at the local drygoods store, then moved to Colorado because of his health, but continued his education by working in various Denver retail stores.

At the age of twenty-two he used his entire savings to purchase a butcher shop in Longmont, Colorado, a small town forty miles outside of Denver, but his refusal to "buy off" the chef at the local hotel with a bottle of whiskey a week as a condition of doing business, lost him the hotel trade and subsequently, his business. Not in the least daunted, he went to work once again as a clerk at the local mercantile company, The Golden Rule, and was immediately promoted to the store in Evanston, Wyoming. In 1902, he became a partner and at the age of twenty-six, opened his first store in Kemmerer, Wyoming. He had to borrow $1500 for his share of the partnership, but he did so well that he purchased full interest in the three-store chain from his other two partners in 1907, and started his own chain of Golden Rule Stores which he envisioned would cover the Rocky Mountains. As we know, he did much more than that.

In 1913, the name was changed to J.C. Penney stores. In an era when the principle *Caveat Emptor* prevailed (especially in the rugged mining towns of Wyoming), J.C. Penney insisted on providing quality merchandise at the lowest possible prices on a cash-and-carry policy. He adhered firmly to the Golden Rule of "doing unto others as you have them do unto you." He practiced this philosophy with his customers, as well as with his employees . . . (or his associates as he always called them). Everyone in the company was given the opportunity to work his way up to a partnership and management of his own store, in effect allowing the company to renew itself from within, providing the most effective means of motivation possible by doing so; this has been an important factor in the rapid and successful expansion of the company.

By the end of 1930, there was a Penney store in almost every town with a population of 5000 or more. By 1959, the company had reached sales of $1.5 billion, and by 1984, the company had more than 2000 stores, located in every state and in Puerto Rico and Belgium; with approximately 167,000 associates and $13 billion in sales. The phenomenal success of the company is directly attributable to the philosophies and principles on which Mr. Penny based the foundation for his first store and his life. His is one of the truly great success stories. Like all great men, J.C. Penney retained his perspective and his humility. Faith and fellowship were practiced twenty-four hours a day, seven days a week and not reserved just for Sunday. For over fifty years, he wrote a regular column for an interdenominational monthly called the "Christian Herald." *Lines of a layman* were taken from those articles and consist of day-to-day reflections on the pursuit and practice of a life lived by one who understood the adage, "What shall it profit a man if he gain the whole world and lose his own soul." J. C. Penney left a legacy of love and admiration that is still reflected by those whose paths crossed his. This was most apparent to us when we were seeking permission to use the article from *Lines of a Layman* and contacted the national headquarters in New York by telephone. We spoke with people who had known and worked with Mr. Penney, who still spoke of him with affection. He touched the lives of all he met, and they became better people for it; the J.C. Penney stores still espouse the "Golden Rule," and it shows.

You should realize at the beginning of your climb, that success can never be bought at the expense of others. Look for opportunities but don't be an opportunist. Be aware at all times of the dignity of others and don't rob a person of his dignity. A spark of the infinite unknown resides in all who have life. When you diminish another you diminish yourself.

The essays in this book. . . . some of the most inspiring vignettes I've read . . . are written by a successful man who had no hesitancy or embarrassment in acknowledging the existence of a higher power in the universe, who is there to be called upon. Call it what you may, but all successful people are in touch with universal principles; some may not even realize it. In *Lines of a layman,* J.C. Penny interweaves the spiritual with the practical by giving rules of management in an off-handed way, rules which can be used by anyone from the executive to the stockroom clerk or maintenance crew to improve their working lives and advance their careers. J. C. Penney was a man of vision who set a goal early and never saw reason to deviate from it. His persistence paid off.

The Meaning of Persistence

To persist means to take a stand, to stand firm, or to go on resolutely or stubbornly in spite of opposition, importunity or warning. The degree of your persistence usually depends upon your motivations and expectancy of reward, or summit feeling. I wanted to climb the Grand Teton in Wyoming. In my first weeks of training, my guides bolstered my resolve by telling me repeatedly that I could do it. I was determined to do it and I was standing firm. I went on resolutely and stubbornly in spite of the obstacle of my own body and lack of skills warning me and importuning me to stop. My guides continued to be supportive. "Try again," they would say. "This time, just extend your right foot a bit beyond your vision of it . . . there is a foothold there for you." I trusted, I persisted, and with time, plus a good deal of trial and error, I stayed the course. More often than I care to admit, a voice inside me kept reminding me that a tight-mid-section and enlarged biceps (the result of my persistence with my rigorous training schedule) couldn't disguise the fact that I was approaching a test of endurance which could be viewed as an opportunity to endure or an obstacle to overcome. . . . I chose the former.

Age Need Not Be An Obstacle . . . Young or Old

I have never given much credence to chronological age. When I was young, I felt older than my years, but as I have gotten older, I now feel younger than my years. In my mind, I'm frozen at about age thirty. I do not acknowledge "burn out" at any age . . . however, the time comes when we all must face the "challenge" of aging. Keep in mind that aging is a natural process of living and should be treated as such. Each age has its own privileges and rewards and each should be experienced to the fullest. I have been the cocky teen-ager, the jock collegiate, the young lover, the apprentice salesman, the young father, the novice company president, the trail-breaking marketing man, the father of teen-agers (that ages you rapidly), the brash young actor taking Hollywood by storm, the stunt-man riding in full gallop down a veritably unridable terrain (the key is not to let the horse in on it), the bon vivant, the sophisti-cate, etc. As I have put the years behind me, I have studied, learned and grown, as we all do. I've watched family relation-ships change as my parents have grown older or passed on. Its all part of the progression that is life. Don't fight it and don't miss any part of it.

Some day I will be too old to make the literal climb up the mountain, but I will never be too old to climb the foothills. I will look to the mountain with satisfaction, knowing I had the courage to climb it and to conquer it. There is probably a good reason why our bodies run down, as it seems to allow us the time to become more introspective and closer to the spiritual sides of our natures, but I believe you should be stubborn and persistent in demanding that your body remain useful to you until it is no longer needed. Start in your youth to accept the fact that age doesn't mean helplessness and decay, but just a different form of productivity. You may have a few aches and pains, but nothing you can't handle. There is beauty in age just as there is in youth if we can get over the prejudices set up by the cosmetic companies. Set up a state of mind and an envi-ronment that will allow you to age gracefully; enjoy each decade of your life for what if offers you . . . do the "teen thing" as you fancy. Don't be confused by your desire to "hang on" to some of your glorious past; its natural and in most cases, healthy and normal; its good to reflect and remember, but don't stay too long or you'll wear out your visit.

Knowing When Persistence Should End

An integral part of persistence and stubborness is knowing when to turn it off. Persistence is merely a matter of taking one step at a time with your eyes firmly fixed on your goals, but when persistence becomes pure stubborness, it becomes negative. Be careful of that. It is not failure to let go when you are going in the wrong direction. Don't ride the tail of the whirlwind because you are afraid to get off. . . . let go and accept a few bruises. Its failure to try to bulldoze your way over the mountain when wisdom dictates finding another route. Be persistent only in keeping your vision always in front of you and in following your star.

During the writing of this book, I have embarked upon a new business venture, wearing a hat I haven't worn for many years . . . retail salesman. I have stayed in the Industry which has been very good to me, marketing swimming pools. I had a vision of a place where a person could go to see exactly how a swimming pool would look in his backyard, in a homelike setting. My marketing sense told me to find a spot beside a busy freeway in bustling Los Angeles. We found just such a spot on one of the biggest windows in the world; this alone was not an easy accomplishment. I finally found the perfect parcel and even the name augered well . . . Recreation Road . . . then the monkey wrenches started appearing. The roadblocks thrown in our way by red tape and other factors would have discouraged even Sisyphus, but it felt right, so we persisted and won out against all odds. (All successful entrepreneurs who read this will identify with the difficulty of trying to convince a bureaucracy that it will be done in spite of them).

After finally getting the sub-division and land lease arranged, the actual building took about forty days . . . another "can't be done" I refused to listen to. The complex is beautiful and sales are strong. Be persistent when it feels right and back off when it doesn't. You will know the difference if you honestly listen to your intuition. Trust yourself and by all means "act out" your doubts . . . dos and don'ts, you'll be surprised at just how good an actor you've become.

Book Title: Lines of a Layman
Author: J.C. Penney
Publisher: Channel Press, Great Neck, New York
Chapter: Obstacles Mean Strength

Obstacles
Mean Strength

Demosthenes, the greatest of all orators, as a boy had an impediment of speech which he conquered by placing pebbles in his mouth and shouting. Beethoven, one of the world's greatest composers, was deaf. Milton, the great poet, was blind. The pages of history record acts of men who have succeeded, in spite of obstacles. With some of them, the handicaps were poverty, ill-health and poor education; others were maimed physically, but even this didn't stop them.

It is a natural thing to want to succeed, but all are not willing to pay the price of success. Such folks have a wishbone instead of a backbone. They are not willing to subject themselves to hard labor in order to plant the seed of their ambition. They want to reap benefits, but without much work. They can see how the law of cause and effect must work for others, but they expect to have it suspended in their own cases. Too many

LINES OF A LAYMAN By James C. Penney Copyright © 1956 by James C. Penney, Publisher: WM. B. Eerdmans Publishing Company, Grand Rapids, Mi. Reprinted by permission of J.C. Penney, Inc.

people believe in pull when they should be thinking about push. There is really no excuse for failure. There never have been such splendid opportunities on every hand. There is no dearth of men capable of handling big things. It takes hard work and years of study to fit one's self for the larger responsibilities of life. Cultivate vision and foresight by having faith in an all-wise, benevolent, over-ruling Power.

CHAPTER NINETEEN

Crises and You

When you accept the "real you," and you begin to make major progress in climbing your mountain, you no longer need to prove yourself to anyone but yourself. You just are. You don't dwell on mistakes. You learn from them and go on from there. You can however, cut down on mistakes.

Usually when you find a cliché, you find a truism going hand in hand with it. It has become the vogue today to liken our minds to a computer. Even though our minds are so much more complex than a computer, it is a good analogy. Your mind can only take action on what you feed in. It is programed to seek your goals automatically, so program it with positive exciting goals, then listen to the data coming out. You will find it easier to make correct decisions.

On the mountain, a mistake, or error in judgment, can be tragic, so we learn to think things through a little more carefully than we would at sea level. We learn to listen to the mountain and our intuition. The day we started up the "Grand" they were bringing down the body of a climber who unwisely tied his rope to an unsecure boulder and his repel took the boulder with him.

Luckily, in climbing our personal mountain, we are not penalized quite so severely for a mistake, in fact, they become marvelous learning devices for us. We are also able to profit from the mistakes of others, which allows us to progress faster than if we had to make all of our mistakes ourselves.

The most basic mountaineering course teaches us to stay away from overhanging boulders and small caves during an electrical storm. In climbing the Grand Teton that knowledge apparently slipped my mind. A storm started. The large boulders and overhangs looked so safe and sheltering, that I took refuge under one large boulder, but as I stood looking out, watching the streaks of lightning hit the ground, feeling unjustifiably safe and secure, a ball of St. Elmo's Fire started running around the edge of my false sanctuary. The static electricity it generated made my hair literally stand on end. My chest seemed hot to the touch and the metal carabiners on my strap were dancing on my chest. Needless to say, I abandoned my "haven" with all possible speed, and watched from a little safer vantage point the ball of fire cavort around the rocks.

About this time, my guide came running down the hill so fast he was almost out-distancing the furious streaks of lightning flashing around him. When the storm was over and we had survived unscathed, release of our tension showed by laughter that was just a little too raucous over things that really weren't funny. The guide came in for his share of good-natured banter over his championship run down the mountainside. He came right back with this comment. . . . "I know you can't really out-run a lightning strike, but the least you can do is to get the hell out of the area as fast as possible . . . it cuts down the odds." Good advice for many situations. Because of our technological advances, we very seldom come into conflict with the raw forces of nature. Our technology and the "gimmicks" we use to predict, influence or avoid the weather, has robbed us of a chance to be sharpened by hand-to-hand combat with the elements. This has led us to a mistrust of ourselves as individuals, when in actuality, we are basically as "natural" as the animals, and just as "tuned-in" to the deep rhythms of the earth. Again, I say, trust your intuition. We have progressed as a civilization because we have pretty much eliminated the need for day-to-day survival, but we have paid a high price for the privilege of enjoying our sanctuary.

I go to the mountain to renew my personal ties with the earth. I revel in the opportunity to match myself against the forces of nature and to win by meeting the challenges head-on. This is part of our heritage . . . our common bond with our ancestors who pioneered both the physical and psychological world we inhabit.

Of course, none of this occurs to me consciously when I'm climbing . . . the feeling of well-being is just there. Incidentally, that's a good test of rightness . . . that feeling of knowing . . . "this is just the way it should be" . . . an inner sense of awe, if you will. If we listen, nature can speak volumes to us. If we heed the signals, our intuition can guide and motivate us on life's journey.

Immediacy and Relevancy

George and Nena O'Neill's book, *Shifting Gears,* has present-day immediacy and relevancy; its defining of societal conditions, obstacles and challenges that will be encountered by today's climbers is well-researched and presented.

At the writing of their book in 1973, the O'Neills had been married twenty-eight years and were the parents of two children. George O'Neill was a professor of anthropology at City College of New York, with a Ph.D from Columbia University, while Nena was working on her Ph.D., also in anthropology.

They had successfully collaborated on a previous book, *Open Marriage,* an international best seller in 1972.

Through the ages, human nature has not changed very much. To be quite frank, human beings, though complex, are uniformly predictable under different conditions; the differences usually being determined by the mores of the culture. The laws of the universe are ageless and eternal; but there have been only a handful in each generation who have known how to work with the universe to survive and succeed in their particular society. For the most part, the culture of a person's environment is an important factor in the development of human potentials; but on the flip side, one knew and understood the values of that society, his place in it, and the penalties of breaking the rules, therefore, judgment, values and actions could be initiated from that standpoint. (Margaret Mead reported it best of all in *Growing up in Samoa.* I still look in on it from time to time).

George and Nena O'Neill recognize that we are living in a society that is changing so rapidly it is difficult to generate a set of values or code of behavior that will be valid through each change. Just when we think we've got it down pat, it goes around one more time. *Shifting Gears* was written in an attempt to help you find and take a life-stance that works for you. The sub-title is "finding Security in a Changing World," and refers to the last few years as the "Crisis Culture."

The Crisis Culture

Once again we go to the dictionary. I have a preoccupation with definitions, particularly since we are dealing with the print medium. I want to be sure we are all talking about the same thing. Crisis is an emotionally-charged word which means different things to different people for instance, to me it has the connotation of needing quick and decisive action; in reality that is not a part of the dictionary definition which says crisis is an emotionally-significant event or radical change in status in a person's life; the decisive moment; an unstable or crucial state of affairs whose outcome will make a decisive difference for better or worse. I find this definition too flat with no indication of decisive action even hinted at.

Crisis is that decisive period of flux which can make a change in our lives . . . when action is almost always called for.

Thousands of books have been written on the mechanics of dealing with children from birth (and before) through their growing years to adulthood, but few are written for adults, even though they continue these "rites of passage" for the rest of their lives. Maturity is a myth . . . maturity is extinction. To live successfully you must continue to grow as long as you are alive. Growth is what keeps you in the mainstream of life; reflecting on the past is healthy . . . dwelling on it is not.

As we make the transition from one growth stage to the next, there will be times when we are in a crisis state and therefore extremely vulnerable. Learn to recognize these stages . . . Primitive societies had rituals to mark almost every state of transition (birth, puberty, manhood, death and after-death). Prehistorical calendars, attributed to a number of different cultures, were really developed to deal with such transitions, (Life, the earth, the tides, the moon and the sun, etc.) and were heavily influenced by ritual.

In the last two centuries less and less emphasis has been placed on rituals of any sort. These rituals were actually support systems which today might be satisfactory substitutes for the dependency we had upon others. Since we are becoming a transient society, with an average of fourteen moves in a lifetime, close friends who could be relied upon for support and counsel are becoming few and far between. Religious service attendance is down to seven out of every one hundred. Where do our values and support systems come from to see us through a crisis? Good question, and you will find good answers in *Shifting Gears.*

Look to the Crisis Itself for the Solution

Climbing a mountain is a straightforward proposition. There are few extraneous subtleties to confuse the main issue of getting up the mountain and down again safely. When a crisis happens on the mountain, it must be dealt with then and there; there is no putting it off if there is to be a favorable outcome. The afternoon we were caught in the snowstorm and accompanying white-out on Mt. Ranier and could proceed no farther in any direction, we had no choice but to stop and take action for survival. By cutting blocks of snow and piling them up to make a shelter, we were using the very elements that had caused the crisis to solve it. Crisis . . . the decisive moment of survival, yes . . . but we worked with it and around it to successfully complete the descent though we spent a rather tense and uncomfortable night. You will find within each crisis the means of resolving the outcome and making it work for you.

Don't Let the Fear of Making Mistakes Prevent Your Making the Crisis Work for You.

Preoccupation with the past and real or imagined mistakes is a form of egotism you can't afford in your climb towards success. When you accept yourself as you are, you will begin to make major strides in your climb. When you accept yourself as you are, where you are, you no longer have to prove anything to anybody but yourself. You don't need to dwell on mistakes; you accept them, learn from them and go on from there. There are, however, ways to minimize mistakes.

It is also well to profit from the mistakes of others . . . this is not the least overused cliché . . . as you simply don't have time to make all the mistakes yourself.

So again it all comes down to the same thing. How are you looking at the obstacle or the crisis? . . . are you making it work for you or against you? . . . are you growing or vegetating? It is your decision.

Book Title: Shifting Gears
Author: Nina O'Neill and George O'Neill
Publisher: M. Evans and Company, Inc. New York
Chapter: Making Crisis Work for You

Making Crisis Work for You

The Anatomy of Crisis

Out of every crisis comes the chance to be reborn, to reconceive ourselves as individuals, to choose the kind of change that will help us to grow and to fulfill ourselves more completely. This potential, which exists in every crisis, is nowhere better expressed than in the Chinese language. The written character for crisis in Chinese is made up of two equal symbols: one which stands for *danger* and one which stands for *opportunity.* We all know that there is danger in crisis, for it presents us with situations radically different from our ordinary ones—but too often we forget that in crisis there is also the opportunity for change and growth. Out of the insecurity, the anguish and the pain that we experience in the face of danger and the unknown, we can emerge with new vitality and cour-

From SHIFTING GEARS By Nena O'Neill and George O'Neill Copyright © 1974 by Nena O'Neill and George O'Neill Reprinted by permission of the publisher, M. Evans and Company, New York, N.Y. 10017

age. We can be reborn with new strength.

To come through a crisis with increased personal strength and a sense of renewal, though, we have to understand how to make crisis work for us. And we must avoid the myths and fallacies that hang us up and impede our ability to learn and grow. When you focus primarily on the danger inherent in crisis, instead of on its growth potential, you make it far more difficult to deal with—fear and despair overwhelm the opportunity for self-development. We may be only too well aware of the unknowns and the confusion (which we interpret as danger) but we should also recognize the possibilities for growth.

In Chapter Two we talked about crisis largely in negative terms, demonstrating how the crisis culture in which we live affects the individual's ability to deal with the normal, personal crises of adulthood. When a society as a whole is in crisis, we are faced with what can be called a *metacrisis.* Today we seem besieged by such crises, not only nationally but worldwide. War, economic depression, the assassination of a political leader or the loss of credibility in the ethics of our government are all examples of a metacrisis. In this chapter, we want to concentrate, however, on *personal* crisis. If we understand how to make personal crisis work for us, how to shift gears through the normal crises of our lives, then we ought to be better prepared to respond to metacrises as well, when and if we find ourselves faced by them.

Personal crisis can be brought on by the fundamental events of the human life cycle—birth, puberty, marriage, pregnancy, advanced age and death. It can be brought on by a change in the balance of our internal psychic phases. *Divorce,* a change in status, a career switch, moving from one community to another—these developments may also be the occasion for a personal psychological crisis, causing us to question our assumptive state. Our assumptive state is the way we view the world and ourselves in relation to it, it is what we assume or believe to be true, it is how we perceive the realities through our unique subjective perception.

For many people, these personal crises can seem like catastrophes. We tend to react to them with the same types of behavior as we would when faced by a flood or an earthquake—we panic, not knowing where to turn, shaken loose from everything we thought we could count on. In an earthquake, it is the physical bases for our lives that are pulled out from underneath us; in a personal crisis, it is the psychological bases for our lives that are shattered. And yet panic can be eased and anxiety mitigated if we know what to expect. But in either case, physical or psychological, *crisis puts us in a position from which we cannot retreat to what used to be.*

Crisis is the point of no return. It makes little difference whether your crisis is externally caused (your husband dies, you lose your job) or is the result of a gnawing internal awareness that your life is not what you want it to be (your career, though successful, has come to seem pointless, your marriage a dead end). The crises that are generated inside ourselves are often more complex and perturbing than the externally imposed crises, but in both cases you have reached a point where there is no retreat. You no longer have the choice of going back to your old position—your world is irrevocably changed.

At this crisis point you have only one option: in order to deal with the crisis, you must change. It is like being thrown into a river when you don't know how to swim—you have no choice but to learn to swim. And panic, in such a situation, is obviously the worst possible answer. If you have reached a point from which you can't retreat, then you can only go forward. Going forward into the unfamiliar, toward the as-yet unknown new position that you will eventually take, *is a step in growth.* Inherent in being thrust forward into this new situation is the opportunity of crisis, *the opportunity for renewing change and* growth. Crisis can then be viewed not just as danger but as a positive force, as a situation to *utilize* for growth.

We can, of course, when faced with a crisis, try to avoid it. But by the very definition of crisis, avoidance can only make matters worse. The desire to go back or the effort to stay rooted where you are can only be self-defeating. However, if we accept it, recognize its opportunities and learn how to use it as a positive force for growth—one that can increase our capacity for dealing with life from that point onward—then we can better withstand the pain and anxiety that we may have to go through in crisis.

Our culture, unfortunately, teaches us that crisis is to be avoided at all costs, that it brings only pain and danger. No one wants to hear about pain in America—we sweep it under the rug and lock it away where it can't be seen. We want our plays and movies and books to present personal dilemmas only in ways that can be laughed at and therefore dismissed; the common objective of every situation comedy on television is to anesthetize crisis by making it unreal and laughable. And when we are confronted by pain in real life we try to get it out of sight and keep it there.

We are afraid of reality and our society panders to that fear. Living in a mechanistic culture, we have become mechanistic people. Don't do it yourself, we are told, let a machine do it for you: brush your teeth, squeeze an orange, slice a tomato, carve a roast. And just over the horizon is the possibility of producing a child outside of the womb in a glass container, without emotion and without the crisis of birth. Our inner lives have become a reflection of this mechanization, and in this anesthetized existence it is little wonder that we have lost our ability to feel and respond to life. We move like automatons from day to day, even our joys becoming as mechanical as the canned laughter on the tube.

And yet, paradoxically, these very machines that are supposed to protect us from crisis, from reality, only make us more anxious. Our culture denies crisis, pain and imperfection and provides a thousand ways to avoid them, yet deep within ourselves we know this is at odds with our humanity. Between our innate sense of ourselves as individuals and what society would make of us there is a yawning gap, a disparity between reality and fantasy, between a robot world free of crisis and our human needs for growth and change, a gap that can only produce anxiety and new kinds of problems. We are told to put on a facade that everything is just fine (looking good and feeling bad) while at the same time we are being presented with new causes for anxiety every day.

Today we hear a great deal about the mid-life crisis. This crisis is in fact a perfectly normal point of transition into a new phase of adulthood. But because our maturity myth assures us that we won't have any crises in growth if we follow the rules, the natural changes that take place at mid-life become something to fear, and are inflated into a crisis of major proportions. Since our society ignores our needs for change and growth throughout life, it *creates* an unnecessary degree of crisis out of a natural phenomenon of adulthood.

Our culture also denies time as a factor in solving problems or crises. It used to be that we could listen with some comfort to our grandparents when they said, "Time heals all wounds." And although there is truth in that statement, although time does seal over and diminish pain, and can give us the breathing room in which to seek solutions or come to terms with inner growth, we can take little comfort from such ideas in today's world—time is a commodity in short supply. Because the rate of change is so rapid today, because we are presented with so many options, few of us have time to adjust to crisis on a normal timetable. Thus, in our world, it is more necessary than ever before for us to know how to analyze and deal with personal crisis.

Problems, Emergencies and Crises

It is helpful to be able to distinguish among a problem, an emergency and a crisis. As one man we interviewed put it, "A problem is something I can see how to handle when it happens, and I'm confident I can find an answer to it. But crisis, well, with a crisis I don't know the answer, there's no ready-made solution to it." If Phil is told by the dentist that he will have to undergo extensive treatment for his gums or his teeth will fall out, he's got a problem. It means he'll have to fit numerous dental appointments into his working schedule over the next several months. And it means he'll have to juggle his budget in order to be able to pay for the treatments. But these are problems he knows how to deal with; they have a ready-made solution.

If Phil's visiting mother-in-law falls down in the bathtub and breaks a hip, he's got an emergency on his hands. But again, he knows how to deal with it. Both problems and emergencies can be dealt with by using resources we already have or re-combining known methods in some new way to solve the problem. But few of us have any knowledge of the means for resolving a crisis. In part this is because a crisis requires new behavior and we don't know, can't possibly know, what that behavior may be. But it is also because we may not know enough about the *process* of going through a crisis.

Problem solving involves the reapplication of the already known. You can solve a problem on the basis of your already existing assumptive state, or world view. But crisis directly challenges your assumptive state and almost inevitably calls for a change in that state. To resolve a crisis we have to reorganize ourselves, changing our attitudes and our behavior. All of us have certain established sets of attitudes and behaviors—they are variously referred to as perceptive sets, mental sets, feeling sets, emotional sets and resultant behavioral sets. The way you brush your teeth or fry an egg is part of your personal behavior set—and so is the way you react when someone praises you or challenges your opinion or asks you to do a favor for them. Thus the assumptive state for the individual is equal to the sum total of all his sets, which were formed in the first place by the interaction between the person's inner self and his life experience, and by his ongoing interaction with the environment, since both the environment and the self are processes and continuously changing.

When crisis strikes, the old assumptive state may no longer be a sound basis on which to act. To solve the crisis we usually have to change our behavior sets and develop a new assumptive state. We all know that we have to change certain behavior sets, adding and subtracting and modifying them when the situation around us changes. If we move from a New York apartment to a Los Angeles suburb we have to reorganize our behavior patterns, developing new forms of action that correspond to our new environment. You take subways and cabs in New York, but in California you drive a car—you cannot live without a car.

Let us take another example—a new child arriving in a family. The young husband and wife have lived together for several years. They have fully enjoyed their life together, but the husband has become very dependent on her as wife and companion. The baby comes and suddenly there is a crisis for the husband. His assumption has been that he was the most important person in his wife's life. He is still a most important person, but the couple must now expand to take the needs of the infant into consideration. Much as the husband anticipated the baby, although he thought he knew what was involved, he finds it different from what he expected—he feels left out and it makes him angry and confused. His assumptive state has been challenged, and to meet the crisis he must change his state. It may take a short time or it may take years for this adjustment to be made.

In crisis, many people first try to use their old behavior sets in attempting to resolve their situation. Since a challenge to their assumptive state is involved, the old sets will not work— some people have to find that out for themselves, while others recognize the fact from the beginning and move on to seeking new ways of dealing with the crisis. The young husband in our example tries to use the old sets first, and when they don't work, he begins to send hidden messages about his frustration to his wife. "Where are my socks, why don't I have any clean shirts?" he may grumble. "Why do we always have to wait for dinner?" What he is really saying, of course, is that he feels left out, that he has not yet changed his assumptive state to include the baby in it.

In the case of this husband, the challenge to his assumptive state is not a major one, and the resulting crisis can perhaps be solved by mustering new combinations of the old sets of established behavior. The young father will learn, hopefully, that his needs have to be meshed with the child's, and that he can expect new kinds of responses, new expressions of love from his wife, responses that include the child. By forming a new configuration of his behavior sets and reorganizing the elements of his existing assumptive state, he can perhaps solve the problem and grow to some extent.

But usually in crisis, and often when the challenge is a major one, even recombining the old sets won't work. The magnitude of the crisis may require that we develop some new behavior sets, integrate them with the old and arrive at an entirely new assumptive state. If your wife is having a baby and you lose your job at the same time, a major readjustment will be necessary. If we divorce or are divorced we will have to find new ways of viewing our world and our relation to it; in future man-woman relationships we may have to drop some of our old behavior sets and develop new ones. For many people retirement brings on a similar shock, making entirely new sets of behavior necessary to the achievement of continued growth and fulfillment.

When we develop new behavior sets in response to a crisis, we expand and grow. In rising to the crisis, searching for and developing new ways of dealing with life, we become better able to deal with any number of other possible situations more readily. The greater and the more sophisticated our repertoire of behavior sets, the more capable we become. This is one of the ways in which crisis works to our benefit, and why we should not fear it. Crises are an inevitable part of being human —but each crisis we face up to and solve makes us stronger and makes it easier for us to face other inevitable crises in the future.

Many people, when faced with a crisis, confuse cause with effect. Finding themselves in crisis, they tell themselves that they have failed. And since they have failed, they conclude, there is no point in trying anything else. They become convinced that their crisis is evidence of an inability to succeed. They turn their crisis into a cause for inaction. But their crisis should be a cause *for* action, for changing and growing, not for hanging back in fear and defeat. If a young woman tries to become a professional actress and fails, it doesn't mean that she is a failure as a person, or that her life is a failure. It simply means that, at that particular point in her life, becoming an actress was not the best direction for finding fulfillment. The fact that she failed at being an actress shouldn't be a cause for deciding that she can't succeed at anything—it is merely an effect of one choice that she has made. There are many other possible choices to be made in the present and the future, including acting at some future time. Instead of taking her crisis as evidence of defeat, she should *use* it to explore the other options open to her, to discover aspects of herself that have been lying fallow, and to try another approach to fulfillment.

Crisis involves risk; it is a time of danger. But it is also a vehicle for growth. If we refuse to take the risk, then we lose not only what we used to have (for we are beyond the point of going back) but also the future. Crisis is a time of testing— but it is also a time of renewal. Once we emerge on the other side of crisis, once we have shifted gears, we find ourselves filled with renewed strength and courage. People who saw someone during a crisis when he walked around with slumped shoulders, gray face and harried expression, now find him changed. "How marvelous you look," they say. And he looks marvelous because he *has* changed. It is through the meeting of the challenge of crisis that we measure up to life, and more than that, measure up to ourselves and our best potentials. Having conquered one crisis, having run the rapids, we know that when we meet the next one we will be better equipped. Next time we will not be so afraid, next time we will know better that out of the pain and confusion can emerge a better, stronger self.

Coping

Most of us cope with life. To cope means to squeak through, like getting a C on an exam. We don't cop out, we don't fail, but we don't win any gold stars, either. When we say, "I just can't cope with it any longer," it means we throw up our hands in despair and retreat. Coping is a middle way, lying some-where between advancing and retreating. We look at our chil-dren, as they weave their way through the strange mating dances of adolescence, and we say, "Another year or so and they'll be through that stage. I guess I can cope with it that long." Coping does not give us a positive sense of utilizing all our resources, of really coming to grips with a problem, or of controlling and determining the situation (especially not our children). Coping is getting by.

To grow through a crisis is a very different thing from coping with it. Coping has a place as a form of pre-crisis problem solving, on a short-term basis, but if we merely cope with a crisis it will defeat us. With crisis we have to go beyond coping. Yet coping can be helpful in the early stages of crisis, as we try to maintain our equilibrium. Coping is useful in making the best of a bad situation at a given moment. Coping can make us feel better, and it can give us a breathing space until we are ready to face the crisis head on. But it can't solve the crisis for us.

Dr. Karl Menninger, in his book *The Vital Balance,* speaks of *coping devices*—those short-term regulatory devices we use to deal with everyday stress. Some of the mechanisms he describes, along with others, can be listed in various categories:

Physical Reassurance
Eating
Drinking
Smoking
Drugs (from pot to tranquilizers)
Sleeping
Excercise (tennis, golf, jogging, etc.)
Work (cleaning the attic, gardening, etc.

Venting Your Emotions
Blaming others
Taking it out on loved ones
Psychosomatic illness
Crying

Cursing
Laughing it off

Substitutes for Action
Rationalization
Talking it over with friends and family
Watching television
Going to the movies
Going on a buying spree

All of these coping devices can be used to avoid facing the crisis, and often are; some of them, on the other hand, can give us the kind of momentary reassurance we need while we gather our strength to deal with crisis.

We all know that once in a while a good cry does a world of good—it won't solve our problems but it certainly makes us feel better. Being touched and held by a loved one, sharing coffee, hot tea or a drink, or smoking a cigarette at a tense moment can provide us with short-term relief. We can use exercise to avoid a crisis, like the man who plays golf all the time in order to put off a confrontation with his wife; or we can use exercise to let off steam and get our minds working on how to solve a problem or a crisis. Blaming others or developing psychosomatic asthma obviously isn't going to help, and may even make things worse by creating a second crisis on top of the first one. On the other hand, nobody can deal with crisis as effectively in a state of exhaustion as when they are rested —"sleeping on it" is still good advice.

For good or bad, however, we cannot *solve* our crises with coping devices. "If the objective is not achieved," says Dr. Menninger, "a higher price will have to be paid and devices of a more expensive kind will have to be called upon to maintain the vital balance." When coping devices are used to excess or for too long a time, they become *avoidance devices.*

And when we avoid the crisis, we prolong it. Like letting a symptom go too long before going to the doctor, it's tougher to treat. Eventually we will need to move beyond mere coping to actively dealing with the crisis. We then begin to shift gears.

There is a story about a woman who was forced to flee the Nazis during World War II. It was difficult to know what to do or where to go, and time was at a premium. But in this crisis, the first thing she did was to go to a pastry shop, where she sat and drank a cup of coffee and ate one of the richest pastries she could find. *Then* she was ready to escape the Nazis. Coping thus can provide us with a cushioning effect. It gives us comfort when we sorely need it. If we do not use these coping devices to escape the necessary confrontation with the crisis, then we can use them in conjunction with the development of a *crisis-solving set.*

FORMING A CRISIS-SOLVING SET

POINT I:

It is not the nature of the crisis itself that determines its impact but rather our attitude *toward it.* Our attitude is influenced by a number of factors: (1) the extent to which the person's current assumptive state is based upon myths or fallacies such as the maturity myth and the guarantee hang-up; (2) the extent to which the individual really knows what he or she wants; (3) whether the change is self-induced because the individual is seeking such change or it is forced upon him by external pressures; and (4) whether or not the individual has a strategy for dealing with change. These factors in turn affect the duration of the crisis, which we call the *crisis span.*

When we are confronted by crisis, we filter the external events that give shape and form to the crisis through our psychic lens. Whatever passes through that psychic lens is affected—indeed altered—by our personality, character structure, life history, opinions, and our internalized value system. Thus the backdrop against which the crisis is played out is our inner self, and it is not *what* we see that counts, but how we *perceive* what we see.

POINT II:

All of us have a different crisis potential. What may be a crisis for one person is merely a problem for another. In Latin America the loss of a maid for some middle-class women is a real crisis, because everyday life, household tasks and status depend on the maid's work. On the other hand, for a young American career woman who is constantly juggling the immediacies of household, job, and children, the loss of a maid is only one of a series of problems to be dealt with. A job change may become an opportunity for one man, yet devastate another.

All of us have different resources to draw on in crisis; some have more, some less. Some people may have a strong ego that enables them to solve crises more easily than those of us who are less well integrated and organized. The more experienced we are with crisis, the better we *can* deal with it— the growth potential in crisis means that we can constantly enrich our resources.

Because we have different resources we react differently to different crises, and to similar crises differently at different times. A lot depends on your feeling and emotional state at the time. If you are under stress from other quarters when crisis comes, then you may find it more difficult to handle. There are, of course, crisis-prone people—the women who fall apart when the washing machine breaks down, the men who have a screaming fit when the slightest thing goes wrong at the office. There are also those who develop pseudocrises as a way of gaining attention, people a friend of ours refers to as the "wallowers." They seek one-upmanship through crisis, always telling you how bad it is, how they can't cope, how they have more misery than you. They may not in reality be that disturbed or disoriented at all, but they make a career of crisis and it becomes their chief mode of communication with others.

POINT III:

We can learn to distinguish between different types of crises. There are *catalytic* crises—those that are precipitated by external events. Your apartment building is torn down, or your husband is leaving you and you have no job skills to help support yourself, or your employer calls you in and says, sorry Bud, but in two weeks it's over, not because you've failed to do your job properly but because a government contract has been canceled.

There are *recognition* crises—those that are provoked by some internal cause. The first sign of such a crisis may be a general but deep-seated dissatisfaction. Then follows a realization that your old ideas about your relationships, or your work, are no longer good enough. "Crisis?" said a blunt investment counselor. "Why that's what happens after a period of sheer boredom." But there is something other than just boredom that brings on an internal recognition crisis, that pushes us beyond the point of no return.

Catalytic crises, those from outside, hit suddenly out of nowhere. Recognition crises, those from inside us, may also hit suddenly, but usually they have been building for a long time. We may know something is wrong but put off facing it until finally we can do so no longer and must recognize the crisis or come to a standstill. Or we may not have felt that anything was wrong, with the awareness of crisis descending upon us like a revelation. As a general rule, it can be said that the longer the recognition crisis has been building the harder it will hit.

POINT IV:

Sometimes we are faced by more than one crisis at once; when that happens we must sort our crises out and deal with them one at a time. Usually, in fact, when there are several crises at once, they are interrelated. For instance, Peter K. had a job with a large corporation. The corporation had offices all over the country, and in the first ten years of Peter's marriage to Barbara they moved five times, as Peter was assigned to different branch offices in different cities. Then, for the next four years, they lived in Boston, a city that both Barbara and the children liked very much. Peter was informed that he was to be reassigned once again. Barbara said, "No, this just can't go on any longer. If you accept the new assignment you'll just have to go without us. We're staying here." The children who were now in school and had made large numbers of friends didn't want to move either. And the question for Peter was one of deciding which of several crises to deal with first. He was fed up with moving around the country himself, but if he refused, the chances for further advancement within the corporation would be cut back. If he went ahead he would be giving up his family. The crisis he found most devastating, personally, was the idea of living without Barbara. But it became clear to him that the family crisis was solvable only if he dealt with his career crisis. Since the thought of quitting his job with the corporation—crisis though that would be—was less disturbing to him than losing his family, he decided to face up to the job crisis first. He didn't want to leave the corporation, but the crisis of finding a new job with another company that was based in Boston was one he thought he could deal with. The crisis of separating from his family was beyond him.

In this case, the most important crisis, the one that Peter found most disturbing, was *not* the one to face up to first. For another man, under different circumstances, his career might have seemed more vital to him than his family. Such a man might have gone in the opposite direction from Peter, hoping that his wife was just bluffing and would in the end agree to the move. Thus sorting our multiple crises involves knowing or finding out what you really want most. Until you have made that decision, it is difficult to to deal with multiple crises.

POINT V:

Don't panic. Panic is too often our first reaction to crisis. But panic can be kept within bounds if we know what kinds of *anxiety symptoms* we can expect in ourselves when crisis hits. Psychologists have described three crisis phases for individuals faced with severe bereavement; the same phases may occur in other kinds of crisis situations as well.

(1) Physical and psychological turmoil. Disturbances in body function (indigestion, insomnia, palpitations), and of mental mood and intellectual control. You are likely to feel lousy and find it difficult to think straight.

(2) A painful preoccupation with the past. For instance, the man who begins to feel that he has "wasted" the best years of his life in a job he hates, is likely to spend much time belaboring the past, sometimes blaming others for his predicament, at other times running himself down in a self-diminishing way.

(3) A period of remobilization of our resources, with activity in some direction. This is the point at which we can begin to shift gears, leading on to resolution of the crisis and the achievement of growth.

Obviously, the faster we get to this third phase of crisis reaction, the more quickly we will be able to shift gears. Yet many of us get hung up on the first two phases, both of which contribute to a feeling of panic. If we do not experience the truly awful feeling of panic, we may at the very least experience the discomfort of anxiety. Some people do not need a major psychological crisis to experience panic; the contemplation of anything new or unconventional is anxiety-provoking. Yet all of us are familiar with the anxiety we experienced as children facing our first day at school or going to the dentist for the first time. Even as adults the dread and anticipation of the dental chair is frequently worse than the experience itself. But once familiar with what happens after the first few days at school and once reassured (if not *quite* comfortable) after our visit to the dentist, anxiety vanished and we developed, even as children, a mastery over the situation. Knowing what to expect prepares you for knowing how to meet it. Knowing you are not alone helps too. No one lives without some anxiety. Even our supermen astronauts feel anxiety; but they have learned to contain their feelings and think about solutions to problems. They have learned to utilize relationships with their fellow astronauts for support in their times of stress and decision. Few of us can be as controlled and steady under similar circumstances, but if we know that anxiety symptoms are likely to occur in crisis or change we can learn to ride through it, knowing that these feelings will dissipate with mastery of our situation.

POINT VI:

Discover the crisis question. In every crisis we not only reach a point of no return, but we also move beyond certain questions. If a man is sitting in his office questioning himself as to whether or not he should move to another apartment building, and then the building he lives in burns down, he is beyond that question. He is beyond having or making a choice in response to that question. He can't deliberate or vacillate any longer. He *has* to move. When we find ourselves in crisis we may not have been *consciously* asking any questions that pertain to that crisis. But there is always a question implicit in the crisis, and if we can find out what it is, it can be of great help in illuminating the direction we should move in now.

If a man is fired from a job, the crisis question might be, Did I really like that job, was it good for me? He may or may not have asked this question consciously of himself before he was fired. The answer to that question no longer means anything in respect to the old job—by being fired, the man has moved beyond the question. But the answer to that question can mean something in respect to seeking a new job. It can help him to decide what kind of job he now wants. Similarly, a woman who suddenly becomes a widow has an implicit question about her life with her husband that she may or may not have asked: Can I live without him? Can I be an independent person? Once again, she is beyond this question in regard to the life she previously had, but it has a great deal of relevance to the life she will now be making for herself. Thus, by exploring the implicit crisis question, any of us can better understand the changes ahead.

POINT VII:

Go into the crisis. By going into the crisis we mean experiencing it fully, not avoiding it, not trying to defuse it. In order to make a breakthrough to an understanding of the real nature of any given crisis we must keep asking questions. We must face up not just to what we feel, but ask why we feel it. If we take into account the fact that our perception is altered by our personality and character structure, life experience and attitudes, then it is just one step to asking the questions that lead to the real nature of the crisis: Is there anything about my personality that should make me feel the way I do? What past events in my life have a bearing on what I'm feeling now? Is my attitude preventing me from seeing the problem clearly? What is needed of me to change? In what ways can I change?

These are not easy questions, and we can't expect to come up with answers in the first few days, or even weeks. But if we make the effort of asking them, and if we keep asking them, we will accomplish two important things. First, we will be discovering the true nature of our crisis, making it possible to begin the process of shifting gears. And second, we will be making the crisis work for us, because in the course of asking such questions of ourselves we will be learning more about who we are and want to be. Not everything we learn will be immediately applicable to the crisis at hand, but the more we know about ourselves and our relation to the world around us, the more we will grow and the easier it will be to grow.

By going into the crisis, opening ourselves fully to it, we may experience considerable discomfort at first. But those who come through crisis with real change and growth are often those who seem to take crisis the hardest.

POINT VIII:

Don't make snap judgments or look for immediate solutions. Many crises will seem to demand immediate decisions and actions. We may be inclined to strike out blindly after the first shock and panic—or even during it. But don't panic or take rash action. Stop everything for the moment. Recognizing that your perceptions will be altered or impaired by the first anxiety symptoms, it is clearly not a good time to make quick decisions.

If your wife, after years of strife between you, demands a divorce one night and asks you to leave the house, what do you do? Certainly you don't go charging off the next morning to find an apartment and sign a two-year lease that afternoon. More likely you will take a hotel room or stay with a friend for a few days while you get your bearings, until you *know* what direction you want to move in. Or you may decide to sit it out until both of you consider this action more fully.

During the first hours or days of crisis, it would seem wise to ask yourself if what you're doing, the action you're taking, will have short-term or long-term effects. If it's going to have long-term effects, think again—you may not be ready to make that kind of decision yet.

POINT IX:

Do find someone who cares and who can listen to you. When crisis strikes, this point may be the very first one to take action on. Don't panic; stop short, don't do anything rash and do seek out someone to talk to. It may be your mate or someone in your family or a best friend. There is no need for secrecy in our time of deepest need. Just by talking to someone we can defuse our anxiety and clarify some of our confusion and hurt. At times of crisis we especially need the affectionate support of people who care. But this does not mean someone who will insist upon telling you what to do. It does not mean someone who will smother you with compensation, telling you you're perfect and everybody else is wrong. You need a person who cares for you and who can understand you in a compassionate way without offering immediate pat solutions or telling you what to do. Only you can solve your crisis. Other people can help you, but they can't solve your crisis for you. Since they may be able to see your situation more objectively, they *can* give you a different viewpoint. You may pick up clues from other people by asking them about how they handled their own crises. They can't give you an exact model to follow, because they are different people. But you may find some things they have to say about their own solutions to their own crises can be applied to yours.

You may feel that you need professional help and fortunately today there are many helping professionals who understand the nature of our personal and social crises. Crisis intervention centers are located in some major hospitals and mental health centers; they provide many techniques for immediately coping with the crisis. In a variety of ways, therapists can help us meet our crises in positive ways that promote growth. But even the best professional cannot solve your crisis for you. All they can do is to help *you* to solve your crisis for yourself.

POINT X:

Try something new. You are now ready to begin shifting gears. Trying something new is equivalent to the step of experimentation in shifting gears. The points we have been making in these last few pages apply primarily to the early steps in the process of shifting gears: awareness, evaluation and exploration. Now it is time to move forward, to take action and to grow through our actions.

To realize our full potential as human beings we must continue to grow throughout our lives. And crisis, unsettling though it may be, gives us our greatest opportunity for growth. We grow in many subtle ways even when our lives are at their smoothest. But when we are in crisis and our entire being is focused on resolving the crisis, we can take a great leap forward. When we want to learn a new language, or how to drive a car, or to use a pocket calculator, we make a conscious effort to change and to expand our skills. With emotional habits, it's harder to learn something new, but the rewards can be enormous. Not only can the conscious effort to change lead to a resolution of the particular crisis, it can also lead to a new sense of one's self and a new confidence. We grow by meeting our crises head on, by letting go of our past ways of looking at the world and finding new ways that expand and enrich our interior selves.

Crisis is a distilling process out of which we can emerge more completely ourselves. Like metal tempered in fire, the impurities can be burned off. We can come through the ordeal true and clean, with the vital core not only intact but tempered to a greater strength. As a friend said to us, "I only truly know someone in a crisis, and then I know him in a minute." But not only can we know others most truly when they are in crisis—we can know ourselves most truly in crisis if we take advantage of it fully and make it work for us by exploring ourselves as deeply as we can.

CHAPTER TWENTY

Overcoming Mental Blocks

Perhaps the most important obstacles you must overcome are
not those placed in your path by nature, or experience but
those which come from within your own psyche—your inhibi-
tions, fears and anxieties.

At the writing of his book, *Targets,* in 1981, Dr. Leon Tec
was the director of Mid-Fairfield Child Guidance Center in
Norwalk, Connecticut. He is a diplomate of the American
Board of Psychiatry and Child Psychiatry; a fellow of the
American Psychiatric Association and of The American Group
Psychotherapy Association, and serves as a consultant on sev-
eral hospital boards.

His first book, *The Fear of Success,* was a study of one of
the most common reasons for failure. We have such a fear of
the unknown that we would rather continue where we are
than risk the dangers (as we see them) in change, even if it
means success. He has written numerous articles and has been
the personality behind a successful and informative radio program.

Targets goes one step beyond *Fear of Success* to show you how to overcome your apprehensions and get started on your road to success. According to Dr. Tec, "Targeting" is an ability we all have, "the ability to direct behavior to recognized predetermined objectives." He tells us that this behavior is related to . . . but distinct from . . . the process we normally call "establishing goals." It is also related to . . . but distinct from . . . the process we use to pursue these goals. Targeting is the means through which these two processes of establishing and pursuing goals, are unified into one effective behavioral strategy. He suggests that you think of it as a process that organizes behavior in a way that enables you to get the most out of yourself, regardless of your objectives or your talents and skills. As a means of showing you how to accomplish this, Dr. Tec discusses such things as awareness, planning, scheduling, doing things you don't like to do, persistence as opposed to obsessions and the old stand-by, overcoming obstacles.

At the end of each chapter, you are presented with exercises you can use to test yourself as to your habits, thinking, practices and patterns. I'm always amazed at the effectiveness of self-appraisal and even more amazed at how seldom we practice it. The exercises, called "target practice" by Dr. Tec, make the book worth its weight in gold. We think we know ourselves, but its not until we start testing ourselves, (as we should all make a point of doing) that we find just how little we know about ourselves, our abilities, our education or our motives and motivations.

How Do You Test Yourself?

The role of the American Indian in the turbulent building of our country was that of friend or adversary, depending on the tribe, its leaders, others involved, or the circumstances. It was a culture in which bravery and resourcefulness were the cornerstones of their societal code of behavior. The Indians honored and admired anyone, friend or foe, who displayed those qualities. In order for a tribal boy to achieve recognized manhood, he had to undergo numerous physical tests of skill and danger; the lessons learned to pass those tests were the education that would allow him to live and survive in his society and environment.

Louis L'Amour, the consumate story teller of adventures, writes of ordinary, but courageous men and women involved in events which test them to the fullest. In his book, *To the Far Blue Mountains,* the hero, Barnabas Sackett, has finally been bested by some young Indians warriors of the same ilk he has been coming up against for thirty years or more. No hard feelings on either side, that's just the way life was. The old chief of the young warriors' tribe, upon hearing of Sackett's death, says sadly to himself, "Who now is left to test our young men? Who now?"

Just as our species is a problem-solving animal, finding great satisfaction in solving a good puzzle, so we are prone to testing ourselves and others, as part of the process. . . . as a way to see how we are doing. . . . or how far we can go.

Think back to those situations marking your periods of growth. Didn't they involve problem solving and testing? Think about the ways you test yourself now . . . the little ways as well as the bigger, more obvious ones. I climb mountains to test my physical fitness, my courage, my intelligence, etc. It is equally hard for a timid people, attempting to overcome that shyness, to test themselves by facing what they fear. We are constantly testing ourselves, consciously or sub-consciously, especially if we feel our skills getting rusty. I have a tendency to do this. I practice my accents on my friends and relatives for the humor and the laughter we all require, then in the same hour will discuss a business philosophy with a peer whom I use as a sounding board before that philosophy becomes part of the mountain. Get involved with the various parts of your personality . . . don't settle for a one-dimensional you.

I have to admit I love a good practical joke . . . not the "pie in the face" kind, but those with some imagination behind them. The way I do them is a real test of my ingenuity and skills. For example, a friend of mind, Bill Danforth owns an island in the St. Lawrence Seaway. It has become traditional for him to host a fishing party once a year for a group of his college buddies, all of whom have done extremely well in their professional worlds; they are a fine and fun group of men whom I am pleased and privileged to count as my friends. They gather together each year to spend a well-earned week of laughs and relaxation.

The year I was first invited to join them, I knew only one other person in the group, our advertising man, William Young (who invented the Harvey Wallbanger), so the three of us cooked up an elaborate gag; even though it had all the elements of a bad paper-back novel.

Jolly Island is situated virtually on the United States/ Canadian border of the Thousand islands in upstate New York; it was late September and the St. Lawrence river was cold. At 5:30 A.M. in a dense fog, my boat slid into the boat house. I could see the lights of the big house looming out of the mist. My attire was that of a New York State Park Ranger . . . no detail was spared . . . the 38 magnum loaded with full charge blanks, hostered at my side; with the flashlight and clip board (bearing California mountain maps) in hand. I approached from the other side of the house to the large sliding doors which fronted the other dock; the house is on a hill top.

One of Bill's guests greeted me . . . more than surprised by my appearance he kept me standing on the porch until I asked for some coffee; within seconds of entering the large living room, the other twenty guests (all men) began to assemble . . . I took my position in front of the large roaring fireplace . . . never removing my mirror sunglasses . . . (intimidating

figure if I don't say so myself). When all of them . . . half-awake
. . . were standing in a circle around the room, I apologized
for having to intrude on their outing, but I would require a look
at some identification; all of them complied. One chap (whom
I had met briefly on a social outing in New York City just a few
short months before), was the only one who was a bit testy
. . . I got past him with a buried sigh and told them we had
evidence that an airplane had left Watertown, New York late
last night, loaded with narcotics . . . and we had reason to
believe it had landed on a near-by Island; (one of the more
than cooperative types, reported to me that he had actually
heard an airplane). I went to the telephone and pretended to
call the Ranger office on the mainland. Pretending to be talking
to my superior, I cupped my hand over the receiver and asked
all of them if anyone of them had any "sophisticated electronic
or camera gear?" Just as they were all nodding their heads no
. . . they almost—looked at Bill Young and said . . . "Well,
Youngie has a camera case." I demanded to see it . . . placing
it on a table at the rear of the room, furtherest from the sliding
doors I had used for my entrance. I opened the case. . . . using
one hand, I picked up the largest lens; tucked into its foam
receptacle was a small clear "baggy" neatly rolled up, which
contained a sizeable amount of white powder (flour); as I
turned to ask the owner sarcastically, if it was "lens cleaner,"
he retorted. . . . "Its herbs, I do all the cooking here." With
that, I meticulously opened the bag . . . tasted the contents
. . . and stated that it was the "finest I had ever come across"
and withdrew my 38. With that, Youngie dashed for the door
and ran down the hill toward the dock . . . a chase was the
order of the day. I lunged through the group and posed on the
porch . . . took aim. . . . warned him and pretended to shoot
him dead. . . . for a few moments even the doctor (in the group)
who examined him believed it. Pre-planted ketchup trickled
down Youngie's mouth as he lay sprawled on the hill halfway

to the dock. To add insult to practical jokery, later I caught a huge muskie, a record which lasted most of the summer . . . and is still the record for that particular group of men.

The next year, with the aid of my two cohorts and the captain of their fishing boat, we once again hit on a great stunt. The stage was set with a small article and picture in the local paper to the effect that Mr. Danforth's annual fishing party was very lucky to have the services this year of a famous French fishing guide, Vinnie LaRogue. I arrived with the fishing boat, complete with wig, beard, pipe, scar, French accent, and a hearing aid so I would have an excuse for not answering any awkward questions. I was able to spend only about an hour learning how to handle the boat, but I was so completely accepted that no one even questioned it when I almost ran the boat up onto the dock and backed over their fishing lines. I then proceeded to spend an entire day with fifteen men I had spent a week with just a few short months before. At their insistence, I even went back to the house with them for supper. When it came time to end the gag, I took off my hat, wig and all, but no one noticed until I finally dropped the accent, and then they all realized I had snookered them again. Luckily, they are all good sports and it was a bit of crazy fun for all of us.

Never stop testing yourself. You may prefer to call it experimentation; it is all part and parcel of the same thing. When you reach an impasse, experiment with different approaches, testing them and yourself.

I believe quite strongly that what you see is what you get, so I try to look at things as I would like them to be. Remember, there is more than one way to judge any situation.

Some Obstacles That May Be Blocking Your Way

Be slow to anger. It's very easy to confuse anger with the aggressiveness that moves towards action, because it is a mover; however, in the long run, it is a non-productive act because of the shock waves it leaves in its wake. Aggression is an urge toward action; when frustrated it can turn into violence, toward others or self. Learn to translate the aggression into productive and creative actions. That's what its for.

Be careful about being too judgmental. It can become a natural carry-over from constantly judging and analyzing the business climate. Don't let it carry over towards people. Perfection is not everyone doing everything your way, but rather all working together, in harmony, to achieve personal growth. Support creative endeavors as much as possible; delegate until it hurts.

Don't get caught up in patterns, especially if they are negative ones. As you do your self-analysis look for patterns. If you find the same sorts of things repeatedly occurring in your life, look for the underlying pattern then change it and the situation will be relieved; growth will take place.

Lastly, a mental block may not be all bad. It may by your sub-conscious telling you to look around, to make sure you are heading up the mountain, and not down it.

In summary, here are some ways, out of the many routes available to you, to get around mental blocks.

1. Experiment with alternatives
2. Test yourself to see where you presently stand (good footing goes a long way)
3. Be aware of negative character traits which lead to dead-ends, such as anger and criticism, and use the positive side of such characteristics.
4. Watch out for non-productive patterns and behavior.
5. Realize that a mental block may be trying to tell you something, and may itself be an answer.

If you're not getting anyplace, and doing it fast, shift gears and focus on your target.

Book Title: Targets. . . . How to Set Goals for Yourself and
Reach Them
Author: Leon Tec, M.D.
Publisher: Harper & Row, New York
Chapter: Overcoming Obstacles to Targeting

Overcoming Obstacles to Targeting

Now that you've read this far, you should be well on your way
to an understanding of the targeting process. It may be that
you've begun to use some of the techniques we've been talking about. But it's also possible that, in trying to incorporate
some of these techniques into your life, you've run into some
obstacles—obstacles that have kept you from achieving the
targets you have established for yourself, in spite of all your
efforts.

What kind of obstacles am I talking about?

Well, for one thing, are you one of those people with a large
library filled with books you've started but never finished?
(Don't worry, you are not alone; there are plenty of us!)

Or are you the sort of person who signs up for two or three
adult-education courses in the fall but by Christmas has drifted
away, lost interest, and is no longer going to class? Is your brain
bursting with ideas and projects—for new businesses, for trips,

From TARGETS: How To Set Goals For Yourself and Reach Them By Leon Tec, M.D.
Copyright ' 1980 by Leon Tec Reprinted by permission of Harper & Row, Publishers,
Inc.

for strategies for living or working—but do you find these targets are never realized, and the ideas, alas, never translated into reality? In other words, are you one of those persons who has no trouble establishing targets, but a lot of trouble following through on them?

On the other hand, you may be a person who has no problem getting things done once you get started, but a lot of trouble getting started. I know many such people—gifted, intelligent, competent people—who are the victims of persistent inertia, who are stalled long before they even get their engines running.

And even if you don't happen to fall into either of these categories, there's a better-than-even chance you often run into certain obstacles that can plague even the most target-minded person. If you are like most people, in fact, you may frequently be victimized by those inexplicable obstacles that interfere with successful targeting, obstacles that are often referred to as "mental blocks."

This chapter is about those very mental blocks, those specific problem areas which can inhibit the targeting process. There *are* means to cope with those obstacles, and this chapter will show you some tested ways to combat them. Read on.

Why Goals Are Necessary

Establishing a target is an act of affirmation. Any time you set up a target, the assumption you make is that you have a good chance of reaching your target. Inherent in that action is confidence in your ability to achieve your goal.

Setting a target also implies a belief in the value of that target or goal.

By the very act of establishing a target, therefore, you have expressed a belief in yourself, an attitude of optimism about life and your chances for success.

On the other hand, not being able (or not wanting) to set targets for oneself is an expression of a negative attitude. A curious characteristic about people who have trouble setting targets for themselves is the way they often rationalize this difficulty. They act as if the absence of targets in their lives were a virtue and not a liability. "I just want to take things as they come," a troubled nineteen-year-old college student used to say to me over and over again when he came regularly to see me two years ago. "I want to live day to day, and enjoy every moment for what it is." In a current phrase, he thought he wanted to "go with the flow."

These are poetic sentiments, I grant you, but this was the same young man who, while hitching a ride one afternoon from Connecticut to New York, discovered from the first driver who stopped to pick him up that he was on the wrong side of the highway. He was, in fact, on his way to Boston. "That's okay," the young man said, "I'll go to Boston instead."

There may be something refreshing in this attitude on occasion, but it is hardly a practical or very reasonable approach to most of life's needs. And buried beneath its seeming casualness is, in reality, a negative approach to just about everything. Life is not so simple that we can all take this *laissez faire*, take-it-as-it-comes approach.

I question whether it is really possible to derive any satisfaction or fulfillment unless there is at least some direction or focus in your life. To make no choices, to set up no goals, is to deprive life of its interest and meaning. The hippies and "flower children" of the 1960s had some valid arguments when they rebelled against the materialistic values of American society, but their failure to establish a true set of *alternate* values led to the collapse of their way of life. Humans are problem-solving animals. We need objectives. We need focus and direction. Most of all, we need the sense of accomplishment that comes from achieving what we set out to do. Without this sense of accomplishment, a true sense of self and of self-esteem is virtually impossible to develop.

What's Holding You Back?

Any number of influences beyond your control can determine whether or not you reach your targets, but nothing can prevent you from establishing the target in the first place—nothing, that is, but yourself. Sounds simple but, of course, it's not. We human beings are complicated pieces of work and much goes into determining how and why we act as we do. Many things prevent us from taking the crucial first step in the targeting process. For some it is a fear of failure and disappointment. Such people have the idea that the more you want something, the more it will hurt if you don't get it. Such people are afraid to risk failure and the supposed hurt it can bring.

Another common fear that interferes with targeting, odd as it may sound, is the fear not of failure, but of *success*. This failure seems to stem from an unrecognized, subconscious feeling that somehow one is not really worthy of the success that on a conscious level one is striving for. Many women in American society have this problem, a consequence of their perceived sense of woman's worth in a society dominated preponderantly by male values, goals, and attitudes. For others, the problem can be a lack of basic self-confidence. The chief symptom of such a lack of belief in oneself is the tendency to exaggerate the difficulty of a target, which discourages such people from even establishing the target.

Finally, there are those people who approach life with a totally fatalistic view. Such people will tell you that no matter what you do, things will turn out the way fate intends them to turn out. Personal effort, they feel, is of little use in a world in which all things are predetermined.

Fear of disappointment, fear of success, a lack of self-confidence, an overly fatalistic view of life—any one of these factors is usually enough to short-circuit the targeting process even before the process has a chance to begin. Any one of these factors can be enough to prevent you from taking the one step that, more than any other, will determine whether or not you're going to solve a problem or accomplish a task. If you are restrained from setting up your own targets by any one of these inhibiting factors, there is no way you will be able to envision that problem or task as a target around which you can construct a target-oriented strategy. But there are various (and proven) ways to counter such difficulties.

Talking Yourself into It

If it is true (and it usually is) that the only person preventing you from establishing targets is yourself, it follows that the only person who can get you out of this dilemma is *you*. Not until you can transcend your fear of failure or success, not until you can develop a certain amount of self-confidence, and not until you can modify your paralyzing fatalism will you be able to break through the barrier that keeps you from taking a more active, more target-oriented approach to your life. The agonizing truth here is that the best ammunition needed to fight these obstacles is itself on the other side of that barrier. This ammunition is the sense of accomplishment that is gained from the experience of reaching a target you've set for yourself.

It is never purely accidental that we fear failure or success, that we lack self-confidence, or that we refuse to believe that we ourselves can be the architects of our destiny rather than the victims of it. These "built-in" attitudes are reactions to past experience. Events in our lives lead us to assume a point of view that reflects our past history. Much of this experience occurs in our lives long before we can be fully aware of it—

when we are children. People with a history of failure are not very likely to have much self-confidence. People who have been hurt and disappointed frequently are not likely to place themselves in situations where additional hurt and disappointment is likely.

These patterns, these learned modes of thought and behavior need not become a fixed part of your life. Not at all! You can control your life and you can do something about old patterns. For if the way you think today is a reflection of what happened to you yesterday and the day before, it is certainly reasonable to suggest that if you take certain steps today—difficult as those steps may be—you can produce a different point of view tomorrow, a point of view that will make it easier for you to take other, similar steps.

There is only one way to deal effectively with obstacles that may now be preventing you from establishing targets for yourself. First of all, you must recognize and acknowledge the source of the problem. And the source of the problem, for whatever reasons, is you yourself. Once you recognize this, you'll be ready to deal with the problem.

It may not be easy. I'm not suggesting that it is. There are undoubtedly some real, well-founded reasons that you think the way you do. But if you experience difficulty in doing what you want to do, there are ways and means to change that situation. And in most cases you should be able to reverse the patterns you want to reverse on your own. Here is an exercise that may help. To do this exercise, you need only a large piece of paper and a pen or pencil.

An Exercise in Target Construction

Start by thinking up a target that you may have thought about in the past but have never acted upon. Maybe it involves learning how to play an instrument, or setting up a physical-fitness program, losing weight, or learning a new language. If you have trouble thinking of a target in this category, try to isolate an area of your life currently giving you some trouble —a relationship you may have, or something involving your job. Set up the solving of that problem as a target.

Now that you have determined a potential target, take a large piece of paper, and write the problem across the top of the page. Divide the rest of the sheet into three columns. Now, head the first column "Why I want to reach this target." Head the second column "Obstacles," and head the third column "Why this is not a real obstacle."

At this point concentrate on the first column. Think hard and list all the reasons you can for why you want to reach this target. Be as specific as you can. Don't even think about possible obstacles at this point.

It's crucial that you *not*—repeat, *not*—deal with the Obstacle column before you finish the first column. Too many people tend to do this in the normal course of their lives. What they do is concentrate on talking themselves out of a potential target before they've even had a chance to ponder the potential benefits and desirable advantages of their targets.

Now, in the second column, list the possible obstacles to your target. Stick to the subject here, too. Don't worry about why an obstacle isn't really an obstacle yet. Simply list as many reasons as you can think of as to why you may not be able to reach the target you want to set for yourself.

Surprisingly enough, if you're like most people you may not have to go any further with this exercise. It will become immediately apparent to you that there are really no major obstacles, no real reasons why you shouldn't pursue the target you want. It may be easy and all too human, for instance, to say "I can't do that," but it's very much something else to come up with specific reasons to back up this defeatist claim. Writing reasons down in a column forces you to focus on specifics. Often such an exercise proves that there really aren't specific reasons for not doing something—none, at any rate, of any real substance. Nevertheless, let's assume for the moment that you have indeed isolated real obstacles. This means that you should now proceed to the next phase of the exercise—examining those obstacles carefully, exploring why in fact they may not be real obstacles.

Oh yes, by posing the question the way we've posed it, I realize we've stacked the deck against the obstacle. That is precisely the purpose of this exercise! The point here is to motivate you to counteract the negative impulses that so far have been preventing you from establishing targets.

Let me give you a hint for the best way to attack the third phase of this exercise. Pretend for the moment that you're someone else—someone whose job it is to talk you into this particular target, a sort of "positive advocate" for targeting. As the "positive advocate," start with the premise that all the obstacles *can* be overcome. Assume that the problem is simply a matter of coming up with the right approach. Most important of all, be sure to deal with only one obstacle at a time. If you find you can't come up with a reason why a particular obstacle isn't an obstacle, go on to the next obstacle.

It's entirely possible that when you have finished this exercise, you will have many more items written in the second column than in the third column. This is to say, you won't be able to come up with reasons to discount the obstacles lying between you and your potential target. On the other hand, it's just as possible that once you begin to scrutinize each obstacle carefully, one at a time, you will realize that none of the obstacles you've been concerned with is insurmountable. And what you'll come to realize is that it isn't so much the obstacles themselves that have been keeping you from establishing targets, but rather the way in which you've been imagining these obstacles, the manner in which you have perceived them. In other words, you have been basing your response to a situation not on what actually is, but on what you *think* is.

For an example of how this kind of exercise might look after you've finished each step, see the chart on page 308.

This exercise is not intended to help you reach your target. Its purpose is to get you to a stage where you are willing to establish a true target for yourself. Will the exercise work for everybody in every situation? No. But if you find it difficult to set targets for yourself, or follow through on them, going through such an exercise could very well reverse the pattern. And once you've had success in reversing a pattern, you should find it easier to generate the kind of target-oriented behavior that feeds upon itself and produces the confidence and self-trust you may now be lacking.

How to Dig In

On the face of it, the easiest part of any target-oriented task should be getting started. Early in a project you don't have to deal with deadline pressure, so you can be selective about which aspect of the target you address yourself to first. Generally, too, you bring to a new undertaking a fresh perspective that you don't always maintain midway through the process or near the end.

At the start you tend to have more energy. You're not as familiar with the target or its attached problems. You're not apt to be bored by it. And yet for some people, getting started, digging in, or getting into the right groove is the single most difficult part of any task. It is a common enough failing, but the problem seems particularly prevalent among creative people. Some writers I know talk as if they'd rather be flogged than experience the agony and frustration they feel whenever they are forced to sit down in front of that first piece of blank paper and commit to type the first words of an article, story, or essay.

One writer describes this agony as his "sharpening pencils syndrome." "I start out in the morning," he says, "by sharpen-

TARGET: Learning How to Play Guitar

WHY I WANT TO REACH THIS TARGET	OBSTACLE	WHY THIS IS NOT A REAL OBSTACLE
1. To have a new interest that will bring me pleasure.	1. I'm not very musical.	1. It doesn't necessarily take great musical skill to enjoy the guitar.
2. I'll be fulfilling a dream I've always wanted to fulfill.	2. Guitars and guitar lessons are expensive.	2. Guitars are frequently on sale; there are also inexpensive lessons available at the Y and other places.
3. I'll be developing an interest that will help me meet people.	3. I don't have the time to devote to lessons and practice.	3. I'll spend less time watching television.
4. If I learn how to play the guitar, I won't be bored anymore on evenings when I don't go out.	4. I've never stuck to any lessons in the past; why should this time be any different?	4. The reason I'll stick to lessons this time is that I will make up my mind to do so. (I'll pretend to be determined.)

ing all the pencils I can get my hands on, even though I never use more than two or three pencils a day. I'll even go looking for pencils when I can't find any more on my desk. Once my pencils are sharpened, I can usually find a few books out of place on my shelves, and so I take a few minutes to put them back where they belong. By this time my coffee needs to be heated up and so I have an excuse to go into the kitchen. Finally, after an hour or two, I've run out of excuses and I manage to sit myself down in front of the typewriter."

Not that this phenomenon is found exclusively among writers. Executives I know report much the same thing in corporate offices each week. "It's like a zoo," reports one vice-president of a food company. "Everybody shuffling back and forth from office to office, visiting, getting coffee, delaying until the last possible moment the actual moment they start work."

In moderation, what I'm describing is a common enough and harmless enough practice—nothing to be concerned about. It's the rare person, after all, who can jump straight into the thick of a task. Most tasks require an "easing in" of sorts. Athletes go through a warm-up routine before the actual competition begins. Singers have to warm up their voices. Dancer have to limber up. It's all part of getting the body primed, getting the blood flowing. The same principle seems to hold true for mental activity as well.

There's also an energy principle at work here. To paraphrase Newton, it takes more energy to generate movement from an inert state than it does to accelerate movement once you're already in motion. The principle holds true for electrical appliances, for automobiles, etc., and it appears to hold true for people as well. Getting started on a task—and, in particular, getting started in the right direction—obliges us to expend a good deal more effort than we have to expend once we've already established some momentum.

Another factor at work in the starting phase is *feedback*.

You are never further away from your target than you are at the very start of a task or project. For many people the distance to the target in itself is a problem. Once we're well launched into a task, we can detect tangible signs of progress. This is positive feedback, and this feedback usually acts to spur us onward, encourage us to further effort. But when there are no tangible signs of progress (which, of course, is always the case in the beginning of a project), we have either to generate our own positive feedback or else get along without it—a difficult challenge for many.

Practically speaking, there is no way you can completely eliminate these characteristics of the getting-started process. The problem of inertia and the lack of positive feedback are givens. You can't rewrite the basic laws of physics. You can't change basic motivational and feedback patterns. But what you *can* do is employ a few techniques that take into consideration some of the difficulties inherent in getting started on the right track—techniques that recognize the special conditions that prevail in the beginning stages of a targeted task.

Not all of the techniques I will suggest here may work for you—much about your choice has to do with your job, your work habits, your personality, and your temperament. Still, by familiarizing yourself with the various techniques, and by experimenting with a few of them, I feel sure you will be able to find one or two that will alleviate, if not entirely eliminate, the problem of getting on track each day.

Anticipatory Targeting

A music arranger I knew discovered that if he left an arrangement in midphrase the day before when he stopped working, it was easier for him to start on the arrangement the next day. I have heard of writers who break off their writing in midsentence the same way. This practice of "starting where I left off"

OBSTACLES TO TARGETING • 311

avoids one of the more persistent problems that arise when you're first beginning in the morning. It's a means of insuring an immediate start when next you pick up the work, because it provides you with a continuing thought line to begin with again.

There is no reason why the same practice can't work for people in other lines of work. Indeed, it does work well for many people. There are variations, too, on the habit of leaving something in midstream so as to ease right back into it when

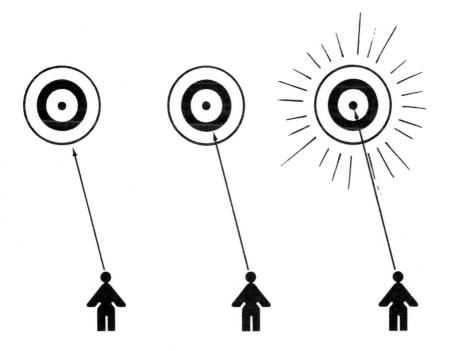

Anticipatory targeting is a targeting procedure for people who have trouble getting started. The answer is "positive grooving"—getting a running start by doing part of a job. Success at one stage creates motivation for going on.

you resume work: "What I do the last twenty minutes or so at work the afternoon before determines how easy it is for me to start being productive the next morning," explains Hal P., a marketing executive who is one of the most productive people I know. He adds, "I don't only write out a list of what I want to do the next day. I try to assemble as many of the things I'll need to get started, so that when I come in the next morning, it's all set. I'm geared for action."

The logic is sound. Tired though you may be at the end of a workday, your mind is still in a more focused groove than it will be first thing in the morning. More's the reason, then, to save at least ten minutes of every workday for setting yourself up for the following day. For myself, I have discovered that it is more difficult for me to organize my thoughts and get into a productive work groove on days when my desk is cluttered than on days when it is in order. I make it a practice, as much as I can, to spend a few minutes in the late afternoon putting my desk in order.

You can apply the same principle to household chores. Remember the cellar so badly in need of clearing out? You've resolved to clean it up, but for two weekends, you've managed to fritter away the morning you've set aside to do the job. Try to change your pattern. This weekend, for a change, try getting everything you need—buckets, rags, cleaning liquids, even the clothes you are going to wear—ready the night before.

Are you a jogger who sometimes finds it difficult to get started on your workout each morning (as many joggers do)? Try to have everything you need—your running shoes, warm-up suit, etc.—set out right by your bed, so you don't have to go searching around for them as soon as you wake up the next morning. Remember, if you give yourself an excuse for not starting (and what better excuse can you give yourself than not being able to find your sneakers?), you're all too likely to use that excuse to put off—and maybe even postpone—the desired activity. *Deprive yourself of easy excuses* and you'll go a long way to limiting the delaying tactics that may be keeping you from getting the most out of your life.

GET DISPLACEMENT TO WORK FOR YOU

There is a phenomenon in psychology known as "displacement" in which one experience has a "carry-over" effect on another experience, even though the experiences are different. When this happens, feelings aroused or reactions caused by one experience may be repressed for the moment, only to surface quite unexpectedly and inappropriately in another situation.

Displacement can work for you or against you. It works against you when a tough day at work puts you in such a sour mood that you start to quarrel with everyone in your family as soon as you get home. But let's examine here how the same phenomenon can work *for* you, especially when it comes to getting you off on the right track in target-oriented tasks.

The idea is to transfer a positive attitude from one situation over to another one—the difficult one. If you have a difficult task ahead of you, purposefully precede that task with an activity you know will leave you with a feeling of accomplishment. The activity doesn't necessarily have to be related to the task at hand. One of the unexpected benefits of jogging early in the morning, for instance, is that it gets your day off on a strongly positive note. You've accomplished something. You've reached a target. You've generated positive momentum. You feel pleased with yourself, and your self-confidence enjoys the boost.

Jogging is hardly the only way to use displacement to good advantage. Another way is to juggle the order of interim targets related to a task or to a job. If you're a businessman who finds it hard to settle into a productive groove each morning, why not deliberately start your day with something you know you can handle easily? Start the day by writing a couple of letters or by putting the finishing touches on jobs that are 95 percent complete. Remember the techniques discussed in the chapter on scheduling. You may not be able to control what you have to do on a given day, but you can control *when* you do it. Arrange your schedule so that an hour or so after you've begun work, you will have something positive to show for your efforts. This small amount of arranged positive feedback can often generate the momentum you need to launch you into the more difficult tasks. It's a warm-up.

Another variation of the same technique involves the setting out of easily accomplished interim targets. Does the mere thought of cleaning out your cluttered attic fill you with exhaustion? Don't think about the whole attic. Look at one corner and set an interim target for yourself involving that corner alone. Have you run into problems organizing yourself for a large dinner you have to get ready for company? Pick out one small part of the meal and complete it. A lawyer I know uses this technique of setting up easily accomplished interim targets. He *deliberately* leaves his desk cluttered the night before. "It usually takes me about fifteen minutes to get everything straightened out each morning," he explains. "And when I've finished, I feel as if I've already done something important and the feeling stays with me throughout the morning."

THE "TOE FIRST" PRINCIPLE

There are essentially two ways you can get yourself started on a task. One method is like taking a running jump into a swimming pool. The other is to ease slowly into the pool little by little, letting the body get accustomed to the water temperature. Some of us are "jumpers," and some of us are "toe firsters." It helps to know what sort of person you are when the time comes to get started on a task.

Carried to the extreme, probably neither one of these approaches is advisable. The "jump first, think later" approach is a sure-fire way of getting the juices flowing in a hurry, but it can also land you on tracks leading to blind alleys. On the other hand, a too cautious "toe first" approach can cause you to waste a lot of time.

Generally speaking, people with a strong measure of confidence and energy, people prepared for the possibility of making a couple of false starts, who are comfortable with the idea of "thinking on their feet" tend to do better with a "jump first" approach to tasks. "Let's quit talking about the script and start acting." Laurence Olivier is quoted as having said on many occasions. "We'll learn as we do." But if you don't fall into this category, don't feel compelled to take this approach. Experiment. Make up your mind one morning on your way to work that you're simply going to plunge right into whatever tasks lie before you at the office. See how you do with that approach. Try it for a couple of days and if you find yourself getting bogged down, then try something different until you find the rhythm that best suits your personality. There is nothing wrong with a "toe first" approach—just as long as it doesn't take you *too* long to get into the water.

Mental Blocks and How to Overcome Them

No matter who you are or what you do, no matter how adept you are at targeting, you are still likely from time to time to run into the phenomenon commonly known as a "mental block."

Being mentally blocked means, simply, getting stuck or being bogged down in a task for no apparent reason. As the term implies, the problem begins with the mind but its effects extend to physical activities, too. It can happen when you're trying to figure out a problem, or when you're writing a report. Everyone has heard of "writer's block," when a writer can't seem to get through a particular writing assignment. But the same thing can also happen when you're at a dance lesson or trying to learn a new chord on the guitar. Suddenly, you run into an invisible wall. You know what you want to do—you have a target—and there doesn't seem to be any reason why you *can't* do what you want. You have the ability and the means at hand. Still, no matter how hard you try you can't make any progress. Like a car mired in a mud bank, your wheels spin and spin but you stand still.

Many theories have tried to explain why and even how mental blocks occur. Sometimes they occur because of a drop in energy level—a drop you may not be aware of. You get mentally fatigued. If there is some doubt in your own mind about what you're doing, some conflict about your task, that could be another reason.

At other times mental blocks occur because of an overload of stimuli. Too much happens at one time for your brain to process all the information efficiently. Imagine a superhighway at rush hour on a morning when four lanes are suddenly forced to converge into one lane because of an accident. A similar jam-up occurs in the brain when we subject it to too much at one time.

What can you do in such moments when you get "blocked?" There are two different strategies that can work with mental blocks, but it's difficult to say which one will work best in which situation. One of them might be called the "battering ram" approach. You simply marshal all your energies, lower your head, and try to crash through the block. If the block is a mild one, the battering ram approach will work. Sometimes, in fact, this is the most practical and most sensible tactic to use.

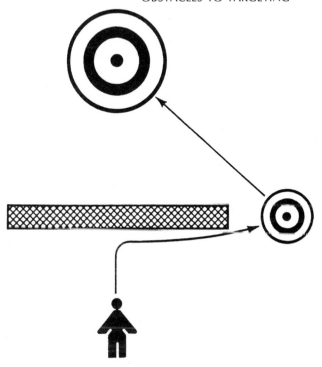

Positive sidetracking is a way to achieve a target that is obstructed. It involves nothing more complicated than going around the obstruction, usually by means of a subsidiary target or targets that show the way. The trick is to keep the main goal in mind.

But if the block is more significant, the battering ram approach will not only *not* work, it will worsen the situation. The more you try, the more impenetrable the invisible wall will appear, and the more frustrated you'll get trying to get through it.

When this happens, when a block doesn't yield to the application of more effort, here's something you can try: It's a technique I call *positive sidetracking.*

POSITIVE SIDETRACKING

Of all the tools you have at your disposal in your targeting arsenal, none is as potentially useful as the ability to use positive sidetracking—when the situation is ripe for it. Positive sidetracking means deliberately taking yourself off the track leading you toward your originally intended target and moving off in another direction altogether. True, by doing so you are taking yourself away from your intended target, just as if you were being victimized by a diversionary target, which we discussed earlier. But the difference between getting side-tracked by a diversionary target and positive sidetracking is that when you sidetrack you are conscious and aware of what you're doing and why you're doing it. You also control how long the sidetracking will continue. You don't lose sight of your target. You simply have made a decision that you feel is necessary for the best interests of ultimately achieving your target.

Positive sidetracking can vary from an activity of only two or three minutes to a strategy involving several weeks. The coffee break is a classic illustration of positive sidetracking. You take a break, getting off your original track for a different one, but you do not stray so far off the primary track that you can't easily resume your initial position. A broader illustration of positive sidetracking is the three-week break from tennis that the Swedish champion Bjorn Borg likes to take each year. "I go away for three weeks and try not to even think about tennis," Borg once said. "I don't bring my racquet, and I don't go near a court."

The need for positive sidetracking varies, of course, from person to person and from situation to situation, but it's safe to say that all of us need to try it from time to time. The problem is that some people are so intensely concerned about reaching a target that they fail to recognize when they are spinning their wheels without getting anywhere. Guilt and group pressure frequently inhibit us from making a positive sidetracking move when the situation warrants it. Too many of us take too literally the adage, "When at first you don't succeed, try, try again." The adage is sensible enough on the surface but not very effective if what we really need is a little time to recharge our batteries. I'm not suggesting here that the minute you begin to sense any resistance to your efforts in a given task you immediately take a break or figure out something else to do. Just try to stay aware of the trap of "overtrying." Keep in mind the image of Br'er Fox pummeling the tar baby in the Uncle Remus story. The more he struggled, the more he became stuck. There is a stage in just about every difficult task where trying *harder* becomes counterproductive. You have to develop the sensitivity needed to tell when this stage is reached.

One of the most reliable barometers is your state of mind. Listen to yourself. Bjorn Borg knows it is time to do some positive sidetracking when he begins to lose his sense of self-control on the court. A journalist friend knows it's time when she starts making typing errors. Any change in your state of mind—getting angry, feeling frustrated, getting bored—can be a sign that it's time to pull back for a moment or two, time to regroup, time to recharge your mental batteries. In certain situations you may not have the luxury of a positive sidetracking alternative, but such situations are generally fairly rare. What is to stop you, for instance, from getting up from your desk when things are going poorly and doing five minutes of stretching or calisthenics? Nothing is stopping you—nothing, that is, but the false sense of urgency that makes it difficult for you to take your eyes away from the target for even a few minutes.

I said it earlier in the book, but I'll repeat it here: It isn't only the amount of time you spend on a task that will determine how successful you are in accomplishing that task. It's also the *quality* of effort expended. Two hours of effort, bisected with fifteen minutes of positive sidetracking, can frequently do more in the way of real accomplishment than four hours of "solid work." Keep the principle of positive sidetracking in mind no matter what you're doing. And don't be afraid to use it when the time seems right.

CHAPTER TWENTY-ONE

Make the Extra Effort

The main thing you can rely upon from the mountain is being forced beyond your "comfort zone."

In one of my climbs in Yosemite National Park, we encountered instant weather in a fierce fall storm. It rained and it hailed. Later, in the safety of our base camp, I asked myself "Why, at my age, did I take up a hobby reserved for twenty- and thirty-year olds?" I've asked myself that several times since . . . and have always been satisfied with my subconscious reply . . . "Because I want to."

As an amateur athlete, I know you must stretch and push yourself beyond your physical limits in order to develop your body. You must go beyond your "comfort zone." This applies to all aspects of life. As a salesman, I know you have to go beyond what you think you can do in order to reach for higher performance goals. As a business man, I know you have to exercise and stretch your imagination in order to develop creativity.

Most of us prefer staying in our comfort zone . . . sitting

comfortably on the patio, sipping a cool drink to refresh ourselves after a short tramp around the foothills, watching those "crazy idiots" trying to make it up the face of the cliffs overlooking the hotel. Safe?. . . . yes, but where is their growth? For growth you must go beyond your comfort zone.

Reach Beyond The Ordinary

In order to reach beyond the ordinary, to scale extraordinary heights you must be willing to make the extra effort even if you are tired, discouraged or afraid. It is that maximum exertion at the last optimum moment which can make the difference between success and failure.

Terry Cole Whittaker is, as anyone knows who has seen her television show, a bubbling dynamo of enthusiasm who totally embodies the philosophy she preaches. She is a California phenomenon, whose wide following is rapidly growing in spite of her departure for Hawaii.

California seems to have developed a reputation as the "kook-factory" of the nation, home of innumerable "crackpots." This is because there is a sense of freedom in our California lifestyle that leads to and allows for experimentation. Several respectable and responsible organizations have arisen and flourished in this climate, with a message that says, in essence, you are free to do anything you wish to do, so long as you do not hurt anyone, including yourself. Too many persons try to follow the first part of this philosophy with no regard for the second part, not realizing that as you give you receive . . . good or bad. You must take the responsibility for your own actions.

Terry Cole-Whittaker started her ministry in the Church of Religious Science; as she developed her own methods of teaching universal principles, she attracted a large following to her church in La Jolla, California. Her congregation increased from fifty people to two-thousand in three years, attracted by her enthusiasm and message; it took two services in a renovated movie theater to accommodate all who wished to attend the weekly Sunday services. A Terry Cole-Whittaker service charges you up for an entire week.

She is regarded as an innovator in the field of human resources development, management leadership and goal achievement with clients such as Rockwell International, General Foods, Bank of America, Xerox Corporation and General Dynamics. Her positive methods have stimulated thousands to recognize and utilize their potential to reach higher and higher personal goals. She has developed seminars and home study courses, using modern technology such as video cassettes to give her audience the sense of her personal involvement and personality in each seminar.

Think-Positive Principles Will Not Be Accepted By All

The "think-positive" principles that we have been presenting in this book are consistently misunderstood by those who have trouble with the concept of taking personal responsibility for their actions and where they are. It's much more comfortable to be able to blame it on outside influences or on an all-powerful, wise Father/God. Those who believe in the nobility of poverty and suffering cannot understand a philosophy that says poverty is a "sin" because it means you are not using your religion properly. Many do not understand a philosophy that says" I must see to my own motives and correct the faults in myself before I can cure the ills of the world." (and yet if everyone did that, the world would be Utopia). These are all facets of accepting the responsibility for your own life and living it the best way you know how for yourself, and thus by extension, for those you come in contact with. No one can be happy if those around him are unhappy. This is the concept of the statement that is the title of the book, *What You Think of Me Is None of My Business.*

In the early part of this year, at the height of her successful ministry and career, Rev. Cole-Whittaker decided to relocate to Hawaii; she is setting up a retreat center for those who wish to follow an in-depth program of self-awareness. She continues to direct the organization set up to present the seminars and home teaching courses, as well as continuing with her writings. She has published one other book called *How to Have More in a Have-Not World.*

What You Think of Me is None of My Business is drawn from her studies in theology and humanism, as well as her counseling sessions. It is her contention that human troubles and failures are the result of misperceptions, influenced by the barrage of false belief systems that become incorporated in the individuals life game plan. Getting rid of faulty belief systems is the key to success. Her book explains how a person can get rid of these obstructing beliefs that run counter to the laws of the universe.

Each exercise in self-awareness, included in the book, asks you to observe how you feel about a given belief, to choose to accept responsibility for that belief, to give up blame for it, and then will give you a technique to use to overcome that particular obstacle. These techniques give you just one more excellent way to test yourself and experiment with ways to facilitate your growth. Belief systems examined during the course of the book are: how do you get the power to accomplish your goals, your right to abundance, guilt, persistence, good health, relationships, sex, competition and whether or not you accept your limitations. It is a very thought-provoking book written for today. I recommend it highly.

Going Beyond an Obstacle and Overcoming It

I've chosen the chapter "Going Beyond Your Comfort Zone" because this often becomes an integral part of the road to success. How you handle it is the key. A resurrected cliché going around says "When the going gets tough, the tough get going." True! You do what must be done without being a crybaby. If you moan and groan the entire time you're working your way through a place beyond your comfort zone, if you make it, you may find you have paid too high a price for it in the loss of respect, friends, business contacts and even family; like the boy who cried "Wolf," people soon tire of the complaints and discord and just stop listening to you. You take the risk of leaving yourself open to a long, very lonely, climb indeed, with most cries for help going unheeded.

Everybody needs a place where he can let down his hair a little, where he can do some grumbling and complaining; however, when you do pause along the route to reflect, don't lash out at others. The child in us will always be looking for a place where it is safe to stick our thumbs in our mouth and nestle down for sympathy when we are tired or hurt. That's all right, just don't let it become a habit or a crutch . . . and above all, keep the child away from the workplace. The adult which might tolerate a temper tantrum in a child, will not accept it in another adult.

Quite often, we are our own worst enemy. We make a hard job harder by repeatedly telling ourselves just how difficult the task is and what a toll it is taking on us (usually to anyone who will listen). We should instead take the attitude that we are knowingly and purposefully going "beyond our comfort zone" to accomplish our goal; by accepting it in that light, we will be able to remain more cheerful (no one expects you to smile and laugh all the time . . . only an imbecile does that, but happiness and laughter eases any burden); getting more rest (if needed) is as much a subjective need as it is a physical one . . . "rest as needed" not because it is time to rest. Incidentally, many people find they are more creative with less sleep at night and small rest sessions during the day.

Each author in this book says the same thing in one way or

another. "Your attitudes and judgment values are what make the difference." If you continue to verbalize or believe that "the whole world is against me" or "I must work/earn by the sweat of my brow" or "work is hard," that is the way it will be for you. Wouldn't it be better to say, "Everyone I come in contact with contributes to the accomplishing of my goals in a way advantageous to both of us" or "The universe is on my side," or "Work is a vital part of human living, necessary to body and soul." There is little growth in a life wasted with trivia.

When you start on a path of negative thinking, it can get out of control unless positive action is taken to change its course. You can and should take that necessary action. Just as the insubstantial mass of a small snowball, at the beginning of its roll, is easy to demolish, so it is easier to demolish the snowball of negative thinking in its early stages. When either one of them has grown out of proportion, it is more difficult to turn or halt. When you're "picking up steam" do it to go uphill, not down.

Keep a Healthy Body

Don't ignore the demands of your body. Whether or not we realize it, many of our problems that may seem to be emotional or business related, could be the results of, or complicated by health problems we may not even be aware of. Keep in tune with your total being and you can listen to your body as well as your intuition. Good health is a natural state and is heavily influenced by your belief systems and your thinking. During the building of our new business (the pool display park), everyone on the staff, from the boys digging in the trenches, to me and my assistant, went "beyond our comfort zone." All of us worked from first light to dusk under the rather grueling conditions imposed by the physical labor associated with the actual construction, the mundane, but mentally grueling, necessity of keeping track of a plethora of details, plus the necessity of constant supervision of both men and materials; on top of it all, this most difficult session took place on one of the hottest Julys on record.

At one time or another, all of us may have started to get sick, but since we really didn't have the time right then, we ignored it, therefore no time was lost as a result of illness. When the job was completed, the summit feeling of completeness and accomplishment plus a chance to get caught up on our rest, kept us all well. While we are more in control than we think we are, starting out in good physical condition makes the going easier. Be ready in case you must go beyond your comfort zone.

The Extra Effort Is What Puts You Over the Top

Book Title: What You Think Of Me Is None Of My Business
Author: Terry Cole-Whittaker
Publisher: Oak Tree Publication, La Jolla, Ca
Chapter: Going Beyond Your Comfort Zone

Going Beyond Your Comfort Zone

Risk is a necessary element in your self-development. It's absolutely necessary if you are to realize your God-given potential. In fact, your willingness to risk is a measure of your willingness to live life to its fullest. The dictionary defines risk as "the chance of injury, damage or loss . . . the chance of the failure of your expectations." What the dictionary doesn't say is that, behind each of those chances, is the *opportunity* to learn and gain the fulfillment of your desires.

When you think of risk, you often feel threatened or fearful. Fear and risk seem to go together, like ham and eggs or peaches and cream. A sort of natural pairing, it would seem. Actually, as we shall see, risk can be a way of overcoming fear. The bottom line is: if you are going to have any fruitful activity in your life at all, you must be willing to risk.

We avoid risk for four reasons. First, we fear that we will get what we think we want, only to discover that we didn't want

Reprinted with permission from WHAT YOU THINK OF ME IS NONE OF MY BUSI-NESS by Terry Cole-Whittaker, published by Oak Tree Publications, 1979 it all. Second, we fear failure and believe failure so painful we won't even try. Third, we fear we will lose what we already have. People spend a lot of energy trying to keep what they have and avoid what they fear. And fourth, we fear we will be successful and that we will not be able to handle our success.

A pernicious by-product of fear is immobility. The phrase "frozen with fear" is usually associated with a traumatic event like war, physical assault, or accident, but such immobility can be an ingredient in our daily lives. We become frozen mentally and physically when we think of taking action to change our lives. There is a part of us that wants to keep things just the way they are, no matter how unhappy we are with them. To cling to the familiar, we will pay almost any price.

An extreme example is the story my great-grandmother used to tell of a woman whose husband beat her regularly. When asked why she didn't leave the man, the woman replied: "I can't leave. I don't know what I would do out there." This woman was unwilling to risk going "out there" for fear that it would be worse than where she was.

To one degree or another, we all do this, over and over again. No matter how painful the familiar, we put up with it because we fear the new. We call this unwillingness to risk "security."

To transcend fear, you must be willing to risk. You must be willing to go beyond your comfort zone. While comfort zones differ among us, the comfort zone is essentially the level of our past experiences. It falls somewhere between the lowest and the highest good you can accept for yourself. We are all familiar with the convict who, after years of imprisonment, is finally confronted with freedom and doesn't want to leave the security of the prison walls. In a way, we are all like the prisoner. We remain in the familiar situation, even when it falls short of happiness and fulfillment, because we are afraid to expand our comfort zone.

We forget that life is to be *lived.* Life is about full self-expression and self-fulfillment. To live fully, you must expand and grow, and that requires risk. When we settle for the familiar, for safety, it's because we've forgotten that God is our only security. Growth and change can be exciting when we depend on the Source rather than on our mates, our friends, our government—on people, places, and things.

There is no lasting security in the physical or material world: people change, money devaluates, governments collapse, companies retrench and fail. Nothing is constant in the physical world. Our quest for security in the physical world is doomed because the world is designed for change.

The only constant is God and the spiritual world. When you realize that God is constant and that you are an individualized expression of God, you can create what you want regardless of what's going on around you. You are free to risk, to give up what's comfortable and familiar in favor of that which is satisfying, fulfilling, and exciting.

Some people are willing to settle for dull, boring, drab, and unfulfilling jobs in the name of security. Others are adventurers who welcome the challenge and excitement of risk. Many of my management seminars are conducted for people who work totally on commission. They have no regular salary, no pension plans, no unions. If they don't produce, they have no income and soon, no job. Yet they love their work. They accept the excitement of challenge. They are willing to risk, and many have been richly rewarded for their risk.

On the other hand, look at the ones who spend a lifetime working for the government because it offers security. Those who are there because of the benefits, the job security, lack aliveness. I have a girlfriend who works in a veterans' hospital. She hates her job but won't leave it because of the benefits and job security. She's a lovely, talented woman; but we don't spend much time together any more because I've gotten tired of her complaints, and she finds my willingness to take risks uncomfortable.

As Henry David Thoreau wrote in *Walden,* "The mass of men lead lives of quiet desperation." This describes a tragically large number of people. These are the people who have given up on life. Immobilized by fear, they are suffering death in small doses. Each one fails to recognize that *action cures fear.*

You must be willing to confront your fears and go through them or they will continue to run your life. I can remember when I was terrified of public speaking. Even in school I was afraid to raise my hand or speak in class. Yet today I earn the major part of my income speaking to large crowds. What's more, I enjoy it!

Looking back I realize I was afraid people would criticize me and tell me my ideas were no good. I was afraid I was going to lose. But I survived and learned an invaluable lesson: a good way to handle this fear, or any other, is to do so in small increments or small doses. First, I tried speaking to small, familiar groups; and in the beginning my body literally shook with fear. But I survived and kept speaking, gradually to larger groups. And gradually I learned to enjoy the excitement and, as a result, my speaking improved. I even learned I could survive the loss of approval when I spoke poorly. To learn *that* was exciting in itself.

When we think we have lost or failed, we tend to exaggerate the experience. If we're honest, we realize that we don't fail all of the time and that, in most of those failures, there are positive lessons for growth. Clearly, there are more people who have accepted us than have rejected us. Yet, we take those few rejections, allow ourselves to be immobilized by fear, and resolve never to get in such a position again.

We take the loss of a job as a signal to find job security rather than to look for a job where we can express ourselves and thereby succeed. We lose an investment and use that as an excuse not to invest rather than as a lesson about how to invest wisely.

I know a man who lived a high-risk style of life. Through his risks, he created a huge financial institution. A company with a heavy investment in his enterprise went bankrupt and set in motion a domino effect, which eventually brought down this man's own business. He lost virtually everything. Now he lives his life very conservatively, risk-free. But he doesn't have very much either. He's afraid to risk again. His belief system informs him that he risked once and lost and that never again can he face the disillusionment of the collapse of his dreams. His attitude is to live with what he has, devoted to the old concept that a bird in the hand is worth two in the bush. A lot of us believe that. Only thing wrong with that concept is that not even *that* is safe because circumstances are always changing.

Of course, many people who have earned large fortunes tell how they first went broke—and often more than once. But they dared to risk again. They listened to their true selves and went on to win. Those opting for safety negated their inner selves, and most are bitter and blame others or the world for doing them in. They don't seem to realize that they still have the power within themselves to create exactly what they want, if they will only risk it.

Risk is exciting; but more than that, risk stimulates aliveness in the person taking the chance. Through risk, we have the opportunity to experience the kind of success that develops our certainty of how the universe works. By experiencing, going through your fears, you can learn that you master the world. Avoid risk and be run by fear, and you allow the world —the environment and other people—to control you.

The willingness to take risk simply means you are willing to go out beyond your familiar niche. There is a first time for everything, and we often feel the sense of risk (and fear) on those occasions. When you first tried walking, you fell. But you were close enough to your higher self to know that walking would expand your life. So you were willing to risk falling until you got it right. Then, as with all new things, you succeeded. Walking worked, and you were comfortable with what had been a scary situation.

So, figure out exactly what you want. This is necessary so that you will recognize it when it comes along. And when it does, as it will, you must be willing to go for it. Be willing to risk. Know that action overcomes fear and that you can go for your goal in small steps.

SELF-AWARENESS STRATEGIES AND EXERCISE

Observe

Notice those times when you are willing to take a risk. How do you feel? What's involved in the risk? What do you think you will gain? What do you think you will lose?

How do you feel about others who take risks? Do you support them or do you discourage them? Why?

Notice those times when you are unwilling to risk. What are you afraid you will lose? Do you avoid challenges because of fear? Are you afraid to ask for what you want? Do you think people will leave you? What are you really afraid of? Why?

Choose

Accept yourself the way you are. If you are unwilling to take risks with people, say, "I choose not to risk with people." If you feel fear, say: "I choose to feel afraid." "I choose to not expand." "I choose to hide or be safe." Remember, you are responsible for your own life. Take responsibility

Give up Blame

**Create It
the Way You
Want It**

for your feelings and actions about risk.
You don't need to feel guilty if you are unwilling to take risk now. You are in the process of changing your life, and it won't help if you make yourself wrong. Learn to risk in small steps.

Others are no the reason you are unwilling to risk. If you are afraid that someone will leave you, that's your fear. And if they leave you, then let them go. When you blame others, you are giving up your power.

Take a look at the way you want to be, the way you want to feel about risk. Visualize situations in your past where you wish you had taken a risk. What would you have done? What would you have said? How would you have felt if you had taken that risk? What would the result have been?

Picture risk situations that you think may come up in the future. What is the result you want? Imagine asking for and getting that result. What will you say? What will you do? Think about how you will feel when you get the result you want. See yourself already having achieved your goal. Write a specific affirmation that says exactly how you want to respond in risky situations. Read it aloud at least twice a day.

CONCLUSION

Reaching
Summits and Truths

The rock or obstacle you must climb over today on your way to the top of the mountain may be the rock you must stand on tomorrow to reach your next plateau. There is purpose and orderliness in all things; let the joy of the climb carry you onward and upward. When you stand in the rarefied air at the top of the world, you will know it was all worth it . . . and if you should pause a moment to ask "what's left?" . . . there's always the stars.

I hope you will utilize this book to climb your own mountain in your own way, at your own speed and toward your own destiny. No one can do it for you. How could I possibly describe to you what its like to watch a sunset on the snow from a mountain saddle at fourteen thousand feet? There are no words to describe the stars as seen from the top of the world, magnified and multiplied against the black sky of creation. How can I make you feel the wind at my back and the warmth of a small fire to take away the chill of the night as we rest at our basecamp? How can I share the awesome anticipation of the night before the final pitch to the summit? These are my mountain summit feelings, similar to the ones I felt when I achieved my first million dollar month with the Sealed Air Solar Pool Blanket and the day I discovered I held a record for earning the highest commission ever paid to a commissioned salesman in one month. Nor can I explain to you the emotions I feel in looking at our new Pool Display Park, seeing the beautiful reality which will bring a luxury into the average person's budget that sprang, practically overnight, from an idea held in my mind. In fact, it is better that I cannot explain my optimum feelings for you must find your own "summit feeling."

Here are some of the suggested steps for climbing your own mountain. Decide upon your motive for climbing. It could be for the pure joy of it, for the challenge and the adventure, for the reward, for all of these or none of them, but do establish your motive.

Assemble your climbing gear and carry with you the traits of enthusiasm, self-reliance, commitment, honesty, love, laughter, dependability and desire. You won't get far without them.

Learn the best way to get started and how to chart a route your capabilities can handle; then start your climb.

The one thing you must be prepared for when you start your personal climb is change. Expect it and accept it without fear and with enthusiasm. Remember how long it took you to develop bad habits and to get where you are. Luckily, when you are consciously working on change, it comes much quicker. Immediate change can start taking place, especially when you look for and recognize every successful demonstration which takes place as a result of your conscious attempt at change, and give thanks for it . . . Express appreciation to yourself and the universe. One word of caution; once you start using the principles suggested herein to become more proficient at acheiving positive and rewarding results, if you should drop back into a negative way of thinking, you will experience negative results at an accelerated, or more proficient, rate also. The principle does not distinguish between good or bad, it just creates. If you find yourself having trouble thinking positively, don't judge yourself, just work through it. Even when you are doing things right you have a lot of accumulated habits to clear out to make room for new behavior and thought patterns. Remember that an obstacle is a plateau on the way to the summit; therefore, you can find the necessary means to surmount it and make that final push to the mountain-top.

You have the innate knowledge and skill to create. Use it to create the things that will bring you the most satisfaction, with a full realization that you will experience "summit feelings" time after time along the way. There will be those magic moments when you find yourself immersed in rainbows and feel the "color electric" wrapped around your stay at the summit, rainbows to take along with you. There will even be those moments on the peaks, when you feel such strength and power, you know that if you would only reach out a little further into the star-strewn skies, you could capture and hold that fragile beauty in your hands. Reach and partake of all life has to offer you, keeping always in mind; however, that the greatest joy is in the climb itself, not in reaching the summit.

Right now, resolve to take your own life into your own hands, and accept responsibility for it. You can build your dreams and achieve your desires. You can accept life on its own terms and live it with gusto. The choice is yours. Trust Yourself! Trust the Universe! Climb Your Own Mountain. YOU CAN DO IT!

Bibliography

Adams, A.K. ed. HOME BOOK OF HUMOROUS QUOTATIONS. Dodd, Meade & Company, Inc. 1969. Publisher: Binghamton, N.Y.; Vail-Ballou Press, Inc.

Branden, Nathaniel. THE PSYCHOLOGY OF SELF-ESTEEM. Los Angeles: Nash Publishing Corporation, 1969

Bristol, Claude M. THE MAGIC OF BELIEVING. Englewood Cliffs, N.J.: Prentice-Hall, Inc. 1970

Brussel, Eugene E. ed. DICTIONARY OF QUOTABLE DEFINITIONS. Englewood Cliffs, N.J. Prentice-Hall, Inc. 1970

Burns, Robert C., and S. Kaufman. ACTIONS, STYLES AND SYMBOLS IN FAMILY DRAWINGS: AN INTERPRETIVE MANUAL, New York: Brunner/Mazel. 1972

Caplan, Gerald, ed. PREVENTION OF MENTAL DISORDERS IN CHILDREN. New York: Basic Books, 1961

Cole-Whittaker, Terry. WHAT YOU THINK OF ME IS NONE OF MY BUSINESS. LaJolla, CA: Oak Tree Publications, 1979

Coué, Emile. BETTER AND BETTER EVERY DAY. New York: Barnes & Noble, Inc. 1961

Cumming, John and Elaine. EGO AND MILIEU. New York: Atherton Press,

1969

Darling, Lois and Louis, A PLACE IN THE SUN: ECOLOGY AND THE LIVING WORLD, New York: William Morrow, 1968

Dyer, Wayne W. YOUR ERRONEOUS ZONES. New York: Harper & Row, Publishers, Inc. 1976

Ekman, Paul, and Wallace Friesen, UNMASKING THE FACE. Englewood Cliffs, N.J: Prentice-Hall, 1975

Fox, Emmet. LOVE. Marina del Rey, CA: DeVorss & Company

Fromm, Erich, THE ART OF LOVING, New York: Harper & Row, 1956

Goble, Frank G. THE THIRD FORCE, Grossman, 1970

Greenwald, Harold, ed., ACTIVE PSYCHOTHERAPY. New York: Jason Aronson, 1974

Hill, Napoleon, and W. Clement Stone. SUCCESS THROUGH A POSITIVE MENTAL ATTITUDE. Englewood Cliffs, NJ: Prentice-Hall, 1960

Ittelson, William H. and Hadley Cantril. PERCEPTION, A TRANSACTIONAL APPROACH. New York: Doubleday, 1954

Kiev, Ari. A STRATEGY FOR SUCCESS. New York: Macmillan Publishing Co., Inc., 1977

Kipling, Rudyard, IF. New York: Doubleday

Kneelan, Tim. WILDERNESS SURVIVAL. Seattle, WA: Tim Kneelan and Associates. 1984

Kopmeyer, M.R. THOUGHTS TO BUILD ON. Louisville, KY: Success Foundation, 1970

Kopp, Sheldon B. IF YOU MEET THE BUDDHA ON THE ROAD, KILL HIM: Palo Alto, CA: Science and Behavior, 1972

Lair, Jess, I AIN'T MUCH BABY—BUT I'M ALL I'VE GOT. Garden City, NY: Doubleday, 1972

L'Amour, Louis. TO THE FAR BLUE MOUNTAINS. New York: A Bantam Book, 1976

Lindemann, Erich. SYMPTOMOLOGY AND MANAGEMENT OF ACUTE GRIEF, American Journal of Psychiatry, 1944

Maltz, Maxwell, PSYCHO-CYBERNETICS. Englewood Cliffs, NJ: Prentice-Hall, 1960

Masserman, Jules, and John Schwab, SOCIAL PSYCHIATRY. Vol. I, New York: Grune & Stratton, 1974

Mayeroff, Milton, ON CARING. World Perspectives Series, edited by Ruth

Nanda Anshen. New York: Harper & Row, 1971

Menninger, Karl, THE VITAL BALANCE, New York: The Viking Press

Miller, Nunnally, and Wackman, ALIVE AND AWARE, (Interpersonal Communications Programs, Inc. 1975

Minuchin, Salvador, and Avner Barcal, PROGRESS IN GROUP AND FAMILY THERAPY. New York, 1972

Norfolk, Donald, THE STRESS FACTOR, New York: Simon and Schuster, 1977

O'Neill, Nena, and George O'Neill. SHIFTING GEARS. New York: M. Evans and Company, 1974

Peale, Norman Vincent, ENTHUSIASM MAKES THE DIFFERENCE. Englewood Cliffs, NJ, Prentice-Hall, 1960

Penney, James C., LINES OF A LAYMAN, Grand Rapids, MI., William B. Eerdmans Publishing Company, 1956

Peter, Laurence J. THE PETER PRESCRIPTION. New York: William Morrow and Company, Inc. 1972

Ponder, Catherine. THE DYNAMIC LAWS OF PROSPERITY. Englewood Cliffs, NJ: Prentice-Hall, 1962

Prosser, David C. PEEL YOUR OWN ONION. New York: Everest House, 1979

Puzo, Mario, THE GODFATHER, New York: Putnam, 1969

Rau, Neil, and Margaret Rau, ACT YOUR WAY TO SUCCESSFUL LIVING, Englewood Cliffs, NJ: Prentice-Hall, 1966

Shain, Merle, WHEN LOVERS ARE FRIENDS. New York: Harper & Row. Publishers, Inc., 1978

Sheehy, Gail, PASSAGES, New York: Dutton, 1976

Tec, Leon, TARGETS, New York: Harper & Row Publishers, Inc., 1980

Tyhurst, James, THE WALTER REED SYMPOSIUM ON PREVENTIVE AND SOCIAL PSYCHIATRY. Washington, DC: Government Printing Office, 1958

Watzlawick, Paul, THE LANGUAGE OF CHANGE: ELEMENTS OF THERAPEUTIC COMMUNICATION. New York: Basic Books, 1978